Adolescents,
Work, and
Family

Understanding Families

Series Editors: *Bert N. Adams, University of Wisconsin*
David M. Klein, University of Notre Dame

This book series examines a wide range of subjects relevant to studying families. Topics include parenthood, mate selection, marriage, divorce and remarriage, custody issues, culturally and ethnically based family norms, theory and conceptual design, family power dynamics, families and the law, research methods on the family, and family violence.

The series is aimed primarily at scholars working in family studies, sociology, psychology, social work, ethnic studies, gender studies, cultural studies, and related fields as they focus on the family. Volumes will also be useful for graduate and undergraduate courses in sociology of the family, family relations, family and consumer sciences, social work and the family, family psychology, family history, cultural perspectives on the family, and others.

Books appearing in **Understanding Families** are either single- or multiple-authored volumes or concisely edited books of original chapters on focused topics within the broad interdisciplinary field of marriage and family.

The books are reports of significant research, innovations in methodology, treatises on family theory, syntheses of current knowledge in a family subfield, or advanced textbooks. Each volume meets the highest academic standards and makes a substantial contribution to our understanding of marriages and families.

The National Council on Family Relations cosponsors with Sage a book award for students and new professionals. Award-winning manuscripts are published as part of the **Understanding Families** series.

Multiracial Couples: Black and White Voices
Paul C. Rosenblatt, Terri A. Karis, and Richard D. Powell

Understanding Latino Families: Scholarship, Policy, and Practice
Edited by Ruth E. Zambrana

Current Widowhood: Myths & Realities
Helena Znaniecka Lopata

Family Theories: An Introduction
David M. Klein and James M. White

Understanding Differences Between Divorced and Intact Families
Ronald L. Simons and Associates

Adolescents, Work, and Family: An Intergenerational Developmental Analysis
Jeylan T. Mortimer and Michael D. Finch

Jeylan T. Mortimer
Michael D. Finch
Editors

Adolescents, Work, and Family

An Intergenerational Developmental Analysis

UNDERSTANDING
FAMILIES

SAGE Publications
International Educational and Professional Publisher
Thousand Oaks   London   New Delhi

For information address:

SAGE Publications, Inc.
2455 Teller Road
Thousand Oaks, California 91320
E-mail: order@sagepub.com

SAGE Publications Ltd.
6 Bonhill Street
London EC2A 4PU
United Kingdom

SAGE Publications India Pvt. Ltd.
M-32 Market
Greater Kailash I
New Delhi 110 048 India

Printed in the United States of America

Library of Congress Cataloging in Publication Data

Main entry under title:

Adolescents, work, and family: an intergenerational developmental
   analysis / editors, Jeylan T. Mortimer, Michael D. Finch.
      p.   cm. — (Understanding families; v. 6)
   Includes bibliographical references and index.
   ISBN 0-8039-5124-8 (cloth: acid-free paper). —
ISBN 0-8039-5125-6 (pbk.: acid-free paper)
      1. Adolescence.   2. Teenagers—Family relationships.
3. Teenagers—Employment—Psychological aspects.   4. Work and
family.   5. Parent and teenager.   6. Intergenerational relations
I. Mortimer, Jeylan T., 1943- .   II. Finch, Michael David.
III. Series.
HQ796.A33544   1996
305.23′5—dc20   96-10001

This book is printed on acid-free paper.

96   97   98   99   10   9   8   7   6   5   4   3   2   1

Sage Copy Editor: Joyce Kuhn
Sage Production Editor: Michèle Lingre

Contents

Preface

The Youth Development Study began as an extension of research on the impacts of adult work on mental health and psychological development. It is well known that work experiences in adulthood, particularly occupational self-direction and autonomy, but also stressors and uncertainties, have pervasive effects on individual psychological functioning (see Mortimer & Lorence, 1995, for a review of this literature), extending well beyond the work sphere. That is, these dimensions of work experience influence not only job satisfaction, work commitment, and other psychological orientations to work itself but also affect quite general attitudes and dispositions, including orientations to self and others, depressive affect and well-being, and the person's basic stance toward change. Our earlier work, drawing on longitudinal data from the 1973-1977 Quality of Employment Survey (Lorence & Mortimer, 1985; Mortimer, Finch, & Maruyama, 1988), indicated that the effects of work autonomy on central orientations toward work—job satisfaction and work commitment—were greater for younger workers under the age of 30 than for those who were older.

There are two plausible explanations of this pattern of diminishing response to work as persons grow older. First, according to the "impressionable years" hypothesis, adolescents and young adults are particularly receptive to environmental influence. After initial views about work or other matters are crystallized, the individual avoids the strain of cognitive dissonance by selecting associates and experiences that are likely to promote the same orientations and ideas. Moreover, because acquisition and maintenance of the work role is such a highly important marker of the transition to adulthood, it may be particularly salient to the young person. It is the vehicle through which financial independence is obtained from the family of origin, and it is a key dimension of most adults' identity. In fact, the future work role is a major, desired component of the young person's future "possible self" (Markus, Cross, & Wurf, 1990). Early jobs provide experiences that give the young person a sense of moving toward this "possible self": One learns about how to get and keep a job, how to earn and manage money, and how to build work-relevant interpersonal skills.

In contrast to this developmental approach, a second explanation of increasing stability as persons age focuses more on environmental pressures for change. That is, young people are particularly likely to change in response to environmental forces because these experiences are new to them. Heightened self-awareness generally occurs in unfamiliar environments (Hormuth, 1984), and youths often find themselves in new work contexts, given the frequency of job changes in the initial phase of the work career. Although individuals may be malleable and responsive to changing circumstances throughout the life course, environments tend to stabilize after early adulthood. As a result, there is less impetus for the older person to reconsider and to adapt to changing circumstances, so there will be less change.

If, indeed, young people are particularly reactive to new environments, and if they are now being introduced to the paid work role early in the teenage years, adolescent work experience—first in the family setting and later in the more formal workplace—is potentially an exceedingly important influence on socialization relevant to work and to development more generally. What do young people learn in the work setting? How do work experiences influence their sense of competence and confidence in themselves, their work values, and their goals in life? Does the young person encounter stressors at work that engender feelings of strain and depressive affect?

The Youth Development Study was initiated to examine when the processes through which work influences the personality begin and to assess whether responses to the various dimensions of work are the same for adolescents as have been found among adults. Thus, we began with an interest in the life course and came to the conclusion that a focus on youths was essential to understand the full developmental implications of work experience. Most important from the perspective of this volume, we began to address how adolescent work experiences—including work in the context of the family as well as the paid workforce—affect relations with parents and other features of family life.

Our perspective on development is multifaceted: We examine changes across both individual and historical time in adolescents' participation in the family economy and in paid work; changes in adolescents' sense of competence as they contribute to the family division of labor; some adolescents' increasing resilience as they find sources of social support and "comfort" in the work setting; shifts in parent-child relationships in reaction to adolescent paid work; and the links between plans and attainments as adolescents begin to make the transition to adulthood.

Chapter 1 begins this book by summarizing our earlier analyses that demonstrate the importance of work quality and context in developing a sense of adolescent competence as well as other psychological orientations that likely contribute to success in life.

In Chapter 2, Pamela J. Aronson and her colleagues point to competence and efficacy as key outcomes of the parents' own prior work experiences when they were adolescents. Surprisingly, although the kinds of work that contemporary adolescents and their parents did are quite different, the perceived implications of that work experience are found to be very much the same. Kathleen Thiede Call, in Chapter 3, shows how work in the household can contribute to a sense of competence when conditions in the family are favorable and, in Chapter 5, how positive work experiences can buffer the person from deleterious family stressors that otherwise diminish competence and self-esteem and have other ill effects. In Chapter 4, Michael J. Shanahan and his colleagues also demonstrate how adolescent paid work can contribute to positive family relationships, which Seongryeol Ryu and Jeylan T. Mortimer in Chapter 6 find are important in the transmission of a key dimension of orientation to the future: preference with respect to occupational rewards. Finally, Ellen Efron Pimentel, in Chapter 7, highlights the significance of efficacy in enabling adolescent aspirations and preferences to be effectively realized.

These are some of the intergenerational, developmental linkages of work and family elucidated in the analyses presented in this book. In the concluding chapter, we consider fruitful directions for future research on work, family, and adolescence in light of our findings thus far.

Acknowledgments

This book grew out of a collaborative research project, the Youth Development Study, directed by Jeylan T. Mortimer and Michael D. Finch, from 1987 to the present. This research project is supported mainly by the National Institute of Mental Health (MH42843). Supplementary support has been provided by the National Institute on Aging (which enabled the data collection and analyses reported in Chapter 2 on intergenerational patterns of adolescent work and family) and by the National Center for Research on Vocational Education. Besides the co-investigators, contributors to the volume are collaborators who were once graduate student research assistants on the project (e.g., Pamela J. Aronson; Kathleen Thiede Call, who is now Assistant Professor in the School of Public Health, University of Minnesota; Seongryeol Ryu; and Michael Shanahan, now Assistant Professor at Pennsylvania State University), postdoctoral associates (Ellen Efron Pimentel, now Assistant Professor at the University of Illinois, Chicago), or undergraduate student research assistants (Carol Zierman and Michael Hacker). In addition, Glen H. Elder, Jr., Margaret Burchinal, and Rand D. Conger collaborated with Michael Shanahan in the comparison of adolescent earnings and family relationships in the urban (St. Paul, Minnesota) and rural (Iowa counties) settings.

Although none of the chapters has been published elsewhere, the introductory chapter, which presents a summary of Youth Development Study findings regarding the connection between work and adolescent psychological development, draws heavily on earlier publications. The authors are very grateful to David Klein and Bert Adams for the many helpful comments they made with respect to each chapter and for their patience during the years it took for the idea for this book to become a completed manuscript.

1

Work, Family, and Adolescent Development

JEYLAN T. MORTIMER

MICHAEL D. FINCH

I t is increasingly recognized that individual development is influenced by multiple environmental contexts, each impinging simultaneously on the person (Bronfenbrenner, 1979, 1986). However,
researchers generally examine them separately. Developmental psychologists, in their studies of children and adolescents, view the family
as the crucial context for the developing child, with the school and
peer group assuming greater importance in adolescence. Sociologists
give primary attention to the work sphere, examining adult development as a function of work experience (Kohn & Schooler, 1983;
Mortimer, Lorence, & Kumka, 1986). Although each of these "microsystem" contexts has direct consequences for development, because
they are often experienced at the same time there is potential for important connections between them at the "mesosystem" level that give
rise to questions about their consequences across contextual spheres.

A good deal of scholarly attention has been given to the linkages
of work and family in adulthood (Cherlin, 1988; Hood, 1993;
McLaughlin et al., 1988; Moen, 1992; Voydanoff, 1987). In fact, the
extensive sociological interest in the impacts of work experience on
psychological functioning is driven largely by the recognition that

1

work influences the family through its effects on the worker's attitudes, orientations, and personality. The most prominent example is Kohn and Schooler and their colleagues' pathbreaking research on work and personality that began with the study of work experience and parental values (Kohn, 1969). Individual reactions to the challenges and opportunities as well as the obstacles and stressors experienced in the workplace have major repercussions in the family setting (Eckenrode & Gore, 1990; Menaghan, 1991; Piotrkowski, 1979; Wharton & Erickson, 1993).

There are critical gaps in these bodies of literature. First, the potential developmental implications of working in adolescence have been neglected, despite the fact that the majority of young people simultaneously work and go to school. In prior generations, American youths' paid work experience prior to leaving school was rather restricted; when they did have paid jobs, their work was often sporadic and informal, after school or on weekends, and typically in the homes of neighbors, relatives, and friends. More formal jobs (in nonhousehold settings) might be held during the summer months, but most adolescents did not perform this kind of work when school was in session.

In contrast, almost all U.S. adolescents now work at some time during high school. A national study by Manning (1990) showed that 70% of 16- to 18-year-olds were employed during the preceding month and that 61% of 10th graders and 90% of students in the 11th and 12th grades were employed at some time during the school year. Bachman and Schulenberg's (1993) study of 71,863 high school seniors in the annual "Monitoring the Future" surveys showed that 75% of boys and 73% of girls did paid work; among the employed, 47% of the boys and 38% of the girls worked more than 20 hours per week.

In view of the great prevalence of teenage employment, the demands (and rewards) of work must be taken into account in studying the experience of adolescence. What kinds of work do contemporary adolescents typically perform, and how does their experience of work differ from that of prior generations? The adolescent of today must add work to all the other role obligations and activities that are typical at this time of life—as student, family member, and friend. How does this trend influence adolescent mental health and development?

Second, little is known about the developmental linkages between work and family in adolescence. We need to know more about how adolescents contribute to family economic strategies (Moen & Wethington, 1992) and about how relationships between parents and their children are altered in response to adolescents' changing involvement in household and paid work. Socialization to work begins in the household when children and adolescents are assigned chores and often paid according to the extent and quality of their performance. We know little about the implications of these work experiences in the family, whether they are salutary or detrimental with respect to children's growth.

It is well known that the adult work role can act as a stressor to the family. Adolescent work could also possibly contribute to family problems. However, adolescents' employment could serve as a signal to parents that their children are making progress toward the acquisition of adult roles, and their employment, in fact, might contribute either directly or indirectly to the family economy. In these circumstances, adolescents' working might have a positive effect on parent-child relationships. Furthermore, when activities in the workplace are going well, employment could serve as a buffer to stressors deriving from change and disruption in the family setting.

Third, we know little about how adolescents think about their future work and family lives and about how their developing aspirations and plans influence their behaviors as they make the transition to adulthood. At the same time that adolescents are working and adapting to changes in their families and other social environments, they are likely to be engaged in thinking and planning about these domains of life in the future. Moreover, the fact that parents' own jobs extend into the family sphere may likely influence their adolescent children's developing values about work. This book attempts to address these important and multifaceted issues.

Prior Literature and the
Debates Surrounding Adolescent Work

In contrast to the extensive literature on adolescent socialization in the family, school, and peer group, relatively little systematic study of adolescent work has been conducted. This research, mostly concerned with paid work, has yielded divergent findings and sparked much controversy. In the first camp in the debate about adolescent work are those who conclude that working is "good" for youths. According to this view, employment in adolescence poses special opportunities for growth and development. In the second camp are those who argue that teenage employment during the school year is detrimental, especially when it occurs in large doses; therefore, hours of work should be strictly monitored. Elsewhere (Finch, Mortimer, & Ryu, in press) we have reviewed these arguments, evaluated the evidence, and posed a third, and what we consider a more plausible, position: that the consequences of the transition to part-time work depend, preeminently, on its quality, its meaning, and the context in which it occurs. Consequences of employment for adolescent development and mental health are crucial in considering how adolescent work affects the family, for if working influences adolescent personality development, it surely will affect orientations and behaviors in all the major contexts of experience, including the family. As a backdrop to the present study of the intergenerational and developmental linkages of work and family, we summarize the arguments and relevant empirical findings here.

- *The transition to part-time work is beneficial.*

The transition to part-time work may indeed signify to the adolescent, as well as to parents and others, progress in moving toward the adult work role. Despite the age-segregated character of some adolescent workplaces, many working adolescents do have frequent contact with adult coworkers. The performance of workplace tasks, in cooperation with adults, could promote a sense of contribution, being "grown up," and even egalitarianism. The adolescent's work experiences, both good and bad, might serve to clarify both work values and preferences for future jobs. Exposure to diverse work environments likely encourages thinking not only about the self with respect to future occupational goals but reflection on issues of great significance for vocational development: "What kind of job would I like to have in the future?" and "What am I good at?"

Furthermore, the adolescent may acquire skills on the job that, while seemingly mundane from the perspective of an adult, could be highly salient: for example, the knowledge that one is able to find a job, meet supervisors' expectations, and accept responsibility. From this perspective, what is learned, even in a so-called menial job, may be quite consequential: how to relate to supervisors, cooperate with coworkers, deal with customers and clients, manage money, be on time, and even gain task-related skills (e.g., learning to use a cash register or a computer) that are transferable to other jobs.

Employed adolescents may also learn to better manage their time so as to effectively juggle the multiple roles and responsibilities of worker and family member as well as student and friend. They may come to realize that such conflicting responsibilities and time demands, particularly with respect to work and family, are pervasive in adult life; their growing capacities to handle these circumstances in adolescence could promote a general sense of efficacy, a self-image of being able to meet the challenges of adult life (Elder & Caspi, 1990).

Consistent with this salutary view of working, most parents approve of the increasing autonomy and independence that derive from their adolescent children's employment (Phillips & Sandstrom, 1990). Parents see their children's jobs as providing opportunities to take responsibility and to manage time effectively. Although Greenberger and Steinberg's (1986) study of students in four California high schools generally emphasized negative consequences of adolescent work (outlined below), these researchers found that teenage employment was associated with self-reported punctuality, dependability, and personal responsibility and with girls' self-reliance. Moreover, employment is sometimes found to have positive consequences for academic achievement. D'Amico's (1984) analysis of the National Longitudinal Studies youth data showed that employment at low intensity (less than 20 hours per week) lessened high school dropout rates. Moreover, adolescent part-time work has positive consequences for employment and income in the years following high school (Steel, 1991; Stern & Nakata, 1989).

- *The transition to part-time work is detrimental.*

In the 1980s, as the findings of Greenberger and Steinberg's (1986) research became increasingly visible, the notion that adolescent work is good was replaced by an entirely opposite stance: that work is bad, placing adolescents at risk with respect to their present health and development, jeopardizing their relationships with family members as well as their peers, and diminishing the likelihood of positive future outcomes. Greenberger and Steinberg argued that in contemporary America, unlike previous eras, youths are unable to acquire work that prepares them for their future occupations. Instead, young people are found in age-segregated youth employment ghettoes, where simple tasks require virtually no training. Moreover, these researchers allege that there are psychosocial costs of adolescent work, as it interferes with the prominent developmental tasks of this period (e.g., identity formation, making close friends, and achievement in school). Accordingly, the predominant tone of much contemporary scientific commentary on youth employment is negative.

Why might working pose such risks to youths' mental health and development? Adolescents who work long hours or at night may be vulnerable to chronic fatigue and exhaustion. Bachman and Schulenberg (1993) studied more than 70,000 "Monitoring the Future" respondents nationwide and found that adolescents' long work hours were associated with unhealthy lifestyles—diminished sleep and lack of exercise.

Greenberger and Steinberg (1986) stressed that young workers prematurely take on adult responsibilities without adequate coping skills (see Greenberger, 1983, 1988). Greenberger (1988) describes adolescent worksites as highly age-segregated; whereas youth workers have ample contact with their age mates, relations with peer coworkers are often rather superficial— the conditions of youth work hamper the development of close and meaningful friendships. Moreover, working adolescents may have less time to spend with their families by having to work through the dinner hour and being unable to participate in family activities on weekends. If working were to disrupt ongoing social relationships, such as ties to peers or bonds with parents, there could be a serious reduction in social support.

Employment might also foster undesirable behaviors outside the workplace, such as smoking and alcohol use. Relationships with older coworkers could introduce adolescents prematurely to substance use —more adultlike ways of handling stress or spending leisure time. Employment then provides the financial wherewithal to support these often costly, unhealthy habits.

Sometimes, the risks of paid work are framed in terms of its "opportunity costs." Greenberger and Steinberg (1986) warn that because work typically consumes so much time, adolescents risk losing a valuable "moratorium" period to explore alternative identities and interests and to develop close interpersonal bonds. Moreover, much of the concern about youthwork derives from a fear that working draws students away from school, promotes behaviors that interfere with learning, and reduces investment in homework and academic achievement. A half-time job coupled with a full school schedule and extracurricular activities could produce role overload and consequent distress.

Those in the "work is bad" camp sometimes compare students who are working with those who are not employed; more typically, they examine differences between those who work more and fewer hours. Investigators (Bachman, Bare, & Frankie, 1986; Bachman & Schulenberg, 1993; Greenberger, 1984; Greenberger & Steinberg, 1986; Steinberg & Dornbusch, 1991; Steinberg, Greenberger, Garduque, Ruggiero, & Vaux, 1982) have linked decrements in adjustment to hours of work, finding that adolescents who work long hours are particularly prone to the use of cigarettes, alcohol, illicit drugs, and delinquency. Indeed, work may provide a new arena for delinquent (even criminal) acts, such as stealing from the cash register.

Employed adolescents have higher rates of school tardiness (Greenberger & Steinberg, 1986) and misconduct (Steinberg & Dornbusch, 1991) than those who are not employed; as hours of work increase, less time is spent doing homework (Greenberger & Steinberg, 1986). Several investigators observe negative associations between employment, or hours spent working, and grades (Finch & Mortimer, 1985; Lewin-Epstein, 1981; Marsh, 1991; McNeil, 1984; Mortimer & Finch, 1986; Steinberg & Dornbusch, 1991; Steinberg, Greenberger, Garduque, Ruggiero, & McAuliffe, 1982; Steinberg, Greenberger, Garduque, Ruggiero, & Vaux, 1982). However, the causal relationship between grade point average and employment is not clear.

Whereas prior studies are, for the most part, cross-sectional, longitudinal data are considerably more useful in ascertaining whether diminished achievement and involvement in school are the antecedents or the consequences of employment. Using longitudinal data from a panel of California and Wisconsin high school students,

Steinberg, Fegley, and Dornbusch (1993) compared students who entered the workforce with those who remained unemployed over a 1-year period. They found that nonworkers in Year 1 who entered the workforce in Year 2 earned lower grades and also spent less time on homework, had lower educational expectations, and expressed more disengagement from school at Time 1 than those who remained nonemployed at both times. This pattern would support a selection argument. That is, students who are less interested, involved, or successful in school choose to enter the labor force, perhaps seeking a new domain in which to demonstrate competence.

Consistent with such selectivity, Bachman and Schulenberg (1993) suggest that a lack of success in school fosters youth employment, which may be one component of a syndrome of "pseudomaturity" or "precocious development" that precipitates hastened transition to adulthood—early involvement in adultlike behaviors like drinking and smoking, and withdrawal from the more dependent, preadultlike student role.

Alternatively, working students' poorer grades could be due to the influence of employment. However, Steinberg and his colleagues' (1993) assessment of change in grade point average, considered as a consequence of employment, yielded mixed findings.

- *The consequences of the transition to part-time work depend on the quality of work experience, its meaning, and the context in which it occurs.*

Given the multifaceted character of adolescent work roles and the rapidly changing developmental needs of adolescents, we believe that both the "work is good" and the "work is bad" perspectives are overly simplistic. The extant literature pays scant attention to the quality of the adolescent work experience. Investigators compare working and nonworking adolescents or, more frequently, measure work experience solely in terms of its quantity: the number of hours worked per week. Adolescents select themselves into employment or are selected by employers, they work a given number of hours per week, and "benefits" or "costs" are observed. Investigators sometimes speculate about possible causal mechanisms. However, as little is known about what actually occurs at work, employment is essentially a "black box."

The findings of research on adults dictate a very different approach. That is, the primary focus is the quality of adult work, particularly its complexity and self-directed character, that has pervasive implications for psychological functioning, the self-concept, and other indicators of mental health (Baker & Green, 1991; Johansson & Aronsson, 1991; Kohn & Schooler, 1983; Mortimer et al., 1986). Given this pattern, we should examine the quality of adolescent work experience and consider its relationship to adolescent outcomes.

It must be recognized, however, that what constitutes a "quality" work experience may be different for an adolescent and an adult. For example, unlike adults, adolescent novices to the workplace may need more direction and clarity of instruction. To new workers, autonomy may be somewhat frightening, given their lack of experience and skill. Shanahan, Finch, Mortimer, and Ryu (1991), in fact, report that decision-making autonomy in youth jobs is significantly associated with youth distress.

In a notable exception to the dearth of research on the quality of adolescent work, Schulenberg and Bachman (1993), using data collected over a decade from "Monitoring the Future" cohorts, report a series of interactions between work intensity and work quality in affecting outcomes. That is, students suffered when they worked in poor-quality jobs for long periods of time—jobs that did not make use of their talents, were unconnected to anticipated future jobs, and were only being done "for the money." These researchers also report many direct benefits of "high quality" work experience in terms of reduced substance use and other positive outcomes.

Furthermore, the broader meaning and social context of working must be taken into account. Given the importance of the family in the lives of adolescents, consideration of the family's reaction to teenage work must take center stage. Because many parents also worked when they were teenagers, one wonders whether they look back upon their past employment with regret or as an experience to be valued in view of their subsequent life circumstances and needs. Parents may see adolescents' employment either as a factor contributing to the welfare of the family as a collectivity or as a source of individual benefit to the teenager. Are parents critical of their adolescent children for wasting their earnings on designer jeans, admiring of their diligence in saving for college, or grateful for their contributions to the family coffer?

Marsh (1991) reports positive effects of employment on grades, but only when the worker is using earnings to save for college. Such use would have major implications for the family, for in the absence of adolescent savings, parents are often considered responsible for footing the bill. Marsh's finding suggests that much depends on the social meaning of adolescent work. When there is high academic involvement and a clear linkage between earnings and future educational attainment, work may even be educationally beneficial and recognized as such by both the adolescents and the parents.

There is evidence from the Depression era that adolescents in economically deprived families who contributed to the family economy by paid work gained a sense of self-confidence and efficacy from helping their families at a time of crisis (Elder & Rockwell, 1979). The positive mental health and subsequent socioeconomic attainment of these young people were attributed to these early helping experiences; caring for others is often thought to be developmentally beneficial (Garmezy, 1988; Hetherington, 1989).

However, Bachman (1983) raises the spectre of "premature affluence" that derives from large amounts of disposable income at a time when the adolescent still lives at home and most basic expenses are being taken care of by parents. He questions whether adolescents can learn realistically about the uses and value of money when much of their income is being spent frivolously. Yet contrary to this rather pessimistic scenario, he presents data indicating that the majority (62%) of students who plan to complete four years of college save at least some of their earnings for this purpose, and almost half give at least some money to help pay family living expenses. These uses of earnings suggest that adolescent employment may have real economic benefit for the family and may be viewed favorably by parents.

An extensive literature documents the mental health benefits of multiple roles in adulthood (Thoits, 1983). Multiple roles provide access to social contacts, diverse activities, and opportunities to cope with challenging problems and tasks. The social support and confidence gained from these experiences can constitute important resources in dealing with future stressors. Moreover, given stressors in any role or social context, social support and positive experiences in other contexts can enable more effective coping. By the same token, positive adolescent work experience could also function as an "arena of comfort" (Simmons, in press) that lessens the experience of stress, and consequent negative outcomes, when there are disruptions in the family or other settings.

Design of the Youth Development Study

The Youth Development Study (YDS) was initiated in Fall 1987 when a sample of adolescents was randomly selected from a list of ninth graders enrolled in the St. Paul Public School District. Consent to participate was obtained from 1,139 parents and 1,139 adolescents, who constituted 64% of eligible cases. Eligibility was defined by enrollment in the school district at the time of the first data collection and by the absence of disabilities that would prevent completion of a questionnaire.

The St. Paul Public School District has a large concentration of Hmong students (9% of the student body) that is reflected in the figures provided above (129 Hmong parents and adolescents provided consent). But because the Hmong are a recent immigrant group with a distinctive cultural tradition, what has become the Hmong substudy of the YDS focuses on issues of acculturation and adaptation. Moreover, Hmong adolescents rarely are employed in paid jobs. Therefore, the analyses presented in this volume exclude the Hmong families and are based on the panel of 1,000 students and their parents that was initially surveyed in 1988 (see Table 1.1).

The 64% response to the letter of invitation is cause for concern because those who agreed to participate could be systematically different from those who refused. For instance, more highly educated parents could be more positively disposed to research of this kind. To investigate this possibility, a probit analysis (LIMDEP) of the decision to participate was conducted, with neighborhood socioeconomic context indicators derived from census tract tapes and other variables from school records assigned to each general sample (non-Hmong) case as predictors (Finch, Shanahan, Mortimer, & Ryu, 1991). Girls were found to be more likely to participate in the study than boys. Of the initial 1,000-member general sample, 524 girls and 476 boys completed first-wave questionnaires. Older students (i.e., older than their ninth-grade peers) were less likely to agree to be in the study.

TABLE 1.1 Youth Development Study[a]

	In School: Full Survey				Mail Survey:			
					Life History	Calendar	Tracking	Full Survey
Grade level	9	10	11	12				
Age	14-15	15-16	16-17	17-18	18-19	19-20	20-21	21-22
Year	1988	1989	1990	1991	1992	1993	1994	1995
No. adolescent respondents	1,000[b]	964	957	933	816	782	799	779
% Retention rate	—	96.2	95.4	92.8	81.3	77.7	79.6	77.5
No. mothers responding	924	—	—	690	—	—	—	
No. fathers responding	649	—	—	440	—	—	—	
% Respondents with at least one parent responding	95.9	—	—	79.1	—	—	—	

a. This research was funded by the National Institute of Mental Health, "Work Experience and Mental Health: A Panel Study of Youth" (MH42843), Jeylan T. Mortimer, Principal Investigator, and Michael D. Finch, Co-Investigator.
b. 1,010 consented to participate in Fall 1987.

Almost all (94%) of the ninth-grade study participants were 14 or 15 years old; 6% were 16 or 17. Most important, no socioeconomic contextual variables predicted participation.

We conclude, on the basis of this analysis, that the sample is representative of the student body in the St. Paul public schools and of the community from which it was drawn. Thus, it includes families of diverse ethnic and social class backgrounds. Excepting the Hmong, the initial study panel was 73.6% white, 10% African American, 4.6% Hispanic, and 4% Asian. Median household income fell in the interval range of $30,000 to $39,999; 62% of the families had incomes at or below this level. Among the parents, 11% had less than a high school degree, 39% were high school graduates, 37% had attended or graduated from college, and 11% had done graduate work or had obtained professional degrees.

The study design is shown in Table 1.1. Questionnaires were initially administered to the students in their school classrooms in Winter and spring 1988. The surveys inquired about work in the family and the paid workplace (as well as in the school setting), including objective kinds of information (e.g., hours and pay), and more subjective and evaluative measures (e.g., about the meaning of work or job satisfaction). We also asked about relations with parents and peers. Finally, widely used measures of self-esteem (Rosenberg, 1965), mastery or self-efficacy (Pearlin, Menaghan, Lieberman, & Mullan, 1981), depressive affect (Ware, Johnston, Davies-Avery, & Brook, 1979), achievement orientations and plans for the future, and questions about problem behaviors—getting in trouble at school, alcohol use, and smoking—were included in the survey instrument. The students continued to be surveyed during the remaining three years of high school, with questionnaires administered once each year in the winter and spring. Students who were not present for either of the two scheduled administrations at their school (and those not attending school, e.g., 10% in Wave 4) were mailed questionnaires using follow-up procedures recommended by Dillman (1983). Of the initial 1,000 participants, 93% were retained over the 4-year period. That is, 93% of those students who completed a survey in Wave 1 also responded in Wave 4 (892 students participated in all four survey waves).

To supplement this self-report data, in the first and fourth waves of the study, parents were mailed surveys in an attempt to discern their perspective on the adolescent work experience. We assessed parents' retrospective evaluations of the costs and benefits of their own early employment—when they were still in school—and their observations of their own children's experiences of work (that is, the child respondent in the YDS). We also obtained the parents' views about adolescent work in general. As shown in Table 1.1, questionnaire data were obtained from the parents of 96% of the adolescent participants in Wave 1 and from 79% in Wave 4.

We continued to follow the adolescents when they left high school, with yearly surveys conducted by mail. During the following four years, they were asked to complete monthly life history calendars, reporting on their residential arrangements, marriage and parenthood, school attendance, and both part- and full-time work experience. The final chapter of this book reports on work and family-related planning and behaviors during the two years following high school. Although there was some panel attrition between Waves 4 and 5 immediately after high school, participation in Waves 6, 7, and 8 has been quite adequate.

The Developmental Impacts
of Adolescent Employment:
Evidence From the YDS

Because detailed analyses relevant to the question of whether work is good or bad for adolescents have been published elsewhere (Finch et al., 1991; Mortimer, Finch, Dennehy, Lee, & Beebe, 1994; Mortimer, Finch, Ryu, Shanahan, & Call, in press; Mortimer, Finch, Shanahan, & Ryu, 1992a, 1992b; Mortimer & Shanahan, 1994; Mortimer, Shanahan, & Ryu, 1993; Shanahan et al., 1991), we only summarize the findings here. Using various measures of work experience, we have compared students on the basis of their work status (employed or not), the hours they worked at each wave, their cumulative work involvement (in formal jobs over the entire four-year period of high school), and, finally, on the basis of the quality of their work experience at each time of measurement. We have examined a range of developmental "outcomes," including indicators of self-concept and mental health (self-esteem, self-efficacy, and depressive affect), involvement in school (grade point average, time spent doing homework), behavioral adjustment (frequency of alcohol use and smoking), educational and occupational aspirations, and measures of the quality of the adolescent's relationships with parents and peers.

Although we have not examined all work features and health outcomes, we can bring a considerable amount of evidence to bear on the question at issue. Here, we report what we have learned about the impact of the transition to part-time work on adolescent development.

At any wave, we have found virtually no differences, considering a wide range of outcomes, between students who work and those who do not. The consistent pattern of null findings with respect to work status supports the conclusion that working per se is neither beneficial nor harmful with respect to the healthy development of youths (Mortimer et al., in press).

We also obtained yearly measures of the intensity or amount of work at the time of each survey administration: operationalized as dummy variables indicating high-intensity (more than 20 hours/week) and low-intensity (20 or fewer hours) employment. The reference category in these analyses consisted of nonworking youths. Intensity of work bore no consistent significant relationship to measures of adolescent mental health, homework time, academic achievement, or relationships with parents and peers (Mortimer et al., in press; Mortimer & Shanahan, 1991, 1994). Apparently, contrary to the notion that work time functions as an "opportunity cost" with respect to more educationally beneficial activities, adolescents in the YDS who worked fewer hours did not choose to invest their "extra" time in homework activity.

However, in a highly stringent analysis incorporating relevant controls (e.g., socioeconomic background, race, family composition) and the lagged outcome, we found that 10th- and 11th-grade students who worked at higher intensity did engage in more alcohol use (Mortimer, 1996). Consistent with the selection argument, that characteristics of the person determine the extent of involvement in employment, prior alcohol use each year (Waves 9, 10, and 11) significantly predicted the number of hours worked in the year following. But selection processes could not "explain away" the impact of more intensive work; the effects of work hours on alcohol use were manifest even when the lagged dependent variable (alcohol usage measured one year previously) was controlled. Considering the congruence of the findings of the YDS, Steinberg's research (Steinberg & Dornbusch, 1991; Steinberg et al., 1993), and Bachman and Schulenberg's (1993) large-scale study, the linkage between working long hours and alcohol use appears to be one of the most robust findings on this subject. However, the contention that work intensity influences mental health, academic achievement, and cigarette smoking did not withstand the extensive controls applied in these analyses.

In summary, our investigation of the effects of work intensity, or the amount of time students spend working, on adolescent developmental outcomes has yielded many null findings. With respect to behavioral adjustment, we find consistent evidence that more intensive work promotes alcohol use. Our studies of achievement (grade point average) yield null findings with hours of work measured each year. Let us now turn to the quality of adolescent work, that is, to the character of the tasks on which adolescents work on, the nature of their interpersonal relationships on the job, and their own accounts of their experiences.

EFFECTS OF THE QUALITY OF WORK
EXPERIENCE ON ADOLESCENT OUTCOMES

We find that employed adolescents who have opportunities for advancement, perceive little conflict between school and work, and feel they are paid well (and thus are appreciated by their employers) increase in self-efficacy over a one-year period (Finch et al., 1991). However, when they experience problems in the job setting (e.g., time pressure, overload, or conflicts between school and work), they express more depressive affect over time (Shanahan et al., 1991). Given that analyses demonstrating these effects incorporated numerous controls as well as lagged variables, we have considerable confidence that the quality of work does matter for adolescent mental health. Moreover, there is evidence that when boys have work that involves mastery of new skills, the quality of their relationships with their parents and their peers improves over time (Mortimer & Shanahan, 1991, 1994). We also find that the opportunity to learn skills on the job has positive implications for occupational value formation. Employed adolescents with such opportunity became more aware of the variety of rewards that work has to offer, affecting both intrinsic and extrinsic value dimensions (Mortimer, Pimentel, Ryu, Dennehy, & Lee, in press). Employed girls with opportunities to help others on the job manifested a stronger sense of self-efficacy over time (Call, Mortimer, & Shanahan, 1995).

If the quality of work is indeed so important, it becomes crucial to know to what extent adolescents actually have high- or low-quality jobs. Contrary to the depiction put forth by Greenberger and Steinberg (1986), we find much evidence that the character of adolescent work is, for the most part, not a cause for concern. Most of our job-quality indicators are positively skewed. For example, only a minority of employed 11th-grade students feel that their jobs do not provide them with "a chance to learn new things" (16%), lack challenges (19%), place them under time pressure (31%), or subject them to role conflict (22%). On the other hand, 70% report that it is "somewhat" or "very true" that the job "gives me a chance to be helpful to others"; 65% say they are "never" or "rarely" held responsible for things that are really outside their control. Only 9% say that their pay is not good, and 71% believe that they could keep their jobs as long as they want.

Of clear developmental importance, we find evidence for a typical adolescent work "career." Initially, young people do informal work in their own households, often taking care of younger siblings and performing household chores. They then do the same kinds of jobs in other households, such as baby-sitting and yardwork. Their first formal paid jobs are often service jobs in the restaurant industry. However, by the last year in high school, adolescents tend to move from this kind of work into more diverse forms of employment. With these changes, adolescents' paid jobs become increasingly complex, involve increasingly more lengthy training, and more supervisory responsibility (Mortimer et al., 1994).

Overall, the perceptions of the students themselves do not indicate wholesale dissatisfaction from work nor widespread exposure to detrimental work environments. In fact, they are quite satisfied with their jobs. Thus, parents' views of their children's jobs and adolescents' own assessments are, in fact, quite positive (Phillips & Sandstrom, 1990).

On the basis of our data, we do not dispute the fact that working, in some circumstances and with respect to certain outcomes, may be bad for adolescents. We believe it is important to specify, when considering whether work is good or bad, what outcomes are at issue. In some respects, there is congruence between our findings and those who are most squarely in the "work is bad" camp—Steinberg, Dornbusch, Greenberger, and their collaborators. We both find that long hours of work foster alcohol use, and this is certainly cause for concern. As we see it, the strongest evidence in support of the "work is bad" argument lies in the area of substance use, particularly alcohol, which is now the drug of choice for adolescents and an important "gateway" drug, preceding more socially unacceptable drug involvement (Kandel, 1989; Wagenaar & Perry, 1994).

However, there is room for difference in interpretation even when findings across studies are essentially the same. For example, both the YDS (Mortimer & Shanahan, 1994) and Steinberg et al.'s (1993) research indicate that youths become more independent of parents when they work more hours. Steinberg and his colleagues view this as an ominous trend—raising the specter of employed students lacking parental supervision and being out of control. Parents and adolescents agree that working has made the students more independent of their families, but the parents in our study consider this a good thing (Phillips & Sandstrom, 1990). Acquiring independence from parents is a normal developmental task in adolescence. Indeed, historical records suggest that productive roles have long been associated with this process.

In summary, investigators have examined different facets of adolescent work (employment status, intensity, and quality) and different health-relevant outcomes, used varying methodological techniques and analytic procedures, and attributed differential importance to null findings. The findings obtained thus far in the YDS, taken in tandem with our review of other studies of the consequences of adolescent work, lead us to believe that it is the quality, social meaning, and context of adolescent work that are most important, not whether a student is employed or not nor even whether a small or large number of hours are committed to work activity each day. That is, consistent with the extensive literature on work experience in adulthood (Mortimer & Lorence, 1995), what happens on the job coupled with the meaning and significance of that work experience for both the self and significant others are the things that matter for adolescent health and positive developmental outcomes. Consistent with this pattern, policymakers, employers, and educators might profitably give greater attention to the quality of adolescent jobs instead of focusing so exclusively, as has been typical up to the present, on work-hour restrictions.

Overview of this Book

Whereas our prior studies have focused on the adolescent and on outcomes that are mostly conceptualized and measured at the individual level, the primary focus of this book is on the changing linkages of work and family life in adolescence. Implied throughout is a developmental concept of the adolescent career: There are typical trajectories of adolescent work in both family and occupational contexts that change through historical time and vary across community settings. Reflecting these are temporal changes in parent-child relationships and individual psychological and behavioral outcomes. Whereas the focus is on adolescent work, we acknowledge that parents also participate in the labor force, and this involvement has important repercussions in the family setting, particularly with respect to adolescent vocational development. Finally, we examine the implications of adolescent attitudes with respect to future work and family life, as well as their emerging sense of competence, for their early attainments beyond high school and their capacity to fulfill their ambitions.

In Chapter 2, Pamela J. Aronson and her colleagues take a broad intergenerational and historical view, describing trends in adolescent employment. The authors investigate claims that the work experiences of young people have deteriorated over historical time. They also examines differences between parents and children in time allocated to household work, in paid work outside the home, and in evaluations of the costs and benefits of paid jobs. Discrepancies between parental comparisons of their own and their children's allocation of time to household chores and the actual time that is reported by each generation in these tasks are particularly interesting.

Despite the characterization of youths as individualistic, they find that contemporary adolescents are contributing a good deal of their time to household labor, a small minority give at least part of their earnings to their parents, and many young people contribute to their household budgets by using their earnings to pay for things for which parents would otherwise be held responsible.

Aronson et al. find definite trends in work experiences that differentiate two parental cohorts (baby boom and pre-baby boom), and continue into the adolescent generation. There is also pervasive gender segregation at work; in fact, differences in the adolescent jobs occupied by each gender were generally greater than the differences between parental cohorts or between generations. Overwhelmingly positive evaluations of earlier work experiences are reported across cohorts, genders, and generations. Parents describe a wide range of different kinds of benefits of youthwork, including the development of responsibility, the "work ethic," money-management skills, social skills, friendship, confidence, and self-esteem. Helping to define work preferences, job-related skills, and other preparation for adult careers were also mentioned. Very few parents indicated any problems or long-term disadvantages associated with adolescent jobs.

The next two chapters extend the investigation of intergenerational helping behavior by examining, in Chapter 3, the developmental impacts of helpfulness for the emergence of a sense of competence in the adolescent child generation and, in Chapter 4, the implications of youth employment and the uses of earnings for intergenerational relationships.

Using the concept of "possible selves," Kathleen T. Call (Chapter 3) draws on longitudinal data covering the four high school years to assess the causal antecedents and consequences of helping—in both the family and the workplace—for the development of competence. Most adolescents are actively involved in anticipation of, and planning for, their future adult family and work roles. According to Call, adolescents may be motivated to perform helping behaviors in the family and work to actualize their future selves as heads of their own households, as parents, and as future workers. From this perspective, one might expect that helping would further a sense of competence. The helpful character of chores and caring tasks is accentuated by their link to indicators of family need, such as family size and household income. Employed students may become more sensitive to such need as they move through high school.

What we learn from Call's analysis is how important the context of household work is for developmental growth, paralleling our prior analyses that highlighted the context and meaning of paid work. She finds evidence that when intergenerational helping occurs in family contexts that promote both independence and a sense of being needed, and involve an anticipatory realization of adultlike possible selves, adolescents' sense of competence is enhanced.

Paralleling Aronson et al.'s analysis of gender segregation in paid work in both parent and child generations, Call provides further evidence of major gender differences in helping behavior, particularly in the last year of high school. Girls are more likely than boys to report helping experiences in both family and paid work environments.

In Chapter 4, Michael J. Shanahan and his colleagues examine differences in the implications of adolescent earnings for family relationships within the contexts of rural and urban ecologies. They note that earnings from paid work confer an adultlike status by providing both material and psychological autonomy and signifying the capacity to enact adult roles in the cooperative context of the workplace. As such, employment and earnings might be expected to enhance parent-adolescent relationships. Moreover, those adolescents who spend their earnings in nonleisure ways and particularly in ways that may enhance the family collectivity (e.g., giving earnings to parents, saving for education or other long-term goals, and using the money for school expenses) might be especially appreciated by their parents and admired for their maturity and growing independence. Shanahan et al. investigate whether these phenomena differ in urban and rural settings, given the greater familism in the rural context and greater emphasis on individualism in urban settings.

Comparing data from the YDS and the comparable Iowa Youth and Families Project, which studied intact families in economically depressed areas of rural Iowa, Shanahan et al. report that adolescents of the same age (9th and 10th grades) are more frequently employed in the rural setting, have greater earnings, and use their earnings much more for nonleisure (i.e., more adultlike) purposes. Not surprising, especially in view of their greater collective uses of earnings, rural youths' relationships with their parents become more positive and adultlike, with greater sharing of advice and more positive emotional ties, when they have more earnings. This pattern was not observed in the urban setting.

This comparison of urban and rural settings again underscores the importance of context, which determines the meanings surrounding adolescent paid work and its implications for family relations. Not only does the experience of employment—the stressors, rewards, and experiences of work—influence the kinds of impacts it will have on adolescent development as well as family relationships (Mortimer & Shanahan, 1994), but the features of the community itself condition the meaning of adolescent work and its implications for family relationships and the family economy.

In Chapter 5, Kathleen Call considers the interrelations of work and family in adolescence in another way. She builds on Roberta Simmons's (in press) and others' conception of an arena of comfort—a context of unconditional acceptance wherein the person does not have to worry about self-presentation, unpredictability in others' responses, or stress.

Call investigates whether adolescent work functions as such a comfort arena when the adolescent experiences strains in the family. She observes that working in adolescence is concordant with life-stage specific needs for autonomy; the more childlike role within the family setting may at this time be a source of strain, especially if parents resist adolescents' emergent strivings for independence. As such, the paid work role may be more congruent with the adolescent's desired "possible self" as adult (see Chapter 3). Given these considerations, she suggests that the work domain may indeed act as an arena of comfort for adolescents when experiencing family stressors.

She finds that indicators of "comfortable" experiences and relationships in the work setting do, in fact, moderate otherwise deleterious effects of strain in parent-child relationships on mental health and adjustment. For example, when adolescents have good relationships with their supervisors, such strain has no significant effects on indices of well-being, self-esteem, and mastery. However, adolescents who lack this "arena of comfort" at work and experience such strains with their parents suffer diminished self-esteem, mastery, and well-being. The character of relationships with friends at work and the presence or absence of work stressors similarly moderate the effects of potentially stressful changes in the family setting.

It is particularly important, given prominent concerns about whether working may diminish adolescents' involvement with, and the quality of this relationship with, parents, to find that working may actually, when conditions are favorable, help children to cope when family life is disrupted. If, as appears to be the case, having an arena of comfort at work strengthens adolescents' resilience, protecting their sense of self-esteem, well-being, and mastery that would otherwise be threatened, they may be better able to deal with further problems in their lives—in both family and other settings.

Chapter 6 examines another facet of the intergenerational linkages of work and family by focusing on the transfer of occupational values from parents to children. Whereas most sociological studies of occupational attainment focus on significant others' influence in the development of educational and occupational aspirations, Seongryeol Ryu and Jeylan T. Mortimer focus on values about the perceived importance of varying occupational rewards. What do adolescents look for when thinking about desirable jobs for the future? Do they mainly want to obtain extrinsic rewards—that is, opportunities to make a lot of money, achieve social status, advance in the hierarchies of work, and obtain financial security? Or do they seek intrinsic rewards—opportunities to fulfill their interests and abilities at work, assume responsibility, and attain autonomy?

Ryu and Mortimer report that fathers who are more self-directed in their work have stronger intrinsic values, and that these values are transferred to their sons through close and supportive father-son relationships. That is, paternal support was found to have different effects on sons' intrinsic values, depending on the character of the father's occupation. This finding highlights the importance of family dynamics as conduits of values. As such, they may have significant implications for understanding intergenerational patterns of occupational choice and mobility.

In Chapter 7, Ellen Efron Pimentel examines other dimensions of adolescents' orientations toward the future, specifically, their aspirations and goals with respect to future educational, work, and family roles. Some have proposed that because of the "destandardization" and consequent unpredictability of the early life course, adolescents no longer can look forward to clearly defined pathways or sequences of education, work, marriage, and childbearing. Rapid advances in technology yield ever-changing occupational opportunities that require different kinds of educational preparation. Traditional family structure is also in a state of change and dissolution.

In modern postindustrial societies, young people increasingly carve out their own "individualized" life courses, moving back and forth between involvements in education, work, and family and combining them in different ways. Because rapid social change and unexpected circumstances may make the best laid plans go awry, adolescents may invest less energy in planning for their futures, as new possibilities can always arise. In this context, the power of expectations, aspirations, and goals to predict subsequent life circumstances may be called into question. However, adolescents' future orientations and planfulness may still assume an important role in educational, work, or family outcomes by creating early constraints on future trajectories. That is, early choices may eliminate some future options, thus restricting realistic chances for change during the subsequent life course.

Moreover, future orientations and planning may assume even greater importance if structured career sequences no longer carry individuals through well-defined trajectories with respect to education, work, or family once they arrive at various career portals or "entry-level" positions. Pimentel investigates the extent to which adolescent expectations and aspirations, with respect to leaving home, marriage, fertility, and education, predict behaviors upon leaving high school, once resources deriving from more or less advantaged family backgrounds are taken into account.

Using YDS data from Wave 4, when most students were seniors in high school, and Waves 5 and 6, two years beyond high school, Pimentel finds that earlier aspirations and plans do indeed have important predictive capacity. Despite claims to the contrary arising from the "destandardized life course" thesis, adolescents in the YDS are generally following through on their residential, family, and educational plans, though not all are successful in realizing early ambitions. The question then arises, what factors distinguish those who are able to fulfill early aspirations from those who are not? Pimentel identifies the sense of efficacy as one such important factor.

In Chapter 8, we look to the future and, in light of the findings presented in this book, identify some perplexing questions that merit researchers' attention.

2

Generational Differences in Early
Work Experiences and Evaluations

PAMELA J. ARONSON

JEYLAN T. MORTIMER

CAROL ZIERMAN

MICHAEL HACKER

Youthwork is certainly not a new phenomenon, as many young people in previous generations had paid jobs before completing high school. We believe that experiences of prior generations are useful in assessing the values of contemporary youthwork. In reflecting on their own past experiences, do parents perceive benefits or costs of their early jobs? Even if the character of adolescent work has changed dramatically, there may still be generic lessons to be learned from virtually all kinds of paid work, irrespective of the tasks involved. For example, learning about responsibility and time and money management are likely salient issues across generations.

However, the early work experiences of previous generations of Americans have been subject to almost no empirical scrutiny. Little is known about how contemporary parents look back on the work they performed when they themselves were adolescents or about whether perceptions of adolescent work experience differ between generations. The purpose of this chapter is to assess generational differences in early work experiences and in perceptions of the benefits and costs of these experiences.

Given changes in the economy and the character of the youth labor market, we expect to find historical variations in typical adolescent jobs and, as a result, differences in the actual experiences associated with youthwork. But despite this diversity, we think there is more reason to expect generational continuity than discontinuity in the evaluation of youth employment experience. Contemporary adolescents generally evaluate their own jobs quite favorably (Mortimer et al., 1994). Moreover, contemporary parents hold quite positive attitudes about their own adolescent children's jobs (Phillips & Sandstrom, 1990). It would be consistent with parents' positive stance to find that they have favorable retrospective assessments of their own past work experience, for if they felt that the jobs they held as adolescents were detrimental, they would probably want to protect their own children from similar harm. Therefore, we expect to find positive retrospective assessments from parents of the jobs they held when they were teenagers that parallel their sanguine orientations toward their children's jobs as well as the adolescent children's positive perceptions of their own contemporaneous work experience.

Because work experience typically begins in the family setting, we begin by considering changing adolescent contributions to the family economy. Specifically, we examine generational differences in adolescents' contributions to household family work. We also compare monetary contributions. Next, we assess generational differences in adolescent workforce participation. The variance in parents' ages allows us to consider the implications of historical change in parents' work experiences by comparing parental birth cohorts. We assess differences by generation and by parental cohort in the occupations of adolescent workers and also variation by gender. Last, we consider generational differences in the perceived benefits and costs of adolescent work experience.

In this chapter, we use data collected in the first, third, and fourth waves of the Youth Development Study (YDS). In Wave 4 (when the youths were mostly 17 and 18 years old), 1,130 parents (690 mothers and 440 fathers) participated in the study by completing and returning mailed questionnaires. For 79.1% of the children, data were obtained from at least one parent. These included natural parents, adoptive parents, stepparents, or other adult guardians living with the child at the time of the data collection.

In this research, we compare parents and children in an aggregate manner, which indicates general changes over time. This strategy may obscure similarities in adolescent work experiences within family experiences and relationships may be important for the intergenerational transfer of occupational preferences and values. The influence of family processes on children's preferences regarding work in adulthood is examined by Ryu and Mortimer in Chapter 6 of this volume.

Changing Adolescent Participation in the Family Economy

Work experience usually begins in the family, where young people first learn about work by doing chores and caring for other family members such as younger siblings or, less frequently, elderly grandparents. Later on, adolescents typically take on "informal jobs" outside their own families but still within the context of private households, often those of relatives, neighbors, or family friends (e.g., baby-sitting and yardwork). Subsequently, they acquire jobs in other, more formal nonhousehold settings (Goodnow, 1988). But because housework constitutes the initial experience of work for most youth, we begin by examining household responsibility.

Although the majority of American children perform some household tasks (Blair, 1992b), the amount and type of household work varies according to family size and composition (Goodnow, 1988; Weiss, 1979; White & Brinkerhoff, 1981a), maternal employment status (Goodnow, 1988; Peters & Haldeman, 1987; Weiss, 1979), the division of labor between adult members of the household (Goldscheider & Waite, 1989), and the sex and age of the child (Duckett, Raffaelli, & Richards, 1989; White & Brinkerhoff, 1981a; Zill & Peterson, 1982).

Social scientists also find evidence of historical variability in children's participation in household work. Zelizer (1985) notes that children's contributions to the family economy are linked to historical changes in the activities and conceptions of childhood. During the 18th century, children were valued for their economic contribution to the family, as they took on considerable work responsibilities on farms, in small business enterprises, and within the household itself. They contributed most, if not all, of their earnings to the family when they worked outside their homes. By the mid-19th century, however, the middle class became concerned with children's education, as educational attainment increasingly determined a child's future worth in the marketplace.

Working-class families lagged behind this trend. Up until the late 19th-century, they continued to depend on their children's financial and household chore contributions. However, with the enactment of child labor laws and compulsory education, their economic dependence on their children likewise decreased.

Zelizer (1985) argues that the value of children became redefined largely because of these institutional changes in the family and the economy. Rather than being primarily viewed as useful labor sources by their parents, between the 1870s and the 1930s children were increasingly "sentimentalized." Whereas children in the past were considered "economically useful," they came to be seen as "emotionally priceless." Zelizer argues that this conceptual change, stemming from altered social conditions, had the effect of further diminishing children's participation in household work.

More recent studies indicate that children are continuing to perform less and less household work (Boocock, 1976; Campbell, 1969). However, increases in divorce during the past several decades, which have generated rising numbers of single-parent families, make adolescent helpfulness in the household all the more necessary (Weiss, 1979). Moreover, poverty, which is concentrated in single-parent, female-headed families, increases family economic need for the adolescent's earnings contributions.

Comparing generations, Thrall (1978) found a lack of consensus among parents about whether today's children actually help more or less around the house than they themselves did. The parents in Thrall's study saw the assignment of chores to children important for two main reasons: to acquire a feeling of being part of the family and as training for when they grow up. However, some families think that their children have more important things to do than chores. When chores were assigned, the sex of the child was an important factor in the types of tasks performed, with traditional gender stereotyping prevalent.

Data from the YDS enable us to compare contemporary adolescents' household responsibility with that of their parents when they themselves were adolescents. The parents of the senior student participants were asked about the household chores they performed when they were teenagers. However, we do not compare that information with data obtained from their children when they were seniors in high school, for 7.4% of the fathers and 6.2% of the mothers did not graduate from high school. These lesser educated parents would likely have been in the full-time labor force (or in the military) by the time they reached the same age (17-18) as the children who were, at the time of the parent survey administration, high school seniors. We use adolescent 11th-grade data for purposes of comparison to better approximate the age period that the parents were likely to reference when thinking about themselves as teenagers.

Adolescents in the YDS were involved in many aspects of household work. Substantial numbers reported cleaning their rooms, cleaning other parts of the house, doing the laundry, washing dishes, and cooking. Table 2.1 reports the distribution of chores and the amount of time spent performing each chore, by gender, for youths in Grade 11. Although both boys and girls report participating in many areas of household work, there is much gender stereotyping in the types of task they perform. For example, girls more often than boys reported washing dishes (75% vs. 53%) and doing the laundry (79% vs. 57%), whereas boys more frequently than girls reported doing yardwork (64% vs. 22%) and taking out the trash (70% vs. 37%). Of those adolescents who performed particular tasks, both genders were quite similar in the number of hours they spent on those tasks, except with respect to caring for younger children. Girls with responsibility for younger siblings averaged almost 14 hours per week caring for them, whereas the boys, on average, spent only 6 hours per week on this task. This pattern suggests that when boys and girls do the same tasks, they generally spend similar amounts of time on them, although there is considerable difference in the type of task performed.

Our findings with respect to intergenerational differences should be viewed with caution, for the questions that the parents and adolescent children responded to were not identical. Parents were asked

TABLE 2.1 Household Work

Task	% Who Report Doing Task		Average Hours Spent Per Week for Those Who Perform Task	
	Girls	Boys	Girls	Boys
Cleaning my room	93.1	84.5	1.6	1.2
Cleaning the house	86.8	74.2	2.2	1.4
Laundry	78.7	56.7	2.9	2.0
Doing the dishes	75.1	53.4	2.0	1.4
Cooking	68.0	62.3	2.6	1.8
Taking care of pets	49.8	53.1	4.0	3.8
Shopping for food	42.3	31.8	1.8	1.3
Setting the table	39.1	35.0	.7	.5
Taking out the trash	37.4	69.7	.6	.6
Yardwork	22.3	63.9	1.2	1.8
Caring for younger children	37.5	23.1	13.8	6.0
Caring for elderly relative	4.7	6.3	4.6	3.1
Other tasks	40.5	44.2	3.8	5.5
n	506	446		

to give overall estimates of the amount of time spent per week on housework when they were teenagers, whereas their children were asked how much time they spent on specific duties. Some of these duties could be carried out simultaneously, such as washing dishes while baby-sitting. Thus, summing the hours spent performing various household chores probably yields an overestimate of the actual time spent.

Nonetheless, there appears to be some discrepancy between perceived generational differences in household work, as reported by the parents, and actual generational differences. The adolescents, on average, report *greater* amounts of time spent on household tasks than their parents did when they were about the same age (see Table 2.2). Considered in the aggregate, mothers report a mean of almost 10 hours per week spent in household chores when they were teenagers; their 11th-grade daughters report doing chores, on average, 14 hours per week. Likewise, fathers spent a mean of 7 hours in household chores per week; the corresponding figure for sons (in Grade 11) is

TABLE 2.2 Household Responsibility

Type of Work	Mean Hours of Household Work			
	Mothers	Daughters	Fathers	Sons
Chore hours				
Mean	9.9	14.2	7.3	12.2
Median	7.0	9.8	5.0	7.6
Care hours				
Mean	—	5.4	—	1.7
Median	—	0.0	—	0.0
n	652	505	419	432

12 hours. Also, daughters spend 5 hours per week, on average, taking care of others; sons report spending almost 2 hours caring for others (this question was not asked of the parents). (Note: These means take into account those who do not do the task and are therefore lower than the figures, tallied for each type of chore separately, reported in Table 2.1.) However, the majority of both mothers and fathers perceive their children as having less household responsibility than they had when they were adolescents. Among the mothers, 75% thought they had more household responsibility than their children, 19% indicated the same level of responsibility across generations, and only 6% said they had less responsibility. (The corresponding figures for fathers were 55%, 30%, and 15%.) Of course, chores are a frequent source of disagreement between parents and adolescents. Under these circumstances, it might be expected that adolescents (and parents, retrospectively) may overestimate the amount of chores they perform, whereas parents may underestimate their childrens' chore contributions to the household.

Adolescent children not only contribute to the family through household work, but those who are employed may also give some or all of their earnings to their parents. The YDS parents reported giving money to their own parents at higher rates than their children reported turning over to them. About a third of both mothers and fathers (30% of the mothers and 33% of the fathers) contributed in this way. Still, significant numbers of the adolescent children also did this—almost

12% of the employed daughters and 16% of the employed sons gave at least some of their earnings to their families when in the 11th grade.

Many YDS adolescents contributed to the family budget indirectly by using their earnings to purchase things that otherwise would have to be provided by the parents. When adolescents spend their earnings on necessities, such as food, clothing, or school expenses, and when they save their earnings for the future (Mortimer, Dennehy, & Lee, 1991), they relieve limited household budgets. Substantial proportions of the adolescent workers contribute to the family economy indirectly by using their earnings in such ways (Mortimer et al., 1991). For example, 46% of employed boys and 41% of employed girls used their earnings to purchase food (Mortimer et al., 1991). Nearly two thirds of the boys and three quarters of the girls used their earnings to buy clothing, and nearly 40% of both genders saved their earnings for future education (Mortimer et al., 1991). Aside from car expenses (with boys spending more of their earnings on their cars than girls), both genders spend their earnings in similar ways (Mortimer et al., 1991). Thus, most contemporary adolescents contribute to the family economy both directly through housework and indirectly by using their earnings to purchase what their parents otherwise would have to buy.

In summary, despite parents' perception that their children do less housework than they did when they themselves were adolescents, these data suggest that adolescents may actually be doing more housework than their parents did at a comparable age. Although children contribute financially to their families to a lesser extent than their parents did as adolescents, they do contribute to the family economy through their chores, by caring for other family members, and by using their savings in ways that contribute to the household budgets.

Workforce Participation

Intergenerational comparisons of adolescent experiences in the paid workforce must be particularly sensitive to historical differences across cohorts. The size of birth cohorts can influence socioeconomic attainment throughout the life course, including job prospects, types of employment, and the work experience itself (Kennedy, 1989). The transition to work also varies in response to economic conditions and social norms. Modell (1989) shows how youths' work experience and work attitudes are affected by the sociohistorical circumstances particular to each birth cohort as it enters the labor force. For example, adolescents born during World War II (Pre-Baby Boom, hereafter Pre-Boom) were greatly sought after by employers as a result of the labor shortage caused by the war and the relatively small size of this cohort. Subsequently, the larger Baby Boom (hereafter Boom) cohort found itself in much less demand:

> By the late 1960's, the national economy was in the throes of gnawing inflation, and the first children of the much enlarged postwar birth cohorts were coming of age, no longer confronting rapidly or surely growing material resources. (Modell, 1989, p. 262)

Besides cohort, gender may also be expected to influence early work experiences. Occupational sex segregation has affected the work experiences of both parents and children as well as earlier generations. Men and women have traditionally held different types of employment in our society,[1] and historical change in the rate of female employment does not necessarily alter adult occupational segregation by gender. As Gross (1971) points out, gender segregation was consistently high between 1900 and 1960, despite the rapid movement of women into the workforce during the postwar period. Two thirds of women (or men) would have had to change occupations in order for the occupational distributions to be equal.

Reskin (1993) shows that sex segregation in the workforce has decreased in recent years, although it still remains high. The first significant decline occurred in 1980, when the index of occupational segregation decreased from two thirds to 59.8. By 1990, the sex segregation index was 57—57% of men (or women) would have to change occupations for the gender distributions to be equal. However, this figure may underestimate the real extent of gender segregation because the locus of segregation has shifted from occupations to jobs. Reskin argues that there are still strong tendencies for men and women to enter sex-typical jobs; women are more likely to be part-time, temporary, or contract workers. What is not known, however, is how gender occupational segregation presents itself in adolescent employ-

ment and the degree to which such segregation has changed histori-
cally and generationally.

Historical change in the character of adolescent work is illustrated
by decennial census reports of the national distributions of employed
youth 16 and 17 years old, by industry (see Table 2.3). Whereas some
industries remained relatively stable (e.g., mining, construction, trans-
portation, wholesale trade, entertainment services, and public administration), others exhibited marked shifts with respect to their shares
of employed youths.

Comparisons across gender and year indicate the persistence of sex
typing along with historical shifts in employment distributions. In
1940, over 60% of males but less than 20% of females were employed
in agriculture. By 1980, these figures had decreased to 7% and almost
2%, respectively. In 1960, almost 22% of the males but only 9% of
the females reported employment in manufacturing industries; by
1980, only 10% of employed males and almost 6% of employed
females were so engaged. In 1940, private household employment was
the mode for 42% of young women but almost nonexistent for young
men—a minuscule 1%. In 1980, these figures declined to 3% and less
than 1%, respectively.

Retail trade was the primary industry that increased its share of
youth employment during this period, with especially large numbers
of both genders employed in eating and drinking establishments. In
1940, less than 15% of male and female adolescents worked in retail
trade. By 1960, more than one third of male and female adolescents
were employed in this industry. By 1980, these numbers increased to
54% of males and 59% of females. Other service industries also
showed growth in proportions of adolescent workers between 1960
and 1970 and then slight decline by 1980.

These shifts in youth employment—away from manufacturing and
farming toward retail sales and service sector jobs—reflect more
general economic trends, as overall employment in service-producing
industries (including retail and other trade) grew from 58% of all
domestic employment in 1948 (U.S. Bureau of Labor Statistics, 1968)
to 74% in 1984 (U.S. Bureau of Labor Statistics, 1985). As a result of
these structural changes in the jobs available during the historical
period under examination, we expect to find differences in the types
of work in which parents, as adolescents, and their adolescent children

TABLE 2.3 Employed Youths (16-17 years old),[a] by Industry: 1940-1980[b]

Industry	1940[c]		1950		1960		1970		1980	
	Male	Female	Male	Female	Male	Female	Male	Female	Male	Female
Agriculture	61.1	18.2	41.0	9.4	20.9	4.5	8.4	1.7	6.9	1.7
Mining	.5	0.0	.5	0.0	.2	0.0	.2	0.0	.3	.1
Construction	2.0	.1	3.8	.3	3.1	.4	3.3	.4	4.1	.5
Manufacturing	12.2	15.9	15.7	14.0	21.4	8.6	12.9	6.9	10.3	5.6
Transportation	2.1	.8	2.5	2.2	1.7	1.9	2.2	2.0	1.7	.8
Wholesale trade	1.0	.8	1.8	1.4	1.9	1.2	2.6	1.4	2.8	1.4
Retail trade[d]	13.9	12.5	22.7	37.7	34.5	37.0	50.5	49.2	54.0	59.1
Gas stations	(1.4)	(.1)	(2.5)	(.1)	(4.4)	(.2)	(7.0)	(.3)	(4.0)	(.4)
Eating and drinking	(1.5)	(4.7)	(2.6)	(9.2)	(4.5)	(10.2)	(13.3)	(17.4)	(23.9)	(31.1)
Other	(11.0)	(7.7)	(17.6)	(28.4)	(25.6)	(26.6)	(30.2)	(31.5)	(26.1)	(27.6)
Entertainment	2.0	1.0	4.5	3.5	3.7	2.6	3.1	2.7	3.5	3.0
Private household	1.0	42.2	1.1	16.3	3.2	23.9	1.0	6.6	.5	3.0
Services (other)	3.9	8.2	6.1	14.7	9.1	19.4	14.8	27.7	14.5	22.7
Public administration	.3	.2	.4	.5	.4	.5	1.1	1.5	1.4	2.0
Total	100.0	100.0	100.0	100.0	100.0	100.0	100.0	100.0	100.0	100.0

SOURCES: U.S. Department of Commerce, Bureau of the Census (1940, 1950, 1960, 1970, 1980).
a. The 1960 Census data represent youths aged 14 through 17.
b. Industry figures for 1990 were not available.
c. In census years 1940, 1950, and 1960, many workers did not report an industry to the Census: in 1940, 2.6% of the males and 3.2% of the females; in 1950, 3.1% and 3.8%, respectively; and in 1960, 7.2% and 8.5%, respectively. The percentages are adjusted to exclude these nonreporters.
d. Gas service stations, eating and drinking places, and "other" are categories within the retail trade industry. Numbers in parentheses represent the percentage of youths employed in these types of retail trade.

35

were employed. Specifically, we anticipate a decrease in the number of workers employed in farming and skilled trades and an increase in those employed in retail trade—primarily restaurant and food establishments and sales jobs.

It should be noted, however, that census figures may not be entirely germane to our intergenerational comparisons, as the census data include youths who are enrolled in high school and those who are not. What is not clear from the census data is the distribution of school-enrolled adolescents employed in different industries. (Comparable data for employed in-school youths, by industry, are not available for these years.) Furthermore, adolescents are frequently employed in informal work settings (in private households), and this type of employment may be underreported in household surveys.

In our analysis of the YDS parent data, we follow the model set by Rossi (1989), who showed how cross-sectional surveys can be used to address questions relating to cohort variability and intergenerational differences in life course experience. Comparing two or more birth cohorts allows for the assessment of the influence of social change (Elder & O'Rand, 1995) and illuminates the interplay between macro-social (sociohistorical and structural) change and individual behavior. Comparing particular birth cohorts of parents suggests the manner in which historical conditions could produce variation in youths' work experience. That is, differences in parental age reflect not only the passage of time but also the different economic conditions under which each made the transition to work.

Obviously, because the children in the YDS were selected from lists of enrolled ninth graders, they are all about the same age. However, the parents gave birth to these children at different ages. They may have begun their childbearing, and spaced their children, differently, so the children in the YDS panel have different birth order in their families (e.g., some are first, some last born). Thus, the parents (and guardians) are found to have a wide age range—from 35 to 71 years of age in 1991. We divide our sample of parents in such a manner as to differentiate the two distinct historical periods in which they experienced adolescence. The majority of the parents (90% of mothers, and 87% of fathers) are members of either the Pre-Boom (born between 1937 and 1945) or the Boom (born between 1946 and 1955) cohorts.

As described by Modell (1989), the life situations, economic opportunities, and social climate in which these two groups experienced adolescence were very different. The Pre-Boom parents were born before or during World War II and experienced adolescence (14 to 18 years of age) during the 1950s and early 1960s. The Boom cohort, born after World War II, experienced adolescence during the 1960s and early 1970s. YDS fathers are fairly evenly divided between the two cohorts: 48.3% in the Pre-Boom and 51.7% in the Boom. However, more mothers (65.1%) fall into the Boom than the Pre-Boom cohort (34.9%). This reflects what Nett (1988) calls the "marriage gradient"; women tend to marry men 3 to 5 years older than themselves (Modell, 1989).

We examined differences between these two parental birth cohorts in the nature of their early work experiences. Parents were asked about their first jobs and to tell us about what may be considered their typical adolescent jobs, the longest jobs which they held during adolescence. Children were asked about their first jobs and the jobs they held at the time of each survey administration. Parents' and children's first jobs are directly comparable.[2] We also compared the jobs reported by the adolescents in the 11th grade to the parents' longest jobs. In the 11th grade, most adolescents in the child generation had work experience and were employed in formal settings. Moreover, comparing parents' longest jobs held as adolescents and children's 12th-grade jobs might be somewhat misleading because, as indicated earlier, at the same age as their senior-year children, more of the parents would have already left school and been a part of the full-time labor force.

With respect to the number of hours worked per week in longest (for parents) and 11th-grade (for the adolescents) jobs, there appears to be some intergenerational decline. When asked to estimate the number of hours worked per week in their adolescent jobs, the mothers reported a mean of 21 hours and the fathers 26 hours. In 11th grade, the girls reported working, on average, 19 hours per week and the boys 22 hours.

Using the *1980 Census of Population: Alphabetical Index of Industries and Occupations* (U.S. Bureau of the Census, 1982a), the parents' first and longest jobs and the adolescents' 11th-grade jobs were coded using the 3-digit occupational classification system. The jobs were then grouped into nine primary categories: informal work, sales, restaurant/

food preparation, laborers, teachers/caring occupations (e.g., day care work), semiskilled, clerical, farmer, and other. Because the sample consists of students within a large metropolitan area, the farmer category was excluded from the children's job classification. With these data, we assess intergenerational change. Gender differences are given special attention; we compare the degree of sex segregation between the two parental cohorts and the children.

MOTHERS', FATHERS', AND CHILDREN'S WORK IN ADOLESCENCE

In Table 2.4 we see considerable gender stereotyping along with intergenerational differences. In their first jobs, girls, like their mothers, are overly represented in informal work (74%), unlike boys, who, similar to their fathers, are less so (32%). Like their fathers, many of the boys report first jobs in sales (23%; most of them are paper boys) and as laborers (19%). In their later jobs, mothers and daughters again show similar distributions, with high concentrations in informal work, sales, and the restaurant and food industry (see Table 2.5). Boys, like their fathers, are likely to be found in sales and as laborers. However, they greatly differed from their fathers in increased employment in the restaurant and food industry.

Table 2.4 illustrates a shift in the type of first jobs held by mothers in the two succeeding birth cohorts. Reflecting the growth in the restaurant industry, there is a definitive trend in restaurant/food work: 4% of Pre-Boom and 10% of Boom mothers had their first jobs in this sector. The percentage of mothers employed in clerical work decreased across cohorts, with almost 10% of Pre-Boom and 6% of Boom mothers employed in this field. There was also a decrease in sales work over time, with 12% of the Pre-Boom and 6% of the Boom mothers in this area.

The trend in succeeding maternal birth cohorts, are magnified in comparisons between the mothers and daughters. Fully 74% of the daughters engaged in informal work in their first jobs. Daughters are also more likely than both cohorts of mothers to be working in the restaurant/food industry in their first jobs, with 13% so employed. Additionally, there is a continuing decrease in initial employment in clerical work (only 1% of daughters). The percentage of daughters

TABLE 2.4   Percentage Distributions of First Jobs of Parents and Children

	Females			Males		
Type of Job	Pre-Boom Mothers	Baby Boom Mothers	Daughters	Pre-Boom Fathers	Baby Boom Fathers	Sons
Informal work	62.4	65.5	73.8	24.2	36.5	32.4
Sales	12.4	6.2	7.4	19.8	16.9	23.3
Restaurant/foods	4.3	10.4	12.6	5.5	10.6	18.3
Laborers	2.9	2.6	2.3	17.6	12.2	18.6
Teachers/caring	5.7	5.4	2.1	5.5	4.2	3.1
Semiskilled	1.4	1.8	0.4	4.9	5.3	2.9
Clerical	9.5	6.0	1.1	4.4	4.8	0.4
Farmer	1.4	1.0	—	17.6	8.5	—
Other	0.0	1.0	0.2	0.5	1.0	0.9
Total	100.0	100.0	100.0	100.0	100.0	100.0
n	210	386	515	182	189	447

TABLE 2.5   Percentage Distributions of Longest Jobs of Parents During
Adolescence and Children's Wave 3 Jobs

	Females			Males		
Type of Job	Pre-Boom Mothers	Baby Boom Mothers	Daughters	Pre-Boom Fathers	Baby Boom Fathers	Sons
Informal work	28.4	18.5	13.9	5.6	7.8	3.1
Sales	24.9	17.5	33.9	13.0	8.9	14.1
Restaurant/foods	18.3	27.1	32.3	8.1	19.4	47.6
Laborers	3.0	3.7	2.6	31.7	30.0	23.8
Teachers/caring	5.3	12.0	9.7	5.6	8.3	3.1
Semiskilled	1.2	3.4	1.3	10.6	9.4	4.0
Clerical	16.0	15.1	5.2	4.3	6.7	0.4
Farmer	2.4	1.2	—	16.1	7.8	—
Other	0.6	1.5	1.3	5.0	1.7	4.0
Total	100.0	100.0	100.0	100.0	100.0	100.0
n	169	325	310	161	180	227

doing sales work in their first jobs is only slightly greater than Boom mothers, with 7% employed in this area.

Not surprisingly, we also find cohort and intergenerational differences in subsequent employment—in mothers' "longest" jobs as teenagers and daughters' jobs held in the 11th grade (see Table 2.5). Whereas the women, across parental cohorts and intergenerationally were increasingly likely to do informal work in their first jobs, the trend was the opposite for later jobs. The percentage of mothers employed in informal work in subsequent jobs decreased across cohorts, with 28% of the Pre-Boom and only 19% of the Boom mothers citing informal work as their longest jobs as adolescents. Daughters' 11th-grade jobs continue this trend, with only 14% in informal work. In contrast, there is a continued increase across cohorts and generations in restaurant and food work. Only 18% of Pre-Boom mothers were employed in restaurant and food work in their longest jobs; this increased to 27% of the Boom mothers and 32% of the daughters (with respect to 11th-grade jobs). There is also a decrease and then subsequent increase in sales employment, with 25% of Pre-Boom mothers, 18% of Boom mothers, and 34% of daughters employed in sales. Generally, these patterns indicate increasing employment in service sector jobs across time.

The two cohorts of fathers also differed in their first jobs (see Table 2.4). There was a substantial increase in informal work, from 24% for the Pre-Boomers to nearly 37% for the Boomers. As projected by the "Job Guide for Young Workers" in 1950 (U.S. Bureau of Employment Security, 1950), our sample also reflects the decrease in farming and skilled labor across generations: Whereas 18% of Pre-Boom fathers were employed in farming in their first jobs, only 9% of the Boom fathers were. The most dramatic increase for males across generations is seen in restaurant and food work, with 6% of Pre-Boom and 11% of Boom fathers employed in this field in their first jobs. This trend continues into the next generation, with 18% of sons' first jobs in restaurant/food work.

Changes in employment trends are similar for fathers' and sons' later jobs as adolescents (see Table 2.5). More males are finding employment in the restaurant and food industry—there was an increase from the Pre-Boom to the Boom fathers, and almost half (48%) of their 11th-grade sons were employed in this area in 1990. The percentage of fathers working as laborers remained fairly constant for the two cohorts—32% of Pre-Boomers and 30% of Boomers. Sons were employed as laborers at a much lower rate (24%), yet this was still a substantial field of employment for sons. As shown in Table 2.5, the trend away from farming and toward the service sector (restaurant/food and sales) is evident in the declining percentage of fathers reporting farming as their longest adolescent job. This category disappears for sons. As indicated, a substantial difference between the two cohorts of fathers with respect to the longest adolescent jobs is again evident.

INDEX OF DISSIMILARITY

The Index of Dissimilarity (Gross, 1971), a measure of the degree of occupational segregation between groups, indicates the percentage of each group's members who would have to change their occupations for the distributions across all occupations to be the same. It is calculated by adding the absolute differences in the percentage of each group located in each occupational category and then dividing the sum by 2. It is typically used to compare gender distributions, but it may also be used for other purposes. As noted earlier in this chapter, in the adult labor force the Index of Dissimilarity between genders was approximately 69% in 1960 and about 57% today (Reskin, 1993). For our purposes, this index was calculated to assess both within-gender differences between parental birth cohorts and generations and gender differences between Pre-Boom mothers and fathers, Boom mothers and fathers, and daughters and sons. It is interesting to note that the indices of dissimilarity tend to be greater for gender segregation (see later Table 2.7) than for historical or generational shifts (reported in Table 2.6), indicating greater differences in occupational distributions between men and women (or adolescent boys and girls) than between parental cohorts (controlling gender) or between same-sex parents and children (with the exception of fathers' and sons' later jobs).

The indices of dissimilarity suggest that historical and generational change has occurred in adolescent jobs, more dramatically for the males in our study. One reason is the large decrease over time in adolescent boys' involvement in farming and the considerable increase in employment in restaurant/food work. Change is most evident when

TABLE 2.6 Historical and Generational Differences in Adolescent Work Experience: Indices of Dissimilarity[a]

	Pre-Boom Fathers and Baby Boom Fathers	Pre-Boom Fathers and Sons	Baby Boom Fathers and Sons	Pre-Boom Mothers and Baby Boom Mothers	Pre-Boom Mothers and Daughters	Baby Boom Mothers and Daughters
First job	18.7	26.0	20.6	10.7	20.0	11.7
Longest job for parents, 11th-grade job for children	18.6	40.6	35.7	19.4	28.2	21.5

a. Indices indicate the percentage of one group that would have to change occupations for the distributions to be the same.

42

TABLE 2.7 Gender Differences in Adolescent Work Experience: Indices of Dissimilarity[a]

	Pre-Baby Boom Mothers and Fathers	Baby Boom Mothers and Fathers	Daughters and Sons
First job	43.5	31.5	42.1
Longest job for parents, 11th-grade job for children	56.6	39.1	42.0

a. Indices indicate the percentage of females (or males) who would have to change occupations for the gender distributions to be the same.

comparing the older, pre-Boom parents and their children. As shown in Table 2.6, in the first jobs held as adolescents, the Index of Dissimilarity is nearly 19 between the Pre-Boom fathers and Boom fathers, indicating that almost 19% of one group would need to change occupations for the distributions to be the same. The dissimilarity indices are greater when Pre-Boom and Boom fathers first jobs are compared with those of their sons: 26 and 21, respectively. In terms of the longest job held as adolescents, the Index of Dissimilarity is again 19 between Pre-Boom and Boom fathers. The indices dramatically increase in comparisons of the fathers and sons: 41 between Pre-Boom fathers and their sons and 36 between Boom fathers and their sons. Overall, the female workers in this study exhibited less pronounced historical and generational differences in both first and longest teenage jobs. Like the males, larger historical and generational differences can be found in the longest jobs held as adolescents.

Indices of gender segregation in employment are shown in Table 2.7. Regarding the first jobs held as adolescents, there is a lessening of occupational segregation by gender across the parental cohorts. The Index of Dissimilarity between Pre-Boom mothers and fathers is equal to almost 44; the corresponding figure for Boom mothers and fathers is 32. This is partially attributable to increasing gender similarity across parental cohorts in the prevalence of informal work, farming, and employment in laborer and clerical jobs. With the next generation's initiation of employment, there is a reversion back to gender segregation, as the Index of Dissimilarity between daughters and sons increases to 42. This increase appears to be most influenced by the heavy concentration of daughters' first jobs in informal work.

Like the first jobs, there is also a decrease in gender segregation across parental cohorts in the longest jobs held as adolescents; the index for the Pre-Boom mothers and fathers is 57, whereas that for the Boom mothers and fathers is only 39. Again, the Index of Dissimilarity drops primarily as a result of the lesser degree of gender segregation in informal and farming work among the Boomers. The extent of gender segregation stabilizes in the next generation at 42 between daughters and sons.

Parental Attitudes Toward Youth Work

We next consider whether parental cohort or early occupational experiences influenced parental attitudes toward their children's jobs. We assessed a wide range of attitudes, including scales representing perceived positive changes in the child as a result of employment, and both positive and negative attitudes toward youth employment in general. The scales were constructed using exploratory factor analysis, with a varimax-rotated solution and principle-axis factoring. Items within each group of questions that did not correlate with the extracted factor were dropped from the scale.[3] Each attitude scale was constructed separately for mothers and fathers (see Appendix A for questions used to construct relevant scales). We also considered other issues (interference with school, school benefits gained through the child's employment, negative change in the child as a result of employment, positive and negative changes in family life, and disagreements with child), but none were found to differ across parental cohorts or early occupational experiences.

Generally, parents had favorable attitudes toward youthwork; the attitudinal measures were quite positively skewed. For example, most parents agreed that adolescent employment in general leads youths to develop good work attitudes and to learn skills not taught in school. The majority of mothers and fathers also approved of their own child's employment (see also Phillips & Sandstrom, 1990). We assessed cohort differences (controlling gender of parent) in parental attitudes toward youthwork in general, as well as toward their own children's employment. We also examined whether there were attitudinal differences between those parents who worked relatively high and low

TABLE 2.8 Baby Boom Mothers' and Fathers' Attitudes Toward Youth Employment

Attitude Scale	Mothers	Fathers	t
Positive change in child			
Mean	26.35	25.02	3.70***
SD	4.01	4.02	
n	367	187	
Positive attitude toward youth employment in general			
Mean	15.26	14.89	2.42**
SD	1.72	1.79	
n	383	195	
Negative attitude toward youth employment in general			
Mean	11.00	10.45	2.65**
SD	2.39	2.29	
n	385	194	

NOTE: SD = standard deviation.
*p < .05; **p < .01; ***p < .001.

numbers of hours in both their first and longest jobs as adolescents. We found no evidence that these cohort or experiential differences contributed toward either positive or negative parental attitudes toward children's employment. We also assessed the relationship between parents' longest job held as adolescents and their scores on the attitude scales (using the nine-category occupational code shown in Tables 2.4 and 2.5). None of these analyses indicated significant differences, indicating that one's prominent occupation during adolescence has little influence on one's attitude toward youthwork.

We also assessed differences between mothers and fathers in their evaluations of both youthwork generally and the effect of their own children's jobs specifically. The general assessments of both were quite positive. Although there were no significant differences between Pre-Boom mothers and fathers, there were some significant differences between Boom mothers and fathers. As seen in Table 2.8, Boom mothers are more likely than fathers to report positive changes in their child as a result of the child's employment. Mothers are also more likely than fathers to report both positive and negative attitudes toward youthwork in general. This suggests that mothers are more aware of both the benefits and costs of youthwork. This may stem from seeing these issues at closer range than fathers, as mothers typically have more contact with the child.

Benefits And Costs
of Workforce Participation

Greenberger and Steinberg (1986) argue that in comparison to previous eras, adolescent work is now unique in terms of the numbers of youths employed and the type of work they perform. Instead of providing continuity in the passage from adolescent to adult employment, they claim that contemporary youthwork, concentrated in sales and service industries, does not prepare adolescents for adult employment. In this respect, student workers today are alleged to be distinctly different from those in the past. Specifically, Greenberger and Steinberg believe that within the past 25 years, adolescent work has declined in educational value, economic significance, and meaningful exposure to intergenerational contact. Consequently, they view contemporary youthwork as less likely to foster salutary developmental outcomes than in the past.

In an attempt to assess these claims, we compare the costs and benefits of youthwork, as seen retrospectively by the two cohorts of parents and as reported concurrently by their children. We used two open-ended items regarding the benefits and problems that parents encountered with respect to their own adolescent employment. We first asked, "In general, taking into account all your jobs, do you think the work you did as a teenager was beneficial for you?" We then asked about whether the work "caused any problems or difficulties for you." Those who responded yes to either question were asked, "In what ways?"

These two questions were coded using the program *Opencode* (Leik, 1986), which enables the creation, editing, and modification of code categories as responses are classified. Responses to the question regarding benefits were coded in 14 categories. Often mentioned were "the job helped me to be responsible," "the job helped me learn how to manage money," and "the job taught me work ethics/values" (see

TABLE 2.9 Perceived Benefits and Problems of Youth Employment for
All Parents and for Respondents to Open-Ended Questions[a]
(percentage describing benefits or problems)

	Mothers		Fathers	
	All	Respondents	All	Respondents
Benefits				
Responsibility	22.2	30.6	21.1	22.2
Money management	19.6	27.0	16.4	17.2
Spending money	17.0	23.4	19.8	20.8
Learned social skills	13.3	18.4	10.2	10.7
Work experience/ skill development	8.4	11.6	10.7	11.2
Confidence	8.3	11.4	6.4	6.7
Work ethics	7.8	10.8	15.5	16.2
Nurturing skills	6.4	8.8	.2	.2
Independence	5.7	7.8	7.7	8.1
Time management	4.9	6.8	5.7	6.0
Met new people	4.5	6.2	4.3	4.5
Learned about life/ shaped future	2.6	3.6	4.6	4.8
Money for college	2.5	3.4	4.3	4.5
Other	5.8	8.0	4.1	4.3
Problems				
Less leisure time	3.6	5.0	2.7	2.9
Less school activities	3.0	4.2	1.8	1.9
Hindered academically	2.2	3.0	3.6	3.8
Fatigue	1.2	1.6	.5	.5
Missed school	.6	.8	2.5	2.6
Too much responsibility	.4	.6	.5	.5
Other	2.8	3.8	3.2	3.3
n	690	500	440	419

a. Open-ended questions concerned with the benefits and problems associated with their own
employment during adolescence. Because parents' responses could be coded in more than one
category, percentages do not sum to 100.

Table 2.9 for a listing of all 14 categories). Seven categories were used
to code responses to the question regarding problems, including "the
job had too much responsibility" and "the job did not leave enough

leisure/social time." Responses to these questions along with those from the adolescent survey questionnaire allow us to compare the perceived benefits and costs of working during adolescence for parents and children.

PERCEIVED BENEFITS AND
COSTS OF EMPLOYMENT FROM
THE PARENTS' PERSPECTIVE

The parents of adolescents in the YDS overwhelmingly responded positively to the questions about the perceived benefits and costs of their own work experience as adolescents. When asked whether their teenage jobs had provided any benefits, 86% of the 596 mothers and nearly 89% of the 409 fathers who responded to this question answered affirmatively. When asked whether they had experienced any problems, 87% of the 594 mothers and 86% of the 411 fathers who responded said that they had not. We examined whether there were differences in the tendency to perceive costs and benefits of adolescent work by parental cohort and parental occupational group (for both first and longest jobs). We found no significant differences. This suggests continuity across cohorts in perceived benefits and costs of youthwork. It also suggests that incumbency of jobs in different categories (as reflected by our simplified code) may not produce different levels of perceived costs and benefits. Parents overwhelmingly, irrespective of cohort and earlier job category, emphasized the benefits of their own adolescent work experience. It could be that there is more variability in the conditions of parental work within these rather crude job categories than across them. However, because we do not have detailed information about the quality of parental youthwork, we cannot address whether differences in early job conditions of the parents would influence these retrospective evaluations.

Parents who answered affirmatively to the questions about benefits and costs were also asked to elaborate on their responses; as noted earlier, their answers were coded into 14 "benefit" and 7 "problem" categories. Percentages indicate the prevalence of response, but because more than one response was possible, they do not sum to 100. Parents' replies certainly emphasized the benefits of their own adolescent work experience. Mentions of perceived problems were relatively rare (see Table 2.9).

For the parents, gaining responsibility was one of the primary benefits of employment as adolescents. Of those who responded to the open-ended questions ("In what ways?"), 31% of the mothers and 22% of the fathers considered the development of responsibility an important benefit of their jobs, as these typical responses indicate:

I learned to be more responsible in many areas of my life.

[It] made me feel more responsible for getting a better-paying job and not calling in sick whenever I felt like it.

It helped me be more responsible for my actions and learn why my parents couldn't always give me what I wanted.

Besides gaining responsibility, another frequently mentioned benefit was learning money management skills, with 27% of the mothers and 17% of the fathers indicating this advantage. For example, two parents said,

I worked many long days and very hard for my pay. I usually spend my money wisely and I'm very conservative.

It made me learn the value of money. I bought all of my own clothes and had a savings account also.

Other parents mentioned learning to appreciate the value of money, learning how to save money, how to budget, and how to make decisions about spending.

Also considered beneficial by more than 20% of the responding parents was the actual spending money earned. Many cited the ability to purchase discretionary items such as clothing or a car or to spend money on activities, including entertainment. Others implied that their incomes may have helped their families. As two mothers put it,

I helped pay my dental, clothing, and entertainment bills.

[I had the] freedom to buy some items I would not necessarily [have] had otherwise.

For some, the use of their own earnings for purchases was a financial necessity. Several mentioned that their families were unable to afford the items they needed, which their adolescent jobs allowed them to purchase. As one mother put it, "It was a very large family of moderate income with none to spare for extra clothing, school lunches and events. I paid for all of my own shoes from the time I was 12."

Thus, the spending money that was acquired from paid work was used to purchase both vital and discretionary items that respondents would not have otherwise been able to obtain. Some mentioned that their adolescent earning capacity increased their financial independence from their parents.

Learning social skills from adolescent work was recollected by 18% of mothers and 11% of fathers. The respondents discussed the greater ease they developed in communicating and interacting with adults. They learned how to get along with coworkers and customers. Some parents mentioned that employment improved their understanding of both the workplace and the adult world more generally. Many respondents also said that learning interpersonal skills helped prepare them for adulthood. As one father put it, "When I was done with school, I didn't have to face the world cold turkey." Other parents said,

All my jobs helped for adulthood to deal with adults and children.

I had a chance to try interacting with the world outside of my family independently.

[A benefit was] learning all the different types of people and their temperaments!

Thus, for some respondents, work was seen as giving opportunities to test new ways of interacting and communicating with others, as providing a basis for understanding what was expected in the adult world, and as helping prepare members of the parental generation for adulthood. Some parents discussed the importance of meeting a wide range of different people or spoke of developing long-lasting friendships. One mother said, "I made friendships that have endured until today (nearly 30 years)."

Besides gaining social skills, some respondents thought they gained valuable work experience. Many felt that their early work experience led to better adolescent jobs, as it helped build a repertoire of skills that enhanced their resumés or job applications. Many also spoke of learning specific skills, such as bookkeeping, office operations, machine use and repair, mechanics, child care, and cooking. Others alluded to other skills they would not have otherwise gained. For example, "I learned skills that are not taught in school." Some parents even found their current job or place of employment through their adolescent work:

I still work for the same company as the director of design.

It was my lifelong profession (55 years).

In short, adolescent work experience and skill development were viewed as quite valuable for adult careers.

For some, work experience helped build confidence and self-esteem. Parents described how work fostered feelings of self-worth and faith in one's own abilities. Some mentioned overcoming shyness and becoming more outgoing and friendly:

It taught me not to be shy, to speak out and up for what I want.

In my relationships with adults (and customers), they treated me more on an equal basis and with more respect.

It taught me I could do anything. It gave me confidence.

It made me able to go out on my own with confidence.

The development of the "work ethic" and work values was also mentioned, including discipline, motivation, commitment to work, respect for others, dependability, accountability, sound work habits, and the ability to follow rules. Many began to realize the necessity of work and the benefits of investing energy in work:

I learned many things at the side of my parents and grandparents—about how good it feels to do a job well, and while they never said it, I know I was important to the farm succeeding.

It made me a better worker. I put everything I had behind all the jobs I had no matter what it was.

[I] developed a sense of pride in the work I did.

It taught the value of a job well done, accountability, respect, and was excellent exercise.

Other less commonly cited benefits were increased independence, learning to manage time, learning about life, providing money for college, and the development of nurturing skills, which was more frequently mentioned by mothers (9%) than by fathers (.2%). Some mothers also mentioned the value of learning how to care for children, anticipating parenthood. As one mother said, "It gave me responsibility and gave me a chance to see what it would be like taking care of my own kids." Some parents emphasized becoming independent. They came to depend more on themselves and to value this increased self-sufficiency. Some stated that their parents also began to view them as more independent people. As one parent put it, "It made me less dependent on my parents and defined me as independent." Some respondents learned how to organize and budget their time as well as how to meet deadlines. In one parent's words, "I learned that purposeful use of time and effort can bring rewards."

Adolescent work was also seen as shaping future plans and goals and as providing a learning experience about life in general. Some parents discussed how their work helped them to realize what they did *not* want to do for the rest of their lives. For others, it helped provide a basis for career decisions. The following responses are illustrative:

I learned to meet expectations, which kinds of work I enjoyed (hated offices, loved the hospital), and the importance of getting a degree after seeing older people stuck in low-wage jobs.

It helped me decide what career field to enter.

Respondents also spoke of the benefit of saving money for college—3% of the mothers and 5% of the fathers. A few parents mentioned that they were able to save enough money to pay for several years of postsecondary schooling.

As indicated by responses to the fixed-response categories, very few parents (13% of the 594 mothers and 14% of the 411 fathers) reported problems with their adolescent work experience (see Table 2.9). One perceived difficulty was the pressure on leisure time. Respondents pointed to the combined pressures of work and school, which sometimes left little time for a social life or the development of friendships. Some parents thought that time spent at work eliminated what they believed should have been "play time":

It robbed me of the normal social activities my peers were involved in.

The 50 hours a week after my ninth-grade year was too much. I should have been allowed to play more.

I had no big problems. I just put work ahead of play, and I think I lost a lot of my teen years by doing this.

Some felt that employment reduced their involvement in school-related extracurricular activities. Sports were frequently mentioned in this context. Others thought that adolescent work had deleterious effects on their academic performance (see Table 2.9). They remembered time constraints resulting from being both a worker and student—there was simply not enough time to complete assigned homework or to study adequately. As three parents put it,

My studies were not done until very late.

I was an honor student until my senior year when I worked six nights a week. I almost didn't graduate.

My schoolwork dropped a grade—not enough time for homework.

A related concern raised by a few parents was that they began to care less about their schoolwork as their jobs increased in priority. One parent said, "It allowed me not to care about school." In this way, a very small minority of parents felt that work hindered them academically both because they had less time to devote to schoolwork and because school became less of a priority.

Other problems were fatigue, missing school, and having too much responsibility. Fatigue, resulting from lack of sleep, was seen as reducing the attention span at school. As two respondents put it,

> I was tired in school—we woke at 4:30 to milk before school.

> I didn't get as much sleep as I should have.

Some missed classes in order to go to work or had to drop out of school altogether:

> In Grades 11 and 12 I left school after the required core courses each day to get to a job. My education suffered because of this. I should have been taking physics, chemistry, etc.

> I was unable to attend high school, as my parents required my help to operate the grain and dairy farm.

Some respondents thought they had been given too much responsibility too soon. As one mother said, "I had too many responsibilities. Dad was unstable, mother worked the P.M. shift—I had five siblings to look after." Although these responses are illustrative of problems that were mentioned about adolescent work experience, very few respondents indicated any problems. Overall, the parents indicate that problems related to youthwork are not prevalent.

Along with these open-ended responses we assessed whether there were historical and experiential differences on the closed-ended cost and benefit questions. Controlling for gender of the parent, there were no significant differences between the Pre-Boom and Boom cohorts as to whether their own youthwork was perceived as beneficial or problematic. There were also no significant differences in attitudes between the nine occupational groupings for both mothers' and fathers' first and longest jobs as adolescents. Thus, parents are generally favorable toward their own youthwork, and do not indicate differences according to cohort or adolescent occupation.

TABLE 2.10 Percentages of Adolescent Children Indicating Benefits and
Costs of Employment in Wave 3

	Girls	Boys
Benefits		
Responsibility	90.2	80.3
Money management	65.7	57.4
Learned social skills	87.7	78.3
Work experience/skill development	43.4	42.1
Work ethics (Follow directions)	73.3	68.1
Independence	75.0	77.7
Time management	78.6	74.5
Learned about life/shaped future	26.2	29.0
Problems		
Less leisure time	49.4	49.0
Lower grades	28.1	24.6
Less time for homework	47.9	48.8
Think about work during class	7.7	11.4
Fatigue	51.2	45.1

CHILDREN'S PERCEPTION OF THEIR JOBS

The benefits and problems that the children in our sample linked
to their employment were similar to those mentioned by their parents.
Like their parents, the children overwhelmingly viewed their jobs as
providing important benefits. For the children as well, problems were
much less prominent. However, whereas the parents responded to
open-ended questions, the children's questionnaire items were in
forced-choice format. Probably largely as a result of these differences,
the percentages of children indicating benefits (and costs) are considerably higher than parents (see Table 2.10). The majority of the
children's questions were in Likert-type scale format; the two highest
possible response categories are combined in Table 2.10. For example,
when there were five response options ranging from "strongly disagree" to "strongly agree," responses of "strongly agree" or "agree"
are registered as agreement. Although direct comparisons between

ages of parents and children are precluded by these differences in response format, general trends can be discerned. Children's and parents' "comparable" responses are shown in Appendix B.

Mirroring the content of their parents' own open-ended responses, children most frequently reported that gaining responsibility was a benefit of employment, with 90% of the employed 11th-grade girls and 80% of the boys responding that their job had helped them to learn to take responsibility for their work. Money management was likewise an important benefit, with two thirds of the girls and over half of the boys agreeing that their job helped them manage money. Another perceived gain was learning social skills; 88% of the girls and 78% of the boys responded that their job had helped them learn how to get along with others. Forty-three percent of the girls and 42% of the boys reported that their jobs provided an opportunity to learn new things. Recognizing the acquisition of basic work skills, almost 73% of the girls and 68% of the boys thought that their jobs helped them to learn to follow directions. Learning time management was another recognized benefit, with around 75% of both genders agreeing that their jobs had increased their propensity to be on time. About the same proportion of both genders thought that their jobs had made them more independent of their families. However, only 26% of the girls and 29% of the boys agreed that their jobs had influenced their career choice. In summary, notwithstanding the differences in questions and response formats, children and parents appear to perceive the benefits of their own youthwork very similarly.

Like their parents, children perceived problems with their employment less frequently than benefits. Still, almost half of both genders perceived that they had less time to spend with their friends because of their jobs. Another prevalent problem for the children was fatigue, with 50% of the girls and 45% of the boys agreeing that they felt drained of energy after work. A substantial number of respondents thought that they were hindered academically as a result of employment, with nearly half of both genders saying they had less time to do their homework as a result of their jobs. Furthermore, around 25% of both genders thought that their jobs had lowered their grades. Some said that they thought about their jobs during class and missed what their teachers said. (Still, analysis of difference in grade point average by employment status and hours of work shows no significant detriment; see Mortimer, Finch, et al., in press.)

Paralleling the analyses of the parent data, we assessed whether there were differences in perceived benefits and costs between occupational groups for both the first and 11th-grade jobs. Again, as in the parent generation, we found no significant differences in the adolescent child data by occupational group in the perceived benefits and costs of adolescent work experience.

Conclusion

Consistent with nationwide trends in youthwork, this study found that adolescent work experiences vary considerably across generations. Although parents perceive their children as doing less housework than they themselves performed during adolescence, the children, to the contrary, report more time doing housework. Although this study suggests that adolescents contribute money directly to their families at lower rates than their parents did, adolescent children continue to contribute to the family economy indirectly through their chores and by using their earnings from paid work to purchase items for themselves (food, clothing, school expenses) that would otherwise likely be the responsibility of their parents.

We found that the types of jobs held during adolescence have changed; the service sector is employing more adolescents now than was reported by the parents. There has been tremendous growth in youth employment in restaurant/food work and a decline in farming. Girls today are less likely to be employed in informal work—after their first jobs—than was reported by their mothers with respect to their own "longest" jobs. Boys are less likely than their fathers in their longest jobs to be employed as laborers. These historical and generational differences are illustrated by the Index of Dissimilarity, which shows that change has occurred more dramatically for males and for later (as opposed to the first) adolescent jobs. For the most part, however, the indices of dissimilarity we computed indicate greater differences by gender than by generation. The changing magnitudes of the indices across cohort and generation—for example, gender segregation diminishes between the Pre-Boom and Boom cohorts and then stabilizes in the next generation—indicate that gender segregation in adolescent employment is responsive to historical change.

Rather surprisingly, although the types of jobs held as adolescents have changed over time, perceptions about these jobs have not changed dramatically. We found virtually no differences across parental cohorts or across parental jobs. Our evidence further suggests that parents and children have rather similar views about the benefits and problems associated with their adolescent work. Overwhelmingly, both parents and children think of their early jobs as more beneficial than problematic. Members of both generations emphasized gaining responsibility, money and time management, social skills, work skills, good work habits, and independence. Neither the parents nor their children indicated problems to the same degree. When they did, the main concerns were fatigue, academic hinderance, and less leisure time.

Overall, however, these findings illustrate positive assessments of adolescent work experiences on the part of both generations. In contrast to Greenberger and Steinberg's (1986) thesis that quality of youthwork has declined with the changing composition of the adolescent labor force, we find that the perceived benefits are overwhelmingly high for both generations. Despite great changes in types of work held by contemporary and prior adolescents, such as the decline in agricultural and apprentice-type positions, contemporary youthwork does not appear to have less value. Both parents and children describe their work quite favorably. This study illustrates the importance of assessing such information from adolescent workers themselves rather than inferring benefits and costs of youth employment from the types of jobs held. Thus, contrary to Greenberger and Steinberg's expectations, we find greater evidence for continuity than for discontinuity in the developmental outcomes of adolescent work experience through historical time.

Appendix A
Questions Used to Compose Attitude Scales

I. *Positive Change in Child*

What changes have you observed in your child as a result of his/her current or past employment?

My Child's Work	Strongly Disagree	Disagree	Agree	Strongly Agree
Has given my child a sense of purpose	1	2	3	4
Has led to a greater appreciation of adult responsibilities	1	2	3	4
Has encouraged more serious planning for the future	1	2	3	4
Has taught money management skills	1	2	3	4
Has taught better time management	1	2	3	4
Has taught good work habits	1	2	3	4
Has lead to greater self-confidence	1	2	3	4
Has taught my child to communicate with adults in a mature manner	1	2	3	4
Has taught my child to take more responsibility for his/her behavior	1	2	3	4

Range from 9 to 36

II. *Positive Attitudes Toward Youth Employment*

Most high school students hold paid jobs sometime before leaving school. How much do you agree with the following statements about teen employment?

When Teens Work	Strongly Disagree	Disagree	Agree	Strongly Agree
They get a chance to practice what they have learned in school.	1	2	3	4
They get a chance to learn skills that are not taught in school.	1	2	3	4
They learn to respect others.	1	2	3	4
They develop good work attitudes and habits.	1	2	3	4
They get to meet people from different social backgrounds.	1	2	3	4

Range from 5 to 20

III. *Negative Attitudes Toward Youth Employment*

Most high school students hold paid jobs sometime before leaving school. How much do you agree with the following statements about teen employment?

When Teens Work	Strongly Disagree	Disagree	Agree	Strongly Agree
They take on adult responsibilities before they are ready for them.	1	2	3	4
They are under too much pressure.	1	2	3	4
They have less time for friendships.	1	2	3	4
They have less time to explore and figure out who they are.	1	2	3	4

Have you generally encouraged or discouraged your child from taking paid jobs while attending high school?

4	I strongly discouraged my child.
3.25	I discouraged my child.
2.5	I remained neutral—neither encouraged nor discouraged.
1.75	I gave some encouragement.
1	I gave a lot of encouragement.

Range from 5 to 20

Appendix B
Parents' and Children's Benefits
and Costs of Employment

Parents' Responses	*Children's Comparable Measures*
Benefits	
Responsibility	"How much has your job helped you to take responsibility for your work?" (Not at all . . . A great deal)
Money management	"How much has your job helped you to manage your money?" (Not at all . . . A great deal)
Social skills	"How much has your job helped you to get along with people?" (Not at all . . . A great deal)
Work experience/ skill development	"My job gives me a chance to learn a lot of new things." (Not at all true . . . Very true)
Work ethics	"How much has your job helped you to follow directions?" (Not at all . . . A great deal)
Independence	"Has your job made you more independent of your family, financially or otherwise?" (Yes/No)
Time management	"How much has your job helped you to be on time?" (Not at all . . . A great deal)
Learned about life/ shaped future	"My job has influenced my career choice." (Strongly disagree . . . Strongly agree)
Costs	
Less leisure time	"Because of my job I see my other friends less often than I used to." (Not at all true . . . Very true)
Hindered academically	"Has your job affected your grades?" (My grades have gotten lower . . . better)
	"Because of my job, I have less time to do my homework." (Strongly disagree . . . Strongly agree)
	"I think about my job during class, so I miss what my teachers are saying." (Strongly disagree . . . Strongly agree)
Fatigue	"I feel drained of my energy when I get off work." (Not at all true . . . Very true)

NOTE: Responses representing these categories were composed of the two highest possible response categories.

Notes

1. Females have been highly concentrated in service sector jobs, whereas males have been concentrated in manufacturing. Yet, as Milkman (1987) states, "Although there have been shifts over time in the specific jobs men and women do the extent of sex segregation in the labor market has changed very little during the course of the twentieth century" (p. 153).

2. Boys' and girls' first jobs started at the mean age of 12.8 and 12.4, respectively. Mothers' and fathers' jobs began at age 13.8 and 13.4, respectively.

3. Reliability coefficients for the variables in each scale were between .73 and .90 for both mothers and fathers. Not unexpectedly, these scales are moderately intercorrelated. The largest associations are between scales representing positive change in the child and positive attitudes toward youth employment for both mothers and fathers ($r = .50$ and $r = .61$, respectively).

3

The Implications of Helpfulness
for Possible Selves

KATHLEEN THIEDE CALL

This chapter focuses on the positive and negative effects of help-fulness in the contexts of family and work on adolescents' feelings of competence. Helpful behaviors are typically referred to in positive terms: Helpfulness is thought to promote personal growth (Goodnow, 1988; McHale, Bartko, Crouter, & Perry-Jenkins, 1990), the acqui-sition or enhancement of practical skills, responsibility, autonomy, and feelings of membership and mastery (Eagly & Crowley, 1986; Elder, 1974; White & Brinkerhoff, 1981a; Zill & Peterson, 1982). However, empirical tests of these relationships are lacking (Goodnow, 1988).

There are several limitations in the research on helpfulness (see Call, Mortimer, & Shanahan, 1995). First, studies of helpful activities are typically descriptive in nature. That is, much of the research focuses on the meaning of household activities (Goodnow & Delaney, 1989; Goodnow & Warton, 1991) or differences in the performance and consequences of household chores as a function of characteristics of the family or the helper (Berk, 1985; Blair, 1992a, 1992b; Eberly, Montemayor, & Flannery, 1993; Kalliopuska, 1992). Second, much of the research is cross-sectional, making it impossible to uncover dynamic relationships between helpful acts and psychosocial function-ing. Together with an interest in the extent to which adolescents are helpful, and the antecedents of helpfulness, I want to examine here the interrelation of helpfulness and adolescents' perceptions of competence over time and provide a theoretical model linking the contexts of adolescent helpful acts and their meaning to the self-system.

Finally, the relationship between helpfulness and self-competence during mid-adolescence has not received much attention, and the few investigations that have been done focus only on helpfulness within the home. Helpful acts and their consequences may be particularly meaningful during middle adolescence, a period when adolescents are trying to gain respect, trust, and a certain amount of independence from those around them (Eccles et al., 1991; Montemayor, 1983; Steinberg, 1990). Also, the majority of adolescents are employed at some time during high school (Manning, 1990; Mortimer et al., 1994); therefore, it is important to understand the implications of helpful acts in the workplace.

The theoretical model I propose to explain the relationship between helpfulness and competence is informed by Markus and her colleagues' concept of "possible selves" (Markus et al., 1990; Markus & Nurius, 1986). According to Markus et al. (1990), self-competence is integrally and reciprocally related to the self-system. A sense of competence in a particular domain requires that individuals not only possess some talent and ability, but to make it meaningful and self-defining, structures (or self-schemas) that represent this ability must exist in the self-system. Self-schemas "integrate representation of the self (past, present, and future) and function to organize the processing of self-relevant information in a given domain" (p. 207). The self-schema—including the image and recognition of one's abilities—motivates one to use these talents and gain a sense of control over them and thereby attain competence. Self-schemas are not simply passive representations of past experiences and behaviors; they determine what information is paid attention to and are responsible for present and future actions. However, the social environment influences what talents and attributes are valued, and consequently, the resultant self-structure (Markus et al., 1990).

Possible selves are representations of the self in the future that help organize and make sense of past and present experiences. Given that they are approaching the transition to adulthood, adolescents may be actively formulating possible selves as parents and workers. Competence is integrally tied to both adult roles. Images of possible selves serve to direct behavior as persons are motivated to pursue and realize their future goals (i.e., to become the person they would like to become or resist what they are afraid of becoming). As possible selves are elaborated and become more explicit, the actions and strategies necessary to achieve these identities are anticipated and simulated in preparation for actual performance (Markus et al., 1990).

Possible selves thus provide a bridge between the self-concept and motivation (Markus & Nurius, 1986). This view of self-concept formation incorporates human agency:

> Development can be seen as a process of acquiring and then achieving and resisting certain possible selves. Through the selection and construction of possible selves individuals can be viewed as active producers of their own development. (Markus & Nurius, 1986, p. 955)

In reference to helpfulness then, adolescents may be motivated to perform household tasks and care for other family members in order to actualize their future selves as heads of their own households and as parents. Similarly, part-time work may nurture or solidify adolescents' possible selves in the career world.

From this perspective, the phenomenological experience of helpful activities is critical in determining their consequences for the self-system. That is, adolescents' ideas and beliefs about their potential for achieving their possible selves and their perceptions about whether the surrounding context will facilitate these goals shape the meaning and interpretation of past and current helping behaviors. When adolescents' helping activities are performed independently, are perceived as building skills, and are interpreted as being useful to and valued by others, self-competence in a particular domain should be enhanced. Such helpful acts signify movement toward adult status, activating an image of a possible self who is responsible and dependable. Skills used and cultivated at home and work should increase adolescents' competence as they gain practical experience and information about their performance that can be applied to future tasks and goals. Effective performance of a task validates one's sense of mastery and strengthens this identity. In contrast, acts of helpfulness that are not considered movement toward desired future roles will not foster the adolescent's sense of competence and may instead evoke images of the self in undesirable future roles (negative possible selves).

In accord with this line of thinking, it is argued here that the relation between helpful acts and their consequences for competence will be shaped by the context and circumstances in which the helpful act occurs. That is, under certain conditions, acts of helpfulness should take on adult-like characteristics. Given their compatibility with desired possible selves, we propose that acts of helpfulness that occur within the context of need and positive interpersonal relations should promote adolescent self-competence. First, helpfulness should bolster competence under circumstances of need, when the adolescent's contribution is adultlike, required, and indispensable. Prior research shows that adolescents who are called on to contribute to their families' welfare and play productive roles as a result of parental divorce or financial crisis experience long-term benefits and gains in mastery and self-reliance (Elder, 1974; Elder, Conger, & Foster, 1990; Hetherington, 1989; Weiss, 1979; Werner, 1987). However, it is also possible that the level of family need and the demands placed upon the adolescent may exceed their abilities to provide relief. This situation may be devastating to an adolescent's emergent sense of competence. Alternatively, when family need is not urgent, helping with chores and other acts may be perceived as "make work," having few positive outcomes.

Second, competence may be enhanced when helpfulness is contextualized by positive interpersonal relationships. Even though adolescence is characterized as a time to disengage from families in the quest for greater autonomy, relations with parents remain critical to self-concept development. Warm and supportive relationships with parents boost adolescents' sense of internal control (Scheck, Emerick, & El-Assal, 1973) and mastery (Gecas & Schwalbe, 1986; LeCroy, 1989; Mortimer, Lorence, & Kumka, 1986), whereas a lack of support and the use of coercive control diminish self-competence (Baumrind, 1975). In a context of negative parent-child relations, the psychological benefits of helpful acts may be eroded. Likewise, it is hypothesized that relationships in the work context may condition the effects of helpfulness on competence. Supervisors who are controlling and unsupportive probably minimize the adultlike character of the work experience and stifle any opportunity for gains in mastery.

What follows is a brief summary and discussion of the key findings from an earlier investigation of the interrelation of helpfulness and competence among 9th- and 10th-grade adolescents (Call, Mortimer, & Shanahan, 1995). This review is provided to familiarize the reader with what is known to date about the relationship between helpfulness and competence and its implications for future possible selves. It serves as an orientation to the analyses that follow that incorporate data from all four years of high school.

Consistent with other studies (Elder et al., 1990; Goodnow, 1988; Weiss, 1979; White & Brinkerhoff, 1981a; Zill & Peterson, 1982), my colleagues and I (hereafter "we") found that 9th- and 10th-grade adolescent participants in the Youth Development Study (YDS) respond to economic and other forms of family need. That is, adolescents from large families, with fewer financial resources, and whose mothers are employed take on more household responsibilities. In agreement with other research (Duckett, Raffaelli, & Richards, 1989; White & Brinkerhoff, 1981), 10th-grade girls and boys spent similar amounts of time doing household chores, but girls were more likely to take on the responsibility of caring for other family members. In the work sphere, girls perceived greater opportunities to be helpful to others. This is likely a result of 10th-grade girls' greater involvement in baby-sitting and other informal work (34% of employed girls as compared to 9% of boys did this kind of work) in which helping others is their primary responsibility.

Using the panel data from the 9th- and 10th-grade adolescents, we discovered that competence and helpful acts are reciprocally related over time. Prior competence was not a significant predictor of helpfulness in the home; however, the more competent girls selected part-time work that provided them with opportunities to be helpful to others. In turn, the chance to be helpful to others at work strengthened girls' competence. We concluded that being helpful at work may bolster adolescent girls' possible selves in the work world.

Furthermore, features of the family context moderated the effect of helpfulness in the home on competence. Doing household chores increased minority boys' competence but diminished competence for white boys. Minority and immigrant status were considered indicators of need in the family. Parents who face discrimination or difficulties in adapting to the host society may rely more heavily on their children for diverse kinds of assistance, and they may cultivate a greater sense of interdependence among family members than is true of more advantaged parents (Nidorf, 1985). In such homes, helping out may be highly valued by family members, which fosters a sense of mastery in the helper. If minority boys see themselves as playing a central part in the maintenance and upkeep of their own homes and the well-being of their families, current acts of helpfulness may be seen as contributing to competence in desired future roles.

In contrast, performing household chores was related to a lower sense of competence for white boys. They may view household chores as "make work," lacking value and taking their time away from activities they deem more important, such as sports, "hanging out" with friends, or homework. For them, helping out around the house may conform to a more childlike, dependent, and therefore negative image of the self. We examined whether the relation between helpfulness and competence is moderated by circumstances within the home and work settings. The family dynamics considered possible moderators of the effects of helpfulness are the quality of the parent-adolescent relationship and the degree of autonomy and choice surrounding the performance of household tasks. Relationship quality composites (measured for both mothers and fathers) are based on five questions about closeness to each parent, enjoyment of joint activities, perceived willingness of parents to listen to the adolescent's "side" of an argument (from Furstenberg, 1981) and parent-child communication about problems and decisions (created for use in this study). Over the four-year period, Cronbach's alpha was approximately .85 for mothers and .86 for fathers. Again, weightings of items were derived from confirmatory factor analysis, which indicated the same measurement structure across time and gender for both mothers and fathers. Adolescent autonomy in the performance of household tasks was indicated by the manner in which parents assigned chores (from Kohn & Schooler, 1974b). Adolescents were asked what the parent does when he (she) wants the adolescent to do household work. Insistence by parents may undermine adolescents' feelings of autonomy; "asking or suggesting" indicates more latitude on the part of the adolescent; "leaving it up to me" signifies the greatest degree of parental trust and adolescent discretion. We interpret the adolescents' perceived freedom to "openly disagree" with their parents about household chores

(Kohn & Schooler, 1974b) as another indicator of autonomy. (However, it could also tap actual disagreement surrounding household work.)

Autonomy and support in the work setting were also investigated as potential moderators of the relation between helpfulness and competence. The measure of supportiveness from supervisors (from Bachman, 1970) is a two-item additive scale rating feelings of closeness and supervisors' willingness to listen to problems (over the four-year period, Cronbach's alpha for this measure ranged between .65 and .70). To obtain measures of adolescent work autonomy, respondents rated the closeness of supervision they experience at work, the supervisor's style in allocating work, and freedom to disagree with the supervisor (Kohn & Schooler, 1974a). The measures are itemized in the appendix.

Results

Before examining the relationship between helpfulness and competence, we describe the extent to which adolescents are helpful to others at home and work. To permit developmental comparisons, the analyses were performed for the cohort of adolescents who responded in all four years to the items concerning household and caring tasks.[2] However, adolescents living on their own, independently of their families, in any given year were omitted from the analyses.[3] The demands faced by adolescents who are living on their own are quite different from those of their peers who are still at home and contributing to the household economies of their families of origin.

Figure 3.1 displays the average number of hours per week the cohort of adolescents performed household chores over the four years of high school. Interestingly, girls and boys start out spending about the same amount of time on these tasks. For both genders, there is a reduction in the amount of time performing these tasks between the 9th and 12th grades. However, for the boys, the decline is much steeper and more consistent, and by the senior year, girls are doing significantly more work around the house than boys are.

It should be pointed out again that our measure of household tasks consists of a variety of chores, primarily reflecting traditionally femi-

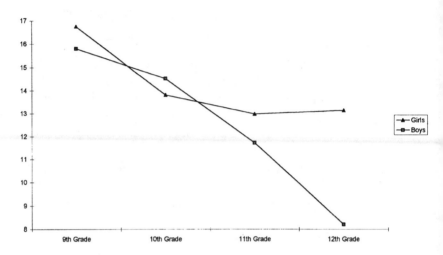

Figure 3.1.   Hours per week performing household chores (cohort analysis).
NOTE: Difference between girls and boys is significant in the 12th grade at the .001 level.

nine tasks and family work (i.e., work performed for the benefit of others), with only two measures each that could be considered masculine or gender neutral and only one task that would be considered self-care (i.e., work carried out for one's own benefit). Although the measures of household tasks available in this study do not allow a more refined categorization of the type of chores performed, Table 3.1 provides a breakdown of the items included in our measure. We find strong evidence of gender differences in the specific types of household chores performed by girls and boys throughout the high school years (73% of the tests of differences are significant). The extent to which adolescents' division of labor at home conforms to stereotypical notions of feminine and masculine work is striking. Girls spend significantly more hours per week than boys cleaning, cooking, doing dishes and laundry, and stocking the refrigerator. This extra effort on the girls' part also applies to cleaning their own rooms, which would be categorized as self-care in contrast to work done for another's behalf (Goodnow & Delaney 1989). Analogously, boys spend at least twice the number of hours that girls do on "men's work," such as taking out the garbage and doing yardwork (which includes shoveling

TABLE 3.1 Hours per Week Girls and Boys Spend Performing Specific Household Chores (significant *t* scores in parentheses)

	9th Grade		10th Grade		11th Grade		12th Grade	
	Girls	Boys	Girls	Boys	Girls	Boys	Girls	Boys
Clean own room	1.78	1.39	1.51	1.14	1.50	1.04	1.21	1.09
	(3.56***)		(2.91***)		(3.94***)			
Clean other parts of house	2.41	1.97	2.13	1.29	1.79	1.12	1.73	1.03
	(2.18*)		(5.10***)		(4.69***)		(5.27***)	
Do dishes	2.25	1.41	1.52	.79	1.28	.79	1.26	.66
	(5.24***)		(4.70***)		(3.83***)		(4.98***)	
Set table	.74	.63	.32	.20	.25	.16	.13	.13
			(2.55*)					
Cooking	1.80	1.39	1.58	1.31	1.62	1.27	1.56	1.34
	(2.66***)							
Laundry	2.19	1.20	2.11	.997	2.41	1.15	2.24	1.13
	(6.65***)		(6.17***)		(7.22***)		(7.94***)	
Grocery shopping	1.07	.70	.68	.46	.83	.40	.67	.48
	(3.08**)		(2.47*)		(4.15***)		(1.99*)	
Take out the trash	.55	1.06	.15	.48	.17	.36	.10	.34
	(5.22***)		(4.47***)		(3.22***)		(3.99***)	
Yardwork	.72	1.99	.41	1.53	.22	1.07	.28	1.01
	(10.01***)		(7.58***)		(8.32***)		(6.74***)	
Pet care	1.74	2.32	1.96	2.37	1.39	2.20	1.28	1.31

*p < .05; **p < .01; ***p < .001.

in the winter). Are girls and boys assigned these specific responsibilities, or do they themselves happen to prefer chores that follow conventions of what is appropriate? Unfortunately, it is not possible here to understand the mechanism involved.

Throughout their high school years, girls spend significantly more time per week caring for other family members. Our composite measure of the amount of time spent in caregiving, to be used subsequently in our analyses, combines hours caring for younger children and

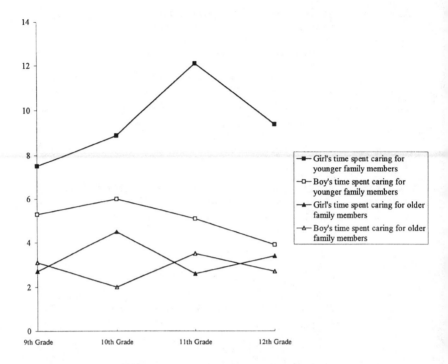

Figure 3.2.   Hours per week caring for family members (cohort analysis).
NOTE: Gender differences in the care of younger family members are significant at the .05 level or better all four years. No significant gender differences exist in the care of older family members.

elderly household members. We separate these tasks here for descriptive purposes. The mean hours reported in Figure 3.2 pertain to adolescents in the cohort who report caring for older and younger family members in a given year. Few adolescents report caring for older family members. For example, 7% of 9th-grade girls and about 9% of 9th-grade boys report caring for older family members, dropping to about 4% of both girls and boys in the 12th grade. As shown in Figure 3.2, girls and boys spend similar amounts of time doing this.

In contrast, girls are more likely to spend time caring for younger family members. Roughly 49% of girls, as compared to 39% of boys, cared for younger family members in the 9th grade. The number of adolescents who care for younger family members decreases over time, but more girls than boys report taking on this responsibility each year

(41.7% of girls and 38.8% of boys in Grade 10; 37.1% of girls and 23.9% of boys in Grade 11; and 29.4% of girls and 22.6% of boys in Grade 12). Of those who do care for younger family members, girls spend significantly greater numbers of hours each week caring for younger members throughout high school (see Figure 3.2). In fact, in the 11th and 12th grades, girls spend more than twice the number of hours caring for younger children than boys do. In most cases, younger family members refer to younger siblings. However, these figures also include adolescents who live at home with their parents and are caring for their own children ($N = 13$ in Grade 9; $N = 22$ in Grade 10; $N = 29$ in Grade 11; and $N = 41$ in Grade 12).[4] For example, about 18% of the 12th graders who report caring for younger family members were caring for their own children in addition, perhaps, to caring for younger siblings.

Most employed adolescents (92% or more of those who have paid jobs over the four years) report at least some opportunity to be helpful at work. One-way analysis of variance reveals that the sense that work provides a chance to be helpful to others varies across occupations. Adolescents working in informal settings, such as baby-sitting or doing yardwork in family contexts, are more likely to feel they are helpful than those who work in formal settings ($p < .05$), such as fast-food restaurants or sales organizations. By the senior year of high school, most adolescents work in formal settings (see Table 3.2). It was found that 12th-grade adolescents who work in teaching, child care, and recreational occupations report significantly greater opportunities ($p < .05$) to be helpful to others than their peers who work in restaurants and the fast-food industry.

Figure 3.3 displays adolescents' mean responses to the question of whether their jobs provide an opportunity to be helpful to others. Throughout high school, girls are more likely to feel they are helpful to others at work. Again, this may reflect the type of work girls and boys have. Girls are more likely to work in informal settings than boys in the earlier years of high school. When adolescents move into the formal work sphere, both genders' work is typically clustered in two industries: (a) restaurant and fast food and (b) sales. However, it is possible that within these industries, girls are in positions providing greater interpersonal contact (with both coworkers and customers) and more opportunities to be helpful to others than boys are.

TABLE 3.2 Proportion of Employed Girls and Boys in Each Occupational
              Category

	9th Grade		10th Grade		11th Grade		12th Grade	
	Girls	*Boys*	*Girls*	*Boys*	*Girls*	*Boys*	*Girls*	*Boys*
Informal	<u>72.8</u>	<u>37.6</u>	<u>36.3</u>	9.7	<u>14.1</u>	3.1	7.1	3.6
Sales	<u>5.1</u>	17.4	12.2	<u>12.1</u>	<u>33.7</u>	<u>14.2</u>	34.8	<u>20.9</u>
Restaurant/fast food	<u>16.5</u>	<u>25.3</u>	<u>40.0</u>	<u>46.1</u>	<u>32.0</u>	<u>47.1</u>	<u>27.6</u>	<u>39.1</u>
Laborers	2.1	11.2	3.3	<u>22.4</u>	2.6	<u>24.0</u>	2.8	<u>19.6</u>
Teachers/recreation/ child care	2.1	2.2	2.9	3.0	9.8	3.1	10.2	5.3
Repairer/operator	.3	2.8	1.6	2.4	1.3	4.0	2.5	8.0
Clerical	.9	2.8	3.3	3.6	5.2	.4	<u>14.0</u>	1.3
Other	.3	.6	.4	.6	1.3	4.0	.9	2.2

NOTE: The three most prevalent job categories are underlined for girls and boys each wave.

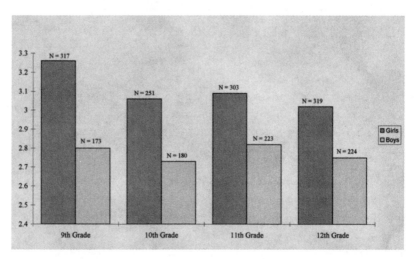

Figure 3.3. Employed adolescents' feelings of helpfulness at work (yearly
means reported).
NOTE: Differences between girls and boys are significant at the .001 level all four years.

    Adolescents may use their earnings from paid work to benefit their
families. Whereas our composite measure of earnings combines four
uses of money indicative of helpfulness, the percentage of those

TABLE 3.3 Adolescents' Use of Earnings: Percentage Responding
"Yes" to Use of Money From Paid Work
(significant t scores in parentheses)

	9th Grade		10th Grade		11th Grade		12th Grade	
	Girls	Boys	Girls	Boys	Girls	Boys	Girls	Boys
Give money to family	5.9	8.4	12.2	14.2	10.9	15.2	8.8	11.2
School expenses	31.8	26.3	43.5	33.3	45.2	32.1	54.2	36.6
			(2.16*)		(3.05**)		(4.11***)	
Save for future education	22.8	22.3	37.7	31.2	41.2	35.3	50.5	47.3
Save for other investments	26.9	33.0	35.7	44.3	42.2	39.7	37.3	42.4
n cases	324	179	255	183	303	224	319	224

*$p < .05$; **$p < .01$; ***$p < .001$.

reporting each earnings use are presented separately in Table 3.3. The most direct helping (giving earnings directly to the family) is rare (between 6% and 15% over the four-year period). However, substantial minorities of high school students use their pay in other ways that are helpful to economically pressed parents: Between 26% and 54% buy school supplies; 22% to 50% save their money for future education; and 27% to 44% save for other investment purposes. Some parents indicated in the first-wave survey that they appreciated their employed children's ability to purchase things that they wanted them to have but could not afford (Phillips & Sandstrom, 1990). Adolescents are equally likely to give money to their families and to save money for future schooling and other investments. However, girls in this panel spend significantly more of their earnings than boys do on school expenses during the 10th, 11th, and 12th grades. The findings presented in Table 3.3 also indicate a development toward greater responsibility and maturity in the use of earnings during high school. Between the 9th and 12th grade, greater proportions of adolescents are spending money on school expenses and are saving money to be applied toward higher education and other future endeavors.

In the next set of analyses, we examine conditions in the family that may encourage adolescent helpfulness over the four-year period of study. We then explore the effect of earlier competence on subsequent acts of helpfulness. Finally, we investigate the contextual moderators of the relationship between helpfulness and competence.

SOCIAL AND PERSONAL ANTECEDENTS OF ADOLESCENT HELPFULNESS

Helpfulness in the family and paid work settings were regressed on gender and background variables reflecting the need for helpful behaviors (i.e., family income, maternal employment, household size, race, and nativity). Again, to allow developmental comparisons, the regressions were performed for the cohort of adolescents who responded to the items concerning helpfulness at home over the four-year period (omitting adolescents who have set up independent households). Because it is typical for adolescents to move in and out of the work force, and to change jobs frequently during high school, we do not perform separate analyses for those who are employed continuously through high school.

Although the background variables account for little variance in helpfulness (R^2s between .04 and .13), adolescents' helpfulness does appear to be responsive to structural aspects of the family and gender (see Tables 3.4 and 3.5). Throughout high school, adolescents from larger families and lower income homes spend more time doing household chores (see Table 3.4). As in other studies (Duckett et al., 1989; White & Brinkerhoff, 1981), we found that 9th- and 10th-grade girls do not spend significantly more time doing chores than boys. However, consistent with the pattern shown in Figure 3.1, in the 11th and 12th grades, girls did more household work than boys when the influence of other background factors are taken into account.[5] Tenth-grade adolescents whose mothers are employed outside the home spend more time on household tasks. Also, in the 12th grade, minority adolescents and those who live in single-parent and other family forms did more chores than white adolescents and those living in two-parent homes.

As shown in Table 3.5, even with the background variables controlled, girls in this cohort spend significantly more time than boys caring for other people in their families. Moreover, adolescents from lower-income and minority homes and from larger households tend

TABLE 3.4 Effects of Social Background and Gender on Helping With Household Tasks (beta coefficients)

	9th Grade	10th Grade	11th Grade	12th Grade
Family income	−.141**	−.124**	−.121**	−.161***
Family composition (0 = other, 1 = two-parent)	−.051	−.062	−.072	−.105*
Household size	.117**	.098*	.085*	.189***
Mother employed	.034	.113**	.049	.069
Race (0 = other, 1 = white)	−.038	−.075	−.032	−.087*
Nativity (0 = foreign born, 1 = U.S. born)	.027	.059	.015	.041
Gender (0 = boys, 1 = girls)	.045	.002	.092*	.224***
R^2	.039***	.046***	.040***	.134***
n of cases	684	692	685	661

NOTE: The background variables are measured in the 9th grade, except family composition and mother's employment status, which are reported each year.
*$p < .05$; **$p < .01$; ***$p < .001$.

TABLE 3.5 Effects of Social Background and Gender on Helping Care for Family Members (beta coefficients)

	9th Grade	10th Grade	11th Grade	12th Grade
Family income (0 = other, 1 = two-parent)	−.151***	−.086*	−.073	−.090*
Family composition	−.014	−.025	−.033	−.093*
Household size	.181***	.154***	.134***	.230***
Mother employed	.019	.028	−.018	.040
Race (0 = other, 1 = white)	−.052	−.102*	−.140***	−.157***
Nativity (0 = foreign born, 1 = U.S. born)	.079*	.091*	.101*	.117**
Gender (0 = boys, 1 = girls)	.103**	.121**	.175***	.141***
R^2	.068***	.060***	.080***	.117***
n of cases	684	692	685	661

NOTE: The background variables are measured in the 9th grade, except family composition and mother's employment status, which are reported each year.
*$p < .05$; **$p < .01$; ***$p < .001$.

TABLE 3.6 Effects of Social Background and Gender on Helping at Work (beta coefficients)

	9th Grade	10th Grade	11th Grade	12th Grade
Family income	.039	.123*	.031	.028
Family composition (0 = other, 1 = two-parent)	.091	.048	.015	−.029
Household size	−.075	−.005	.092	.040
Mother employed	.018	−.065	−.073	−.046
Race (0 = other, 1 = white)	−.077	−.109	−.021	−.048
Nativity (0 = foreign born, 1 = U.S. born)	.079	−.012	.019	.134**
Gender (0 = boys, 1 = girls)	.247***	.188***	.141**	.168***
R^2	.077***	.068***	.040*	.052***
n of cases	400	372	453	462

NOTE: The background variables are measured in the 9th grade, except family composition and mother's employment status, which are reported each year.
*$p < .05$; **$p < .01$; ***$p < .001$.

to spend more time caring for others. In the 12th grade, adolescents who live in single-parent and other family arrangements spend more time caring for older and younger family members. It is interesting that greater caring responsibilities are not required of adolescents when their mothers are employed outside the home. Perhaps these women enter (or reenter) the workforce once their children are old enough to no longer require a lot of attention or supervision or younger children are enrolled in a day care setting and do not require the attention of adolescent siblings. Also, somewhat inexplicably, during the last three years of high school, U.S.-born adolescents spend a greater number of hours caring for others than do foreign-born youths.

Again, in the work sphere, girls perceive more opportunities to be helpful throughout the four years of high school, net of the other influences (see Table 3.6). As discussed earlier, girls' greater involvement in baby-sitting and other informal work in the first two years of high school (for example, 73% of employed girls vs. 38% of boys in the ninth grade) probably provides them with ample opportunities to help. Furthermore, once adolescents move into formal work settings, it is possible that boys are sorted into positions in which a helping component is either not present or not as salient. Tenth-grade adolescents from higher-income families also express this positive appraisal of their jobs. In the 12th grade, U.S.-born adolescents were more likely than minorities to report that they have a chance to be helpful at work.

Finally, the earnings composite was regressed on the background variables and gender. Use of earnings from paid work was not significantly related to the social background factors (nor to competence in analyses of the type described below); therefore, this indicator of helpfulness was dropped from further consideration.

PRIOR COMPETENCE AS A PREDICTOR OF HELPFULNESS

We next assessed whether earlier levels of competence predict 11th- and 12th-grade adolescents' helpfulness. It is possible that more competent adolescents respond to the needs of family members more readily, or they may gravitate toward jobs that enable them to be helpful to others. Indicators of helpfulness in the family and work sphere were regressed on prior competence (one year prior) for boys and girls separately, controlling the background variables. The analyses were performed first for the 11th graders and then using 12th-grade data. In all but one equation, prior competence did not significantly predict helpfulness. Consistent with our earlier research that focused on 10th-grade adolescents, we found that more efficacious 11th-grade girls obtain work in Grade 12 that provides greater opportunities to be helpful (*beta* = .136, $p < .05$). Thus, it appears that competence leads girls to seek out work that provides chances for them to be helpful to others. However, in contrast to our previous findings, helpfulness at work does not affect their sense of mastery.

Next, we examine whether the relationship between helpfulness and competence is conditioned by experiences and relational dynamics at home and at work the last two years of high school. Figure 3.4 presents a general model of the relationships analyzed and described in greater detail in the two sections that follow. Before turning to the results, when examining interaction effects in regression, it is recommended that the moderators be uncorrelated with the predictor and outcome variables (Baron & Kenny, 1986; Cronbach, 1987). Nearly all of the correlations are in the acceptable range ($r < .19$) in both the

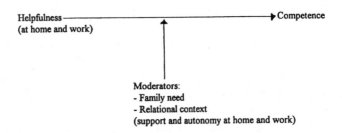

Figure 3.4. A general model of contextual moderators of the effects of helpfulness on competence.
NOTE: All equations control relevant background variables and the one-year lagged outcome variable.

11th and 12th grades. A minor exception is the correlation between adolescents' feelings of competence and perceptions of support from mothers, which exhibits a modest correlation ($r = .24$ in the 11th grade; $r = .23$ in the 12th grade) but should not pose a problem in the analyses.

FAMILY NEED AS A MODERATOR OF THE EFFECTS OF HELPFULNESS ON COMPETENCE

First, we examined whether helpfulness has different effects on competence, depending on family need. Competence in the 11th grade was regressed on prior competence, one indicator of helpfulness (time spent doing household tasks or time spent caring for others at home), all indicators of family need (family income, household size, maternal employment, race, and nativity), and the product of one measure of helpfulness and each need indicator (entered one at a time). Significant interaction coefficients indicate that the level of family need moderates the relationship between helpfulness and change in competence over time. These analyses were performed separately for girls and boys and repeated for 12th graders.

We found that family need does not moderate the relation between helpfulness and competence for 11th-grade girls and 12th-grade boys. However, the effect of doing housework on 11th-grade boys' competence varies as a function of household size ($p < .05$).[6] In the 12th grade, three significant interactions indicate that family need does moderate the relation between helpfulness and change in girls' competence over time: Maternal employment ($p < .01$) moderates the effect of housework on competence; race ($p < .01$) and nativity ($p < .05$) moderate the influence of caring for other family members on competence.[7]

Because beta coefficients for interaction terms are difficult to interpret, regressions were performed separately for each condition of the family need variable that significantly moderated the effect of helpfulness. For example, boys' competence in Grade 11 was regressed on 10th-grade competence, one indicator of helpfulness, and the control variables, separately for families with four (median household size) or fewer members, and for families with five or more household members.

Table 3.7 shows that time spent doing household chores diminishes 11th-grade boys' competence only in smaller households ($z = 3.06$, $p < .01$). We also see that housework negatively affects competence for girls whose mothers were not employed outside the home, whereas performing household chores has no significant effect on girls' competence when their mothers work ($z = 3.51$, $p < .001$). The findings of the analysis for white and minority girls were not robust; that is, the number of hours per week caring for other people in the household was not significantly related to competence in either equation when controlling prior competence and family background. Moreover, the number of foreign-born girls ($N = 16$) is too small to support the conditional analysis. (Correlational analyses indicate that caring for others is positively related to foreign-born girls' competence, $r = .48$, $p < .05$, but has no significant relationship for native-born girls.) The results of these conditional analyses, therefore, are not presented in table form.

THE RELATIONAL CONTEXT AS
A MODERATOR OF THE EFFECTS
OF HELPFULNESS ON COMPETENCE

Finally, we examined whether the effect of helpfulness on competence varies depending on the character of relationships within the

TABLE 3.7 Moderating Effects of Family Need on the Relationship Between Helpfulness and Competence

	11th-Grade Boys				12th-Grade Girls			
	4 or Fewer Family Members		5 or More Family Members		Mother Not Employed		Mother Employed	
	B	Beta	B	Beta	B	Beta	B	Beta
Time spent on chore	-.036	-.164**	.019	.124	-.138	-.439**	.019	.079
Family composition (0 = other, 1 = two-parent)	-.609	-.109	.333	.051	.239	.034	-.027	-.004
Family income	.011	.009	.003	.002	.067	.068	.184	.159**
Mother employed	.224	.029	.735	.116				
Household size					.326	.172	-.066	-.038
Nativity (0 = foreign born, 1 = U.S. born)	-.303	-.022	1.809	.228*	-2.963	-.253	-.324	-.025
Race (0 = minority, 1 = white)	.042	.006	.058	.010	-.414	-.061	-.453	-.067
Competence (one-year prior)	.616	.562***	.398	.402***	.534	489***	.550	.552***
R^2	.322***		.266***		.436***		.345***	
n	202		130		48		312	

NOTE: The background variables are measured in the 9th grade, except family composition and mother's employment status, which are reported each year.
*$p < .05$; **$p < .01$; ***$p < .001$.

family and work settings. First, competence in the 11th grade was regressed on prior competence, one indicator of helpfulness in the home (time spent doing household chores or time spent caring for others), one measure of the relational context (perceived support from mother or father, how the parent assigns household tasks, or whether the adolescent feels free to disagree with the parent about these tasks), and the product of helpfulness and one relational variable. Relevant controls (found in prior analyses to be associated with competence) were included: family income and nativity. The same analyses were performed separately for both 11th- and 12th-grade girls and boys.

TABLE 3.8   Moderating Effects of Family Dynamics on the Relationship
            Between Helpfulness and 11th-Grade Boys' Competence

	Father Insists		Father Grants Autonomy	
	B	Beta	B	Beta
Time spent on chores	−.086	−.295*	.026	.127
Family income	−.027	−.019	−.113	.108
Nativity (0 = foreign born, 1 = U.S. born)	−.373	−.022	.378	.050
Competence (Grade 10)	.841	.622**	.489	.650**
R^2		.416**		.482**
n		62		99

NOTE: Family income and nativity are measured in the 9th grade.
*$p < .01$; **$p < .001$.

In the 11th grade, three significant interactions were identified: For boys, the tactic that fathers chose when assigning household work to their sons moderated the effect of housework on boys' competence (beta = .63, p = .01). The effect of performing household chores on competence was significantly moderated by the level of boys' perceived support from the mother (beta = .371, p < .05), and the impact of caring for others on boys' competence was moderated by support from fathers (beta = −.332, p < .05).[8] One significant interaction was identified in the 12th grade: For girls, the influence of caring for others on competence was significantly moderated by perceived freedom to disagree with mothers about household work (beta = −.252, p = .05).[9]

Each family variable that significantly moderated the effect of helpfulness was divided into two (high and low) categories. For example, the manner in which household work is assigned was divided to reflect differing levels of autonomy granted the adolescent. The first column of Table 3.8 indicates boys who said that fathers just insist that the work be done. In contrast, the second column entails the father asking, suggesting, or leaving it up to the boys themselves. Competence was then regressed on prior competence, hours spent doing housework or caring for others, and the control variables, separately for each moderating condition.

Interestingly, Table 3.8 shows that the negative consequences of housework on boys' competence are present only when fathers are commanding or insistent with their sons when assigning chores ($z = 3.33$, $p < .001$). When fathers act in a way that fosters their sons' autonomy in the performance of these tasks, helpfulness has no significant effect on sons' competence. The results of the conditional analysis for 11th-grade boys' perceived support from mothers, and 12th-grade girls' freedom to disagree with their mothers, yielded no significant effects on competence; therefore, they are not presented.

Besides the moderating effects of family relations on the influence of helpfulness on competence, we found that family dynamics directly impact adolescents' competence. Positive relationships with mothers (perceived support from mothers, autonomy granted in the performance of tasks, and freedom to disagree about housework) significantly increased 11th-grade girls' competence even when prior competence, helpfulness (time spent doing housework or caring for family members), and the background variables were controlled. The same was true for 12th-grade girls: Supportive relationships with mothers, and being able to disagree about household chores enhanced girls' sense of mastery. Interestingly, girls' competence was sensitive to relationships with mothers only. Eleventh-grade boys' feelings of mastery were directly influenced by perceived support from fathers; yet in the 12th grade, boys' competence was responsive to feelings of support from *both* mothers and fathers.

Similar analyses were performed to assess whether the competence-building effects of helpfulness at work depend on the quality of the adolescent-supervisor relationship (as indicated by supervisory support and the degree of autonomy granted to the adolescent worker). Competence (in Grade 11 and 12 separately) was regressed on prior competence, helpfulness at work, one moderating variable, an interaction term (the product of helpfulness at work and the moderator), and the two controls. Although none of the interactions was statistically significant, 11th-grade boys' competence was responsive to positive work environments as indicated by freedom from close supervision by supervisors and the amount of autonomy that supervisors grant in assigning tasks (with the interaction terms dropped, *beta* = .146 and .139, $p < .05$, respectively). Thus, although positive supervisory relationships enhance adolescent competence, the effect of helpfulness at work on competence is neither strengthened nor reduced by adolescents' relationships with the supervisor. The equations were then re-estimated after dropping the interaction terms (in the 11th and 12th grade separately); we found that helpfulness at work does not influence competence.

Summary and Conclusion

Over the four years of high school, the amount of time that adolescents spend doing household chores slowly decreases, presumably providing more time for their studies and other activities that become increasingly important during this developmental period. However, the time spent on these tasks drops off more for boys than girls. Although both genders start out spending about the same amount of time on household tasks, by the 11th grade, girls spend significantly more time on chores (an average of about four hours more per week than boys in their senior year). We also found that girls spend more time than boys caring for other members of the household throughout high school. Blair (1992a) found that the amount of time girls spend on housework decreased with the presence of younger siblings. He speculates that girls are relieved of chores only to be assigned child care responsibilities. Thus, looking at both indicators of helpfulness in the family simultaneously, in agreement with other research (Blair, 1992a, 1992b; Duckett et al., 1989; White & Brinkerhoff, 1981a; Zill & Peterson, 1982), our findings indicate sex-typing in the division of household labor, which becomes increasingly pronounced over time. This is particularly true in the case of caring and nurturing tasks traditionally defined as "women's work."

Furthermore, sex-typing is especially evident when individually examining the items that made up our measure of household chores. Although adolescent girls and boys spend similar amounts of time doing housework between the 9th and 11th grades, a more detailed look at the specific tasks performed is consistent with previous research (White & Brinkerhoff, 1981), indicating that the type of chores done follow traditional sex-typed notions of appropriate tasks. That is, girls spend more time on traditionally feminine tasks, such as cleaning, doing dishes, laundry, and shopping, whereas boys spend more time on traditionally masculine tasks of taking out the garbage and doing yardwork. In another study, Goodnow and Delaney (1989) made a distinction between tasks carried out for one's own benefit versus those for the benefit of others. They found that girls and boys were comparable in the amounts of "self-care" chores performed (i.e., cleaning their own room), but girls performed more "family work" (i.e., cleaning other parts of the home, doing dishes) than boys. Our study revealed that girls spend more time than boys on both self- and family care, with the exception of taking out the garbage and working in the yard. Differentiation among type of tasks deserves more attention than is possible with our measure of household chores, which primarily reflects feminine and family work tasks, with only two measures each that could be considered masculine or gender neutral and only one task that would be considered self-care. Nonetheless, the descriptive analyses reveal pronounced differences between girls and boys.

Most employed adolescents report having an opportunity to be helpful at work; however, girls are more likely than boys to feel they are helpful to others at work over the four-year period. This is likely a reflection of the type of work adolescents have. Work in informal settings (especially baby-sitting, which is more common among girls) primarily entails helping and caring for others. Once adolescents move into formal work settings, girls continue to report more chances to be helpful to others than boys do. Because both genders tend to be clustered in sales and restaurant/food industries, within these industries girls may be in positions that provide a greater social or interpersonal component.

We observed that adolescents' use of earnings reflect greater maturity and responsibility over the four-year period, that is, spending more on school supplies and saving for future education and investments. Any supplies the adolescents do not purchase themselves likely come out of their parents' budgets, and with the rising cost of college education, their savings likely constitute a necessary contribution to the family economy. We found that girls spend more than boys do on school expenses throughout high school. Again, if girls did not pay for their own school expenses, parents would presumably be called on to do so, making this expenditure more valuable. However, it is not possible to distinguish between those girls who do this out of "necessity" and those who simply choose to spend their money this way. Girls may use their earnings toward these practical purchases as a way of establishing independence from their parents, demonstrating that they can take care of some of their own needs. A more direct measure of helpfulness is cash contributions to the family, and this use of earnings is rare among adolescents. Shanahan et al. (Chapter 4, this volume) find that use of earnings does affect father-son relations. Therefore, although use of earnings may have no direct impact on adolescents' sense of mastery, it may affect the relational climate in which helpfulness occurs. Furthermore, in a context of greater need, such as economically strained times or settings (e.g., as experienced during the Depression or in economically depressed rural Iowa), uses of earnings have greater potency as indicators of helpfulness and determinants of competence (see Elder et al., 1990).

It appears that adolescents' helpfulness is responsive to family need, which is consistent with prior research (Elder et al., 1990; Goodnow, 1988; Weiss, 1979; White & Brinkerhoff, 1981a; Zill & Peterson, 1982). Throughout high school, adolescents from lower-income homes and larger families spend greater amounts of time performing household chores and caring for other family members. Understandably, the larger the family, the greater the amount of work required. Families with lower incomes must distribute the burden of work among their members as paying for cleaning and child care services is not a realistic option. Past research led us to believe that adolescents would be called on to do more around the house when their mothers work outside the home (Goodnow & Delaney, 1989; White & Brinkerhoff, 1981). Surprisingly, this was only true in the 10th grade. It is possible that the mothers are working part-time and therefore may not need or choose to reallocate a lot of their housework.

In the 12th grade, adolescents from two-parent homes spend less time on chores and caring activities. It may be that in single-parent homes, adolescents in their final year of high school are seen as achieving adult status. Accordingly, they are expected to take on adultlike responsibilities and are relied on more by their parents (Weiss, 1979). Girls spend more time on household tasks in the last two years of high school. This too may reflect emergent expectations and motivations concerning the performance of these responsibilities, on the part of adolescent girls or their parents, once they reach a certain age. In reference to girls' potential incentives, Duckett et al. (1989) found that girls become increasingly motivated to perform housework as they grow older (whereas boys of all ages reported low levels of motivation in doing chores), describing this as a process of "gender intensification," whereby adolescent girls increasingly define these tasks as both feminine and mature.

We found that girls spend more time than boys caring for others throughout high school even when holding other possible influences constant (i.e., household income, family size, etc.). This is certainly in line with stereotypical expectations of the division of household labor. If girls' possible selves include an image of themselves as caring persons, regardless of its source (some argue that girls are naturally more nurturant and social, whereas others feel this is a result of gendered socialization), this identity will be validated through these actions (Markus et al., 1990).

We anticipated that minority and foreign-born adolescents would be more involved in housework and caring activities than whites and adolescents born in the United States. Only in the 12th grade did minorities perform more household chores than white adolescents, and place of birth was not significantly related to the amount of time spent on chores over the four years of high school. As anticipated, minority adolescents did spend more time per week caring for family members. However, contrary to our expectation, foreign-born adolescents spent significantly less time than U.S.-born adolescents caring for family members throughout high school.

The strongest predictor of helpfulness in the work sphere is gender. Girls are more likely than boys to feel they have opportunities to be helpful to others at work. As explained above, this may be the result of the type of work that adolescents do. From the analysis done here, it is not possible to discern whether early work experiences involve a measure of gender stratification in which girls' work involves a stronger social or interpersonal component as compared to boys' emphasis on activity and production. If this is the case, is this early evidence of gendered work experiences a result of self-selection or sorting?

Having briefly described the patterns of helpfulness at home and work, what are the consequences of these behaviors for adolescents' emerging self-identities and perceptions of competence? Competence and helpfulness appear to be related over time. Our earlier study (Call et al., 1995) revealed a reciprocal relationship: Girls who were more competent in the 9th grade selected work in the 10th grade that offered opportunities to be helpful to others. In turn, being helpful to others at work enhanced girls' competence. Now we find that girls who are more efficacious in the 11th grade obtain work in the 12th grade that provides chances to be helpful to others. However, helpfulness at work does not affect girls' subsequent competence. It seems that with age (or more experience in the work world), girls with a greater sense of mastery continue to seek out work that provides a caring or altruistic component, but this type of work does not influence their feelings of competence.

Possible explanations for this change could be rooted in differences in the occupational structure or the work environment that adolescents experience over time. By the 12th grade, most girls have moved into formal work settings (93% as compared to 64% in the 10th grade): It may be that the acts of helpfulness carried out in informal settings have a greater effect on competence. Acts of helpfulness in informal settings likely consist of watching younger children and doing yard- or housework for neighbors, relatives, and family friends. These are much more sex-typed behaviors for girls and may invoke positive future selves. It is also possible that working for, and being evaluated by, people that they know well adds an element of loyalty and interpersonal involvement that may be more consequential to girls' feelings of efficacy (which is probably absent in the formal work sphere).

We found evidence that the relationship between helpfulness and its effect on competence is shaped by the context and circumstances in which helpfulness occurs. In reference to situations of family need, helping with household tasks diminished feelings of mastery for 11th-grade boys who live in families with four or fewer members but had no significant impact on the competence of boys from larger families. In smaller families, where there is presumably less work to be done, boys may consider their housework contribution unnecessary and unimportant. Furthermore, performing housework has no impact on 12th-grade girls' competence when their mothers are employed, whereas doing household chores diminishes girls' mastery when mothers do not work outside the home. This could be interpreted to mean that when a daughter's helpfulness is not truly "needed," performing these chores is demeaning. When mothers are at home, they are presumably in charge of managing the household, so any work on the daughters' part may be viewed as supplemental and of less value. For both girls and boys, this type of work may be viewed as more childlike and function to evoke and validate negative possible selves in positions of servitude rather than control, leading to feelings of incompetence.

Concerning the relational context of helpful acts, we found that the negative implications of housework on 11th-grade boys' competence are present only when fathers insist that work be done rather than granting some measure of autonomy in the performance of these tasks. Doing housework under these conditions may summon images of submissiveness and weakness for boys as performance connotes obedience, not competency. The relationship between helpfulness and competence was not moderated by the relational quality of the work context.

Although we found some evidence that the relational variables have moderating effects, the relational context at home and at work also has a direct impact on adolescents' competence. The quality of relations with mothers was particularly salient for girls: Positive relationships (as indicated by perceived support from mothers, the autonomy that mothers grant when allocating household chores, and the freedom to disagree about housework) fostered girls' feelings of competence during the last two years of high school. Eleventh-grade boys' competence was related to perceived support from fathers, and in their senior year of high school, boys' competence was responsive to having close and supportive relationships with their mothers and fathers. Thus, we found that parent-adolescent relations continue to be important to adolescent development and feelings of competence throughout high school (Gecas & Schwalbe, 1986; LeCroy, 1989; Mortimer et al., 1986).

In the work setting, being free of close monitoring from their supervisors and having supervisors include them in discussions about work tasks increased 11th-grade boys' feelings of competence. Similarly, our earlier work indicated that 10th-grade boys' sense of mastery was enhanced when they were free of close supervision, and girls expressed greater feelings of competence when they felt free to disagree with their supervisors. Thus, it seems that when supervisors behave toward adolescents in a manner that is consistent with their desire and need for independence, early work experiences foster self-competence (Eccles et al., 1991; Montemayor, 1983; Steinberg, 1990). In conclusion, it is not the number of hours spent doing chores around the house that is important, but the conditions under which they are performed. If adolescents do not interpret helpful acts as valued or indispensable to the welfare of their family or are not allowed some measure of autonomy in carrying out these tasks, they may recall childlike selves that diminish their competence and incentives to be helpful.

Therefore, when helping behaviors take place in positive, independence-promoting relationships, are intrinsically motivated, and help the adolescents work toward the actualization of possible selves, we would expect competence to be enhanced. However, as in our earlier work, we did *not* find that helpfulness fosters competence even in the context of positive and constructive relationships. Why is this? Middle adolescence is a period of growing self-awareness and identity formation (Erikson, 1968). During this time in the life course, adolescents are learning to recognize their abilities and are formulating an assortment of possible selves (Markus et al., 1990). Perhaps they are so familiar with housework and caring responsibilities and these abilities are so much a part of their working self-concept (past and present) that possible selves in this domain are not salient or forthcoming. That is, it may be that only new and challenging experiences give rise to self-reflection and, in turn, gains in mastery. Another possibility is that adolescents recognize that skills in this domain are not highly rewarded, such that helping behaviors are not interpreted as movement toward positive adult possible selves. Under these circumstances, adolescents will not be highly motivated to perform these tasks, and if performed, helping activities are unlikely to enhance feelings of competence.

Many studies attest to the important contributions that adolescents make to the running of their households by helping with household chores and caregiving (Blair, 1992a, 1992b; Duckett et al., 1989; Eagly & Crowley, 1986; Goodnow, 1988; Goodnow & Delaney, 1989; White & Brinkerhoff, 1981a; Zill & Peterson, 1982). Given the prevalence of these activities, it is important that we understand their short and long-term consequences for adolescents. Certainly, perceived competence is only one potential outcome of adolescent helpfulness. Acts of helpfulness in the family and work context may have positive effects on other facets of development not revealed here. Moreover, we may need to turn our attention to other relational moderators, such as the degree of cohesiveness and interdependence experienced in the family and work settings, or the extent to which adolescents feel they should be expected to shoulder certain responsibilities. Further study is needed to understand contextual variations in the interrelations of helpfulness and competence. These patterns may be different in contexts of greater need, such as in rural areas experiencing economic decline or impoverished inner-city neighborhoods.

Appendix
Measures

Competence (standardized lambda coefficients in parentheses)[a]

Each of the following statements was rated on a four-point scale from strongly disagree (1) to strongly agree (4).

	Grade 10	Grade 11	Grade 12
There is really no way I can solve some of the problems I have. (*)	.546	.532	.526
Sometimes I feel that I'm being pushed around in life. (*)	.410	.400	.395
I have little control over the things that happen to me. (*)	.484	.473	.467
I can do just about anything I really set my mind to do.	.250	.244	.241
What happens to me in the future mostly depends on me.	.148	.144	.143
I often feel helpless in dealing with the problems of life. (*)	.540	.528	.521
There is little I can do to change many of the important things in my life. (*)	.464	.453	.448

a. The unstandardized lambdas were constrained to be equal across waves.
(*) = items that were reverse coded.

Indicators of Helpfulness

Family
    How much time do you spend on the following tasks in an average week, including weekends? (Adolescent reported the time spent on each of the following tasks.)

- Household chores
    Cleaning your room
    Cleaning other parts of the house
    Doing the dishes
    Setting the table
    Cooking
    Yardwork (mowing lawn, shoveling snow, etc.)

Laundry
Taking out the trash
Shopping for food
Taking care of pets
Other tasks

• Caring
Taking care of younger children
Taking care of an elderly relative

Work
My job gives me a chance to be helpful to others.
Not at all true (1) to Very true (4)

How do you use money from your job? (circled or not circled)
School expenses (lunches, books, supplies)
Saving for future education
Savings and investments for other purposes
I give money to my family

Moderators

Family
Parental support (The following questions were asked each year separately for fathers and mothers. Standardized lambda coefficients for Grades 11 and 12 are reported in parentheses.)

How close do you feel to him? (.730, .755)
How close do you feel to her? (.665, .688)
Not close at all (1) to Extremely close (4)

How often do you do things with him that you enjoy? (.593, .613)
How often do you do things with her that you enjoy? (.526, .544)
Never (1) to Often (4)

When you are faced with personal concerns and decisions, do you talk them over with him? (.712, .736)
When you are faced with personal concerns and decisions, do you talk them over with her? (.709, .733)
Never (1) to Often (4)

How often does he talk over important decisions that he has to make with you? (.625, .646)

How often does she talk over important decisions that she has to make with you? (.607, .628)

> Never (1) to Often (4)

How often does he listen to your side of an argument? (.689, .712)

How often does she listen to your side of an argument? (.585, .605)

> Never (1) to Often (4)

Does the issue of household work ever come up between you and her (him)?

> If yes, when she (he) wants you to do some household work, what does she usually do?

> She (he) just insists that I do it (1) She (he) asks or suggests that I do it (2) She (he) leaves it up to me (3)

> If yes, when she (he) wants you to do some household work, how free do you feel to openly disagree with her (him)?

> > Not at all free (1) to Very free (4)

Work
Supervisor's support

How often is your supervisor willing to listen to your problems and help find solutions?

> Never (1) to Almost always (5)

How close do you feel to your supervisor?

> Not close at all (1) to Extremely close (4)

How closely does your supervisor supervise you?

> He/she decides what I do and how I do it (1) to I am my own boss as long as I stay within the general policies of my employer (4)

When your supervisor wants you to do something, what does he/she do?

> Usually just tells me what to do (1) Usually discusses it with me (2) Half the time tells me what to do, half the time discusses the work with me (3)

How free do you feel to disagree with your supervisor?

> Not at all free (1) to Very free (4)

Indicators of Need

Income (from parent survey in Grade 9)

What was your total household income in 1987 before taxes?

Under $5,000 (1) to $100,000 or more (13)

Mother's Employment Status (asked each year in adolescent survey)

Have you ever been to her (mother, stepmother, or female guardian who lives with me) place of work?

Does not apply, because she is not employed (0), no (1), and yes (1).

Notes

1. The "other" category contains 66.3% mother-headed single-parent families, 7.7% father-headed single-parent families, 8% joint custody arrangements, and 17.9% living with other relatives, in foster homes, or another arrangement.

2. Adolescents with missing data on these items in any one of the four years were excluded. However, adolescents who did not perform any of these tasks (true zeros) are included in the analyses.

3. The number of adolescents living away from their families is small in any given year but increases with time (one case in the 9th grade, four in the 10th grade, 11 in the 11th grade, and 28 in the 12th grade).

4. The number of girls and boys who are themselves parents and are living at home with their own parents is fairly even in Grades 9 (7 girls, or 1.3% of 9th-grade girls, as compared to 6 boys, or 1.2% of 9th-grade boys) and 10 (10 girls, or 1.9%, vs. 12 boys, or 2.4%). However, girls are more likely than boys to be in this situation in the last two years of high school (in the 11th grade, 23 girls, or 4.4%, as compared to 6 boys, or 1.2%; in the 12th grade, 33 girls, or 6.3%, vs. 8 boys, or 1.6%).

5. Analyses were performed, incorporating the product of each background variable and gender, one at a time in the regression equation. None of the interaction terms was significant, indicating that the effects of social background on helpfulness in the family and work are similar for girls and boys.

6. One of the 12 interactions terms examined (i.e., two measures of helpfulness multiplied by six background variables) was significant (8.3%), which is somewhat better than chance.

7. Three of the 12 interaction terms (25%) were significant, which is better than chance expectation.

8. Of the 12 interaction terms, three were significant (25%), which is greater than chance.

9. Two of the 12 interaction terms (i.e., two measures of helpfulness multiplied by six relational variables) were significant (16.7%), which is slightly more likely than chance.

4

Adolescent Earnings and Relationships With Parents

The Work-Family Nexus in Urban and Rural Ecologies

MICHAEL J. SHANAHAN

GLEN H. ELDER, Jr.

MARGARET BURCHINAL

RAND D. CONGER

Productive activities of the young represented an important pathway to adulthood in early 20th-century America (Modell, 1989). This was especially true in rural settings, where youthwork was highly valued, integral to household economic strategies (Friedmann, 1978; Zelizer, 1985), and one component of the differentiated efforts of family members in response to social change (Clay & Schwarzweller, 1991).

An earlier version of this chapter was presented at the 1995 annual meeting of the American Sociological Association, Washington, DC. Address all correspondence to the first author, Department of Human Development and Family Studies, Pennsylvania State University, 110 Henderson Building South, University Park, PA 16802-6504.

Today, formal employment is quite prevalent among adolescents still in school (Bachman, Johnston, & O'Malley, 1987; Marsh, 1991; Yamoor & Mortimer, 1990) and involves substantial time commitment (Lewin-Epstein, 1981; Steinberg & Dornbusch, 1991). Yet its meaning for the adolescent life stage is uncertain and, with few exceptions (White & Brinkerhoff, 1981a, 1981b), current research focuses on adolescent work in metropolitan or national samples (e.g., Greenberger & Steinberg, 1986; Manning, 1990; Mortimer et al., 1992a, 1992b).

Critics of modern youthwork note the historic trend separating family from work and speculate that contemporary adolescent work experiences contribute to the erosion of parental influence. Consistent with this position is the pioneering research of Greenberger and Steinberg (1986), who argue that youthwork undermines the ability of parents to monitor and control their working children and diminishes the sense of closeness between parents and their adolescents.

Yet youthwork may improve relationships within the family. Evidence from the Great Depression documents that when adolescent work constitutes a genuine contribution to the family's economic strategy, the adolescent's relations with parents are enhanced (Elder, 1974). Adolescent contributions to the household economy are still found in rural settings (Elder, Foster, & Ardelt, 1994), perhaps reflecting the familism thought to characterize the rural family (Flinn, 1982; Willits, Bealer, & Timbers, 1990). Indeed, contemporary evidence indicates that rural young people do more household work than their urban counterparts (Blair, 1992b; Lawrence & Wozniak, 1987). Consistent with these observations, our prior research (Shanahan, Elder, Burchinal, & Conger, 1994) demonstrates that rural adolescents' earnings and spending patterns are associated with improvements in the adolescent-parent relationship.

Are these patterns observed in an urban setting (i.e., the area in and around a large city)? Research based on metropolitan samples shows that adolescent earnings are frequently spent on immediately consumable items such as entertainment (Greenberger & Steinberg, 1986), suggesting that urban adolescent work may not have the same meaning to the family as rural youthwork does. However, earnings imply a degree of discipline and planfulness that is required by youth employment, regardless of ecology. Perhaps because of this, urban parents have a positive attitude toward youthwork, believing that time spent with the family is not undermined and that work does not contribute to family conflicts (Phillips & Sandstrom, 1990).

This chapter examines the dynamic relationships between adolescent earnings and the adolescent-parent relationship, drawing on the urban sample of the Youth Development Study (YDS). Results are compared with our parallel study of the Iowa Youth and Families Project (IYFP) data, a rural sample drawn from farm and nonfarm families in an agriculturally dependent area.

Linking Adolescent Work and Family Relations

Two conceptual models of adolescent work frame this research and suggest different implications of paid labor for family relations. One model, based on the early work of Linton (1942), proposes an age-graded view of adolescence that includes paid labor as part of a normative process in the acquisition of social independence. Another model, based on Erikson's (1959) developmental paradigm, regards paid labor as an acceleration of independence that can result in pseudomaturity, the superficial ability to play adult roles.

Linton (1942) conceptualizes adolescence as a transitory period, marking the movement from childlike to adult roles. The individual is construed as more or less adultlike, depending on the acquisition of symbols indicative of adulthood. Importantly, paid work represents a symbolic right of passage into adulthood: earnings are a readily comprehended signifier that the adolescent can function in an adult domain. From this perspective, parents may see less need for parental monitoring and grant their teenage children more independence as they become adults or at least abandon a childlike identity. The affective quality of parent-child relations may also improve. Finally, as working youths move out of a child identity, both adolescent and parent may be more likely to seek each other's counsel.

However, Greenberger and Steinberg (1986) suggest that adolescent work can promote pseudomaturity, the superficial ability to play adult roles without commensurate, internal differentiation of psychological structures (Erikson, 1959). Maturity requires the development of complex cognitive capacities, including a coherent sense of self and others. The emergence of maturity requires "strenuous introspection" as well as role experimentation and engagement with others.

According to this second view, the monotony and lack of true challenge that mark adolescent work experiences can interfere with this process of internal transformation, deadening introspection and exploratory curiosity. From this perspective, adolescent work experiences can lead to a deterioration of the adolescent-parent relationship. As youths prematurely seek autonomy, they spend less time with the family and more time with peers. Parental monitoring may become problematic and parental guidance a conflict-ridden process, leading to a decline in the affective quality of the parent-adolescent relationship.

Relevant empirical evidence from metropolitan and national samples is inconclusive. The available evidence (Greenberger, Steinberg, Vaux, & McAuliffe, 1980; Manning, 1990; Mortimer & Shanahan, 1994; Steinberg & Dornbusch, 1991; Steinberg, Greenberger, Garduque, Ruggiero, & Vaux, 1982) suggests that hours of work are negatively related to time spent with the family and parental monitoring and positively related to autonomous decision making on the part of the adolescent; the evidence concerning affective ties is ambiguous. In fact, there are several other gaps in prior research that need to be addressed.

First, research has focused on hours on the job as a measure of work intensity, to the neglect of earnings. Yet earnings are consequential for both material and psychological autonomy (Steinberg & Dornbusch, 1991). Paid work typically is characterized by an adultlike, contractual exchange of tasks conducted according to pre-established procedures for monetary compensation, which eliminates the personal nature of children's relationships. Adolescents' uses of earnings are generally subject to their own discretion, reducing financial dependence on parents. Also, the adolescent's work role in formal settings is often coordinated with the efforts of others, including adults, suggesting egalitarianism with older individuals. In fact, Phillips and Sandstrom (1990) found that a substantial majority of parents believe paid work has increased their child's independence in nonfinancial matters.

How earnings are spent is also critical. An important distinction is whether earnings are used for leisure or nonleisure purposes. Nonleisure spending—spending not strongly related to one's immediate entertainment—connotes the assumption of more adult responsibilities, including a sense of independence and concern for others. Earnings and nonleisure spending vividly signify a sense of acquired maturity; the adolescent's status with parents becomes more egalitarian. This heightened adultlike status may be reflected in more consensual decision making, less parental monitoring, and stable to improved emotional ties.

Other linking mechanisms involve the family's favorable regard toward nonleisure spending. This type of spending reduces financial dependence on parents, thereby increasing the parents' ability to achieve important family goals. Parents may "reward" their child because of their self-interest in maintaining the child's nonleisure spending (Hirshleifer, 1993). The group is more functional with these contributions, and so status is accorded the contributor (Ridgeway & Walker, 1994) through a more adultlike parent-adolescent relationship. Contributions to the group's well-being also alter evaluations of distributive justice within the family; the adolescent's increasing contributions are deemed "fair" only because his or her standing in the family has been enhanced. Indeed, Elder, Foster, and Ardelt's (1994) study of seventh graders in the Iowa Youth and Families Project (IYFP) offers preliminary evidence that rural, adolescent work-family connections can have positive implications for development: in the farm setting, mothers' and fathers' perceptions of their son are significantly and positively correlated with the son's earnings.

The fundamental supposition that work experiences alter the character of parent-adolescent relationships or their pace of change through time requires further study. Typically, these relationships reflect many factors and change in dynamic ways (e.g., Laursen & Collins, 1994). Using hierarchical linear equations, we model earnings and adolescent-parent relations as potentially age-dependent phenomena. The unique relationships involving earnings are assessed by taking into account alternative explanations, including gender, grade point average, maturational effects indicated by age, and contextual effects indicated by family composition and nativity (whether born in the United States).

Finally, an emerging body of research suggests that family relationships are interpreted quite differently by individual family members

(Paikoff & Collins, 1991). For example, Carlson, Cooper, and Spradling (1991) observed differences in subjective evaluations of the family environment between mothers and fathers. These evaluations also depend on the child's gender. The work experiences of adolescents may vary in meaning within the family, affecting both how parents act toward the child and how the child acts toward the parents. Although the Youth Development Study (YDS) includes only the adolescents' reports of the quality of parent-child relationships, we can attend to complexity within the family by considering communication from the adolescent to the parent and from the parent to the adolescent.

Comparative Framework:
The Iowa Youth and Families Project

Our prior research (Shanahan et al., 1994) draws on an ongoing longitudinal study of family functioning in an agriculturally dependent, economically distressed region of the Midwest (Conger & Elder, 1994). The initial sample consisted of 451 (215 boys and 236 girls) seventh graders and their biological parents. The youths were from white, predominantly middle-class families. Families resided on farms (34%), in nonfarm rural areas (12%), and in towns with a population under 6,500 (54%). Sample retention has been good across the first four waves of data, with 385 families in Wave 4. During the 1980s, the Iowa families lived in a rural area that suffered its worst economic decline since the Great Depression. Although the economic situation had improved by the late 1980s, the area was still plagued by high rates of business failure, out-migration, declining wages, and low levels of construction (Elder, Robertson, & Ardelt, 1994; Lasley, 1994).

Because the YDS and IYFP were not designed at their inception for comparative purposes, several limitations must be noted. First, the samples were collected at slightly different times and cover slightly different age groups, as shown in Figure 4.1. The urban Minnesota sample began data collection in 1988 with ninth graders, whereas the rural Iowa sample began data collection in 1989 with seventh graders. Strictly speaking, comparisons between the samples are subject to

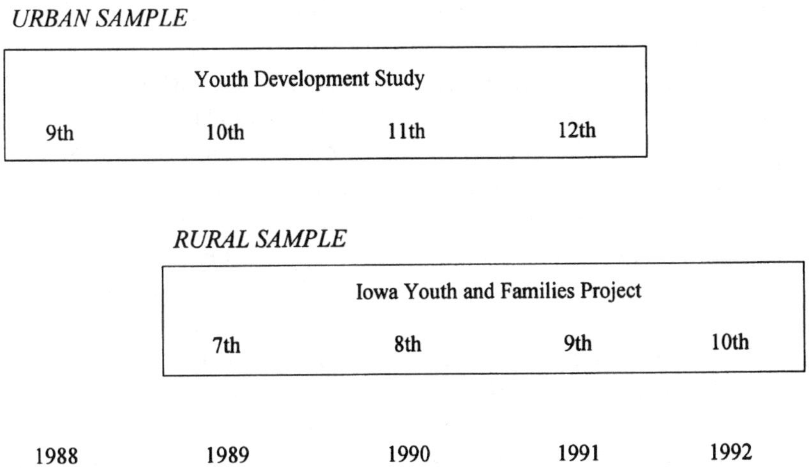

URBAN SAMPLE

Youth Development Study			
9th	10th	11th	12th

RURAL SAMPLE

	Iowa Youth and Families Project		
7th	8th	9th	10th

| 1988 | 1989 | 1990 | 1991 | 1992 |

Figure 4.1.   Comparative design: Data collection dates and grade levels.

confounding influences of age, period, and cohort effects, although such influences seem unlikely given the high degree of similarity along these dimensions.

Second, eligibility criteria differ between the samples. The Iowa sample includes intact families only, with a sibling within four years of age of the respondent. The Minnesota sample does not define eligibility in terms of parent or sibship structure. Finally, although the instruments share common interests and specific items, most comparisons drawn in the present study are based on different measures. Variations in sampling frames and instruments indicate caution in the interpretation of findings.

With respect to the linkage between adolescent earnings and parent-adolescent relationships, results from the IYFP point to three conclusions that can be examined with the YDS data. First, the higher the adolescent's earnings, the more likely is the father to seek counsel from the adolescent. The more money the adolescent earns, the more the father asks about matters that are important and listens to the adolescent.[1] Second, greater adolescent earnings are associated with improved emotional relations with both parents: Earnings are negatively associated with the adolescent's report of maternal hostility and rejection and positively associated with the adolescent's report of paternal warmth. Finally, nonleisure spending is positively associated with warmth between the mother and her adolescent child. As the types of nonleisure spending (e.g., school-related expenses, savings, and future education) increase, relations between the mother and adolescent improve. The interaction between types of nonleisure expenditures and earnings is also positively associated with warmth in this relationship, suggesting that as more earnings are devoted to nonleisure spending, warmth between the mother and adolescent increases.[2]

Thus, results from the Iowa sample support the first conceptual model, that adolescent work induces developmental changes that have positive implications for parent-child relationships. They suggest that paid labor represents an important social mechanism that transforms the adolescent-parent relationship to a more adultlike association, involving more sharing of advice and stable to improved emotional ties. Yet these results also raise the question of generalizability: Would such patterns be observed in urban settings, where youthwork may be less consequential for the family? We turn now to an examination of this issue.

Analytic Strategy

SAMPLE

The analyses that follow use questionnaire data from the YDS, Waves 1-4. Longitudinal studies of adolescents and their families are complicated by changes in family structure. As shown in Table 4.1, roughly half of all YDS adolescents live with their mother and father, biological or adopted, in any given wave of data. Longitudinally, of the 545 adolescents who lived with their mother and father in the 9th grade, 454 were still in this arrangement by the 12th grade. Thus, roughly 45% of the sample lived with their mother and father through the first four waves of the study, that is, from the 9th through the 12th grade. The family composition categories experiencing the most growth are "missing—panel attrition" (0% to 6.7%) and "other arrangements" (from 1.9% to 8.1%), ranging from boarding school to living with a boyfriend and his parents.

TABLE 4.1 Adolescent's Report of Family Structure, Youth Development
Study (frequency/column percentages in parentheses), $N = 1,000$

	Grade 9	Grade 10	Grade 11	Grade 12
Intact, mother and father[a, b, c]	545	504	478	461
	(54.5)	(50.4)	(47.8)	(46.1)
Mother only[b]	229	207	216	210
	(22.9)	(20.7)	(21.6)	(21.0)
Mother and[b, c] stepfather	116	117	107	89
	(11.6)	(11.7)	(10.7)	(8.9)
Father only	22	24	29	36
	(2.2)	(2.4)	(2.9)	(3.6)
Father and stepmother	20	25	27	20
	(2.0)	(2.5)	(2.7)	(2.0)
Joint custody	24	5	19	11
	(2.4)	(2.5)	(1.9)	(1.1)
Relative	17	20	16	16
	(1.7)	(2.0)	(1.6)	(1.6)
Foster parent	4	5	8	—
	(.4)	(.5)	(.8)	—
Other arrangement	19	31	49	81
	(1.9)	(3.1)	(4.9)	(8.1)
Missing, panel attrition	0	36	43	67
	(.0)	(3.6)	(4.3)	(6.7)
Missing, nonresponse	4	6	8	9
	(.4)	(.6)	(.8)	(.9)

a. This category represents "Intact Families," mother and father (biological or adoptive) in the household.
b. These categories represent "Mothers in Diverse Structures." Some additional cases are included in this group by drawing on information provided elsewhere in the questionnaire (e.g., mother living with boyfriend).
c. These categories represent "Fathers in Diverse Structures" (i.e., any male guardian who lives with the biological or adoptive mother). Some additional cases are included in this group by drawing on information provided elsewhere in the questionnaire (e.g., boyfriend living with the mother).

To capitalize on the diversity in family structure, our analyses first focus on intact families (i.e., the presence of both the mother and father, biological or through adoption, in the household), for this group affords a direct comparison to the Iowa data. Thus, our first set of analyses is restricted to the reports of youths who live in "intact families."

We then examine patterns among youths who live with mothers and/or fathers in intact and nonintact family structures. Because over 80% of the Minnesota adolescents are living with their mother at any given time, we focus on this subgroup: youths who live with their mother (by birth or adoption), irrespective of the presence of a male. This second group, designated "mothers in diverse structures," includes mothers in intact families, households with a mother only, and households with a mother and a male guardian (e.g., stepfather or boyfriend).

Our analysis of male guardian-adolescent relationships is restricted to adult males living in households with a mother; thus, "fathers" include biological or adoptive fathers, stepfathers, boyfriends, and other male guardians who live with the biological or adoptive mother. This third group is designated "fathers in diverse structures." Male-headed households (i.e., presence of a male guardian only) are too small in number to provide reliable results.

MEASUREMENT

Work Variables

Annual earnings were calculated drawing on complete work history records constructed for each respondent. This information was based on self-reports of hourly wages, hours worked per week, and months on the job. Annual earnings cover the 12 months immediately prior to the questionnaire administration. Thus, annual earnings for 1988 (the ninth grade) cover February 1987 to January 1988 inclusive. Given the wide range of values reported, the natural logarithm of earnings is used in the following analyses. Based on these same self-reports, current job hours (per week) were calculated. Unlike the Iowa sample, a considerable proportion of the St. Paul youths report no earnings in any given year (26%, 18%, 13%, and 16% in Grades

9 through 12, respectively). The models therefore include a dummy variable (earnings, no earnings) to determine if nonworkers differ from workers.[3]

The models also include hours worked per week on the current job, based on the self-reported work histories. A considerable body of research on the intensity of work has examined hours worked per week in the current job (e.g., Bachman, Bare, & Frankie, 1986; D'Amico, 1984; Steinberg, Fegley, & Dornbusch, 1993), and so we control this factor. Because many of the adolescents were not employed at the time of the survey's administration, we constructed two dummy variables, both having a reference category of zero hours, or not currently employed: low hours (1-20 hours per week) and high hours (more than 20 hours per week). This is consistent with studies based on metropolitan or national samples, which typically define high hours as more than 20 hours per week (e.g., Mortimer, Finch, et al., in press).[4]

Types of nonleisure spending represent the percentage of nonleisure expenditures reported by the adolescent from a list of four possibilities (kept money for future education, saved money, gave money to parents, or paid for school expenses, $0 = no$, $1 = yes$); for example, an adolescent spending some of his or her earnings in three of the four ways would have a value of .75. This construct is a measure of the symbolic mechanism linking spending with the adolescent-parent relationship: The more different types of nonleisure spending, the more fully the adult role is being assumed. Unfortunately, the data do not allow us to examine how much money, or the proportion of earnings, is spent in nonleisure ways. Some adolescents may spend a great deal, or a relatively small amount, but high proportion of their total earnings, on one type of nonleisure spending. Clearly, all three measures are needed and, in this sense, our findings with respect to nonleisure spending are suggestive for future research.

Parent-Adolescent Relationships

We relate earnings to key dimensions of the parent-adolescent relationship, selected on the basis of our prior study that used the IYFP data. The Iowa data allowed for an examination of time spent with the family, as well as counsel seeking, warmth, and hostility from the adolescent to the parent and from the parent to the adolescent; supplemental analyses also examined the adolescent's report of iden- tification with the parent. In the YDS sample, measures of identifica- tion and communication from the adolescent to the parent and from the parent to the adolescent are available; these measures are com- pared with the IYFP results on identification and counsel seeking.

The IYFP measure of identification consists of four items, measur- ing the extent to which the adolescent wants to be like the parent, respects the parent, believes that others respect the parent, and enjoys spending time with the parent. The YDS measure of identification has three items, measuring the extent to which the adolescent wants to be like the parent, feels close to the parent, and enjoys doing things with the parent (1 = *not at all or never*, 4 = *a lot or often*). These items correlate well: The average Pearson correlation coefficient among the three items across the four waves is .55 for identification with father and .52 for identification with mother. The items were averaged to create an identification scale.

The IYFP also contains measures of counsel seeking, four items that reflect the extent to which the individual believes one's own opinions are taken into account (e.g., how often the mother listens to the adolescent's opinions or asks for ideas when solving a problem); the adolescent's report of parents and the parent's report of the adolescent were examined. The YDS data have a two-item measure of communi- cation from the adolescent to the parent, measuring the extent to which the adolescent talks with the parent and believes the parent listens (1 = *never* to 4 = *often*). The average Pearson correlation coefficient across the four waves is .52 for communication with fathers and .52 for communication with mothers. The items were averaged to create a scale of communication from the adolescent to the parent.

The YDS also has one item indicating the extent to which the parent "talks over important decisions that (s)he has to make with you" (1 = *never* to 4 = *often*). As an ordinal measure, the item is not ideal for hierarchical linear models, which are based on the same assumptions as OLS regression models. However, the item is normally distributed and represents the only opportunity to examine communication from the parent to the adolescent.

Family Structure

In models focusing on mothers in diverse family structures, we control the presence of the father versus single-headed household (father present, single-headed household) and the presence of the father versus another male (father present, other male present). In models that focus on adult males in diverse family structures, we control whether that male is the father (father present, other male present).

Control Variables

Finally, the analyses include several control variables: grade point average is based on the adolescent's self-report ($13 = A+$ to $0 = F$); gender is based on school records (female, male); and nativity represents whether the respondent was born in the United States (yes, no).

Appendix A provides descriptive statistics for variables used in the analyses.

METHODOLOGY

This research addresses the extent to which adolescent earnings and nonleisure spending are associated with the adolescent's report of (a) identification with parents, (b) communication to parents, and (c) communication from parents. We approach these research questions using hierarchical models as applied to repeated measures (Bryk & Raudenbush, 1992; Goldstein, 1989; Laird & Ware, 1982). Models estimate the parent-adolescent relationship with both individual growth curves (called "random effects" because they vary between individuals) and group growth curves (called "fixed effects" because they do not vary between individuals).

Our models include an intercept and age effect that vary between individuals (random effects) because we believe that individuals differ significantly in their mean levels of and rates of change in adolescent-parent variables (e.g., identification with parents). To simplify matters, these random effects are not reported in the tables. As expected, all models have significant random effects, indicating that the adolescents differ among themselves significantly in their initial levels and rates of change in the qualities of the parent-adolescent relationship.

Most important, the models also include an intercept and effects of predictor variables that do not vary between individuals (fixed effects). These fixed effects can be interpreted like OLS regression results, although they reflect an adjustment for the random components. These fixed effect predictors include the variables of central interest (earnings, whether employed in the last year, nonleisure spending, current job hours, and family structure) plus controls (gender, grade point average, age, and nativity).

Given the coding of the predictor variables, the fixed intercept represents the mean of the predicted variable across gender, nativity, work status, and family structure categories when all continuous variables are at their mean levels. The fixed effect of the continuous variables can be interpreted as change in the predicted variable associated with change in the predictor. The fixed effect of the categorical variables can be interpreted as change in the parent-adolescent relationship associated with the category coded 1.

Methodologically, these models are particularly appropriate given our repeated measures design. Most important, as opposed to a traditional multivariate repeated measures method, hierarchical linear models (HLMs) permit the inclusion of predictors that change over time. Thus, the adolescent's earnings during each year of the study can be related to adolescent-parent relations longitudinally as a time-varying covariate. Second, an estimation of the combined equation (i.e., the individual and group curves) with ordinary least squares regression would increase the likelihood of a Type I error (concluding that a relationship existed between two variables when one did not) due to underestimated standard errors. HLMs correct these problems and provide better estimates of the fixed effects and especially their standard errors. Third, models based on longitudinal data typically drop cases missing in any wave of data from the analyses; in contrast, as the person-year is the unit of analysis in hierarchical models, all available data are used (Burchinal, Bailey, & Snyder, 1994; Raudenbush & Chan, 1993).

A more complete discussion of hierarchical models as applied to our research questions is found in Appendix B.

Results

We begin with descriptive statistics that describe longitudinal patterns of earnings and spending patterns and then review dynamic models of earnings and family relations, including identification with parents and communication from the adolescent to the parent and from the parent to the adolescent. Models are estimated for intact families, mothers in diverse family structures, and fathers in diverse family structures. Finally, we consider how specific spending patterns contribute to an understanding of adolescent earnings and family relationships.

DESCRIPTIVE PATTERNS

Work Status

In the YDS sample, the percentage of urban youths reporting earnings in the prior year fluctuates between about 74% in Grade 9 and 84% in Grade 11. This is in contrast to patterns observed in the IYFP, in which 92% to 95% of these rural youths report earnings in any given year. For example, about 92% of the Iowa youth report earnings in the 10th grade, compared with 79.5% in the Minnesota sample. Thus, paid work is more prevalent in the rural sample, despite its younger composition. The mean number of hours worked per week is about 11 in Grade 9, increasing to about 20 in Grade 12 in the urban sample.

Most of the rural adolescents report income from work in private households, the service sector, and on farms. Based on an examination of cross-sectional patterns, Mortimer and her colleagues have observed an "adolescent career" in the urban sample: Adolescents start working for pay in private households, then branch into the service sector (especially restaurant work), and later assume a variety of jobs. Cross-sectional distributions suggest that such careers are less likely in the rural sample—the major job categories are stable across the four years of study.

TABLE 4.2 Longitudinal Pattern of Annual Earnings, by Gender (dollars, means, and standard deviations)

	Grade 9	Grade 10	Grade 11	Grade 12
Panel A: Youth Development Study (urban)				
Earnings (in dollars)				
Male	436 (788)	700 (1,039)	1,110 (1,275)	1,162 (1,297)
Female	599 (1,202)	775 (1,012)	1,135 (1,317)	1,212 (1,036)
Panel B: Iowa Youth and Families Project (rural)				
Earnings (in dollars)				
Male	765 (685)	1,127 (1,102)		
Female	435 (446)	612 (631)		

Earnings

Table 4.2 (Panel A) presents descriptive statistics for annual earnings between the 9th and 12th grades by gender for the YDS sample, including persons who have no earnings. A repeated measures MANOVA with gender as a between-subjects factor and wave as a within-subjects factor examines changes in earnings. The analysis includes those students reporting an income of zero, for a subsample size of 890 students per wave. There is a significant main effect of wave, $F(1, 888) = 1118.10, p < .001$, indicating that earnings increase substantially from the 9th to the 12th grades. The main effect of gender is not significant, $F(1, 888) = 2.16, p = .14$, indicating that girls do not earn substantially more than boys. The gender-wave interaction is also insignificant.

A repeated measures MANOVA was also estimated for all four waves of the Iowa data (data for the two comparable waves of data are presented in Panel B of Table 4.2). Those results indicate that the rural boys earn more than the girls and that earnings increase substantially from the 9th to the 10th grade. A significant gender-wave interaction shows that boys' earnings increase at a significantly faster pace than girls'.

As shown in Table 4.2, 9th- and 10th-grade rural boys' earnings are markedly greater than levels found among their urban counterparts. However, the difference may reflect the greater percentage of adolescents reporting no earnings in the urban sample. In fact, when both analyses are restricted to youths who report earnings in all four waves, the mean levels of earnings are still higher among rural boys: For example, among 10th graders, rural boys earn $1,154 on average, when compared with $1,066 in the urban sample.

In descending order, 10th graders' earnings can be ranked according to gender and urban-rural ecology: rural boys, urban females, urban boys, rural females. This appears to reflect the structure of job markets. Rural boys have considerable opportunities in the labor-intensive, patriarchical societies of agricultural America. Indeed, a considerable percentage of boys indicate farm work as the primary source of earnings (ranging from 40% to 60% through the four waves of data); many also indicate farm work as a secondary source of income (ranging from 15% to 35% through the four waves). Personal services (e.g., baby-sitting, yardwork) and service sector jobs are commonly available for urban youths. Rural females are less likely to earn money baby-sitting, perhaps because of longer distances between households and larger families (increasing the likelihood that child care will be assumed by siblings).

Spending Patterns

Data were also collected from the adolescents on how their earnings were spent. Although wording differs slightly, this information was collected from both the urban and rural samples. Leisure spending is common in both settings. As shown in Table 4.3, spending on "entertainment" is common among those reporting earnings and somewhat more prevalent in the rural sample. On the other hand, spending on media-related equipment is considerably more likely in the urban sample. Some caution needs to be exercised in this comparison because the urban question includes bikes and sports equipment. However, these results show that leisure spending is quite common in both samples and suggest that media-related spending is more common in the urban sample.

More interesting are types of nonleisure spending, which include whether the adolescent kept money for future education, saved money, gave money to parents, or paid for school fees (the item responses were 0 = *no*, 1 = *yes*). Within the urban sample, nonleisure expendi-

Table 4.3 Spending Patterns: Intact Families
(percentage yes among those reporting earnings)

	Youth Development Study				Iowa Youth and Families Project			
	9th	10th	11th	12th	7th	8th	9th	10th
Entertainment[a]	61.7	69.9	70.6	75.5	88.8	91.6	92.9	93.4
Media[b]	64.5	66.6	64.1	66.9	20.6	27.5	27.9	25.5
Future education[c]	24.6	38.4	47.5	55.8	na	22.4	23.4	22.9
Savings investments[d]	28.6	40.8	44.2	44.5	75.7	74.1	64.4	68.8
Family[e]	4.5	8.1	9.1	9.6	26.4	38.0	31.5	34.3
School expenses[f]	25.0	32.7	38.1	45.9	34.1	29.7	35.1	39.4

a. YDS: "For movies, entertainment, dating, clubs"
    IYFP: "Used it for spending, like movies, games, snacks, etc."
           (wording changed slightly through the four waves of data)
b. YDS: "To buy other things—like records, tapes, sports equipment, stereo, TV, bike, etc."
    IYFP: "Bought a TV, VCR, boom box, or things like that"
c. YDS: "Saving for future education"
    IYFP: "Put money in a college fund"
d. YDS: "Savings and investments for other purposes"
    IYFP: "Put money into savings, bonds, a CD or other investment"
e. YDS: "I give money to my family"
    IYFP: "Give some or loan some to your parents to help out"
f. YDS: "School expenses (lunches, books, supplies)"
    IYFP: "Pay for necessities like school fees, school lunches, etc."

tures increase markedly over time across all four categories. Savings for future education more than doubles (an increase from about 25% to 56%) between the 9th and 12th grades, as does giving money to families. These changes are not observed in the rural sample, although nonleisure spending patterns are quite high already by Grade 7.

Tenth-grade urban students save more for future education, when compared with the rural sample (38% vs. 23%); some of this difference may be due to the wording of the question in the rural sample, with its limitation to a college fund. However, the 10th-grade Iowans are more likely to save and invest earnings and to pay for school expenses; moreover, they are over four times more likely to contribute money to the family. Some of this difference may be due to wording in the Iowa sample, which includes money both as contributions and loans. However, rural adolescents are more likely to spend money in ways not related to their immediate gratification, when compared with their urban counterparts.

DYNAMIC MODELS OF EARNINGS
AND FAMILY RELATIONS

The tables that follow report estimates from a series of hierarchical linear models. The reported results include the fixed intercept and fixed effects of predictors.

Intact Families

Table 4.4 presents estimates for the adolescent's report of identification with parents and communication to and from the parent. The fixed intercepts represent mean levels of these variables across levels of the categorical variables (e.g., gender), with all continuous variables at their mean levels. Given that all the outcomes have a range from 1 to 4, the magnitude of the intercepts (e.g., 2.87 for identification with mother) indicates that parent-adolescent relationships are positively skewed. A similar pattern was observed among the Iowa adolescents.

The fixed effect of the continuous variables can be interpreted as change in the predicted variable associated with change in the predictor. For example, the association between age and identification with mother ($b = -.03, p < .05$) reflects differences in identification with mother as a function of differences in the mean age and the observed age. Thus, the fixed effect of age is negative and significant, indicating that a 1-year increase in age from the grand mean of age (17.49 years) is associated with a small decrease in identification with the mother, controlling all other variables.

The adolescent's age and report of identification with the father are negatively, significantly associated ($b = -.03, p < .05$). A similar pattern is observed in the Iowa sample, suggesting that identification with the parent decreases slightly with age regardless of ecology. Age patterns of communication are insignificant, suggesting negligible change in how often adolescents talk with their parents and vice versa. This pattern was also observed in the Iowa sample.

Importantly, earnings have no additive effects on any of the dependent variables in the YDS sample: The relationships between earnings and identification and communication patterns are essentially zero. Further, no significant patterns are observed between qualities of the adolescent-parent relationship and whether the adolescent reports any earnings in the prior year. Interestingly, however, low work hours are

TABLE 4.4 Earnings and the Parent-Adolescent Relationship, Intact Families, HLM Estimates (unstandardized coefficient/standard error in parentheses)[a]

| | Mothers | | | Fathers | | |
| | | Communication | | | Communication | |
Fixed Effects	Identification	Adolescent to Parent	Parent to Adolescent	Identification	Adolescent to Parent	Parent to Adolescent
Intercept	2.87***	2.85***	2.72***	2.61***	2.43***	2.35***
	.06	.07	.08	.07	.08	.08
Age	−.03*	.01	−.03†	−.03*	.01	−.03
	.01	.01	.02	.01	.02	.02
(ln) annual earnings	−.01	−.01	.03	−.02	.03†	−.02
	.01	.02	.02	.01	.02	.02
No earnings[b] (1 = 0 earnings)	.00	.01	.07	−.08†	−.06	−.08
	.04	.06	.07	.05	.06	.07
Low hours versus not employed	.03	.02	.02	.03†	.07**	.07*
	.02	.02	.03	.02	.02	.03
High hours versus not employed	.02	.03	−.03	−.02	−.04	−.10*
	.02	.03	.04	.03	.03	.04
Gender (1 = male)	.02	.07*	.10**	−.14***	−.08*	−.07*
	.03	.03	.03	.03	.03	.04
Grade point average	.04***	.03**	.02†	.04***	.05***	.02†
	.01	.01	.01	.01	.01	.01
Nativity (1 = foreign)	−.04	−.10	−.03	−.01	−.06	.07
	.06	.06	.06	.06	.06	.07
n	1,527	1,529	1,531	1,522	1,529	1,529

a. Table omits random effects.
b. All dichotomous variables are effect coded (1, −1); the difference between the categories coded 1 and −1 is twice the size of the coefficient.
†$p < .10$; *$p < .05$; **$p < .01$; ***$p < .001$; two-tailed test.

associated with greater identification with father ($b = .03$, $p < .10$) and better communication from the adolescent to the father ($b = .07$, $p < .01$) and from the father to the adolescent ($b = .07$, $p < .05$). In fact, high hours are *negatively* associated with communication from the parent to the adolescent ($b = -.10$, $p < .05$), documenting a curvilinear association between work hours and the adolescent-father relationship based on a 20-hour-per-week cutoff.

In the Iowa sample, earnings are significantly associated with greater identification with the mother and more counsel seeking from the father. Current job hours are not associated with these outcomes. In the urban sample, earnings have no association with adolescent-parent relationships, and hours are associated with father-adolescent patterns. The different salience of current job hours and annual pay could reflect the greater seasonality of employment in rural settings, which may prompt family members to draw on yearly earnings, not current job hours, as an indicator of work involvement.

Grade point average is an important covariate of all parent-adolescent relationships studied. Grades are consistently and positively related to the children's relations to parents. This pattern is also observed in the Iowa sample, indicating that grades and parent-adolescent relationships are significantly interrelated across urban and rural ecologies.

The fixed effect of the categorical variables can be interpreted as change in the parent-adolescent relationship that is associated with the category coded 1. Mutual communication between the adolescent and the mother is significantly greater among the boys; on the other hand, all father-adolescent relationships are significantly lower among the boys. In the rural sample, relationships between gender and communication with mother were zero but were positive and significant with the father. Thus, being a male is associated with better communication with the father in the rural sample but worse communication in the urban sample (cf. Steinberg, 1990, pp. 265-266).

Mothers in Diverse Family Structures

Table 4.5 presents results for the adolescent's report of identification with the mother and communication to and from the mother, including cases with and without a male present. Because the analysis

TABLE 4.5 Earnings and the Parent-Adolescent Relationship,
Mother Present: HLM Estimates
(unstandardized coefficient/standard error in parentheses)

	Communication		
Fixed Effects	Identification	Adolescent to Mother	Mother to Adolescent
Intercept	2.83***	2.82***	2.81***
	.06	.07	.07
Age	−.02*	.00	−.02
	.01	.01	.02
(ln) Annual earnings	−.01	−.01	.03
	.01	.02	.02
No earnings[a] (1 = 0 earnings)	−.01	.00	.04
	.04	.05	.06
Low hours versus not employed	.01	.01	.01
	.02	.02	.02
High hours versus not employed	.01	.02	−.04
	.02	.03	.03
Gender (1 = male)	.01	.05†	.07*
	.02	.03	.03
Grade point average	.04***	.03***	.02†
	.01	.01	.01
Nativity (1 = foreign)	−.02	−.08	−.05
	.05	.05	.06
Dad versus single mother (1 = Dad)	.14***	.14***	−.06
	.03	.04	.04
Dad versus other male present (1 = Dad)	−.08*	−.10	−.07
	.03	.04	.05
n	2,125	2,130	2,133

a. All dichotomous variables are effect coded (1, −1); the difference between the categories coded 1 and −1 is twice the size of the effect.
†$p < .10$; *$p < .05$; **$p < .01$; ***$p < .001$; two-tailed test.

includes single-headed households and households in which there is a male who is not the father, the sample size increases. The patterns observed in Table 4.4 are replicated in Table 4.5. Nevertheless, Table

4.5 and supplementary analyses address whether family structure is systematically related to change in parent-adolescent relationships and whether family structure moderates the relationships between earnings and parent-adolescent relationships.

The additive effects of the family structure variables on parent-adolescent relationships are significant. The presence of the father versus a female-headed household is associated with greater identification with the mother ($b = 2 (.14) = .28, p < .001$) and greater communication from the adolescent to the mother ($b = 2 (.14) = .28, p < .001$). (Given the dichotomous coding of the family structure variables, the actual effect size is twice the coefficient; see Appendix B.) It may be that adolescents are more apt to see intact families as resources. However, it may also be that single mothers, because of greater work responsibilities, are not as available as mothers from intact families.

Comparing the presence of the father with the presence of another male (e.g., a boyfriend or stepfather), the presence of the father is associated with a decrement in identification with mother and communication from the adolescent to the mother. This pattern runs contrary to previous findings suggesting that child-parent relationships are less salutary in nonintact families (Cherlin & Furstenberg, 1994) and should be interpreted with caution.

An examination of interactions between earnings and hours, on the one hand, and family structure variables, on the other, reveals insignificant results: Neither earnings nor hours are more highly associated with the adolescent-mother relationship, depending on family structure.

Fathers in Diverse Family Structures

Table 4.6 presents results for the adolescent's report of identification with the resident male and communication to and from the resident male, father or otherwise. Again, the general pattern of results from Table 4.4 remains unchanged. The relationship between the presence of the dad (versus another male) and identification with the father ($b = .2 (.18) = .36, p < .001$) is positive: Not surprisingly, adolescents identify more with their biological or adopted father than with other males present in the household. A similar result is obtained for communication from the father to the adolescent ($b = 2 (.13) =$

TABLE 4.6 Earnings and the Parent-Adolescent Relationship,
Father Present: HLM Estimates
(unstandardized coefficient/standard error in parentheses)

Fixed Effects	Identification	Communication	
		Adolescent to Father	Father to Adolescent
Intercept	2.44***	2.37***	2.26***
	.07	.08	.08
Age	−.03	.00	−.05
	.01	.01	.02
(ln) Earnings	−.02	−.03[†]	−.01
	.01	.01	.02
No earnings[a] (1 = 0 earnings)	−.07	−.07	−.05
	.04	.06	.07
Low hours versus not employed	.03[†]	.06*	.05[†]
	.02	.02	.03
High hours versus not employed	−.01	−.03	−.06[†]
	.02	.03	.04
Gender (1 = male)	−.15***	−.10**	−.10**
	.03	.03	.03
Grade point average	.04***	.04***	.03*
	.01	.01	.01
Nativity (1 = foreign)	.03	−.03	.10
	.06	.06	.06
Dad present versus other male (1 = yes)	.18***	.06	.13***
	.03	.03	.04
n	1,906	1,914	1,916

a. All dichotomous variables are effect coded (1, −1); the difference between the categories coded 1 and −1 is twice the size of the coefficient.
[†]$p < .10$; *$p < .05$; **$p < .01$; ***$p < .001$; two-tailed test.

.26, $p < .001$). Adolescents are more likely to discuss important matters and believe that they are being listened to by their biological or adopted father.

Consistent with findings for mothers in diverse structures, we find that neither earnings nor hours are more highly associated with the adolescent-father relationship, depending on family structure.

SPENDING PATTERNS AND THE PARENT-ADOLESCENT RELATIONSHIP

Thus far, no significant, additive associations have been observed between earnings and identification or communication with either the mother or the father. Yet qualities of the parent-adolescent relationship may be contingent on how earnings are spent. Nonleisure spending—spending not strongly related to one's immediate gratification or entertainment—may indicate the assumption of more adult responsibilities, including a sense of independence and concern for others. It may be that nonleisure spending has an additive relationship with aspects of the parent-adolescent relationship or mediates or moderates the effect of earnings.

To examine these possibilities, we enter types of nonleisure spending and its multiplicative interaction with earnings into the equations presented in Tables 4.4 through 4.6. Types of nonleisure spending represent the percentage of nonleisure expenditures reported by the adolescent from a list of four possibilities (kept money for future education, saved money, gave money to parents, or paid for school fees). The multiplicative interaction term is a proxy for the amount spent in nonleisure ways (see Note 2).

The results (not shown) indicate that the purpose for which earnings are spent is associated with the father-adolescent relationship. Within intact families, nonleisure spending significantly and positively predicts identification with father ($b = .28$, $p < .01$) and communication to and from the father ($b = .44$, $p < .001$ and $b = .33$, $p < .05$, respectively). However, the interaction between nonleisure spending and earnings is significantly and *negatively* associated with communication to the father ($b = -.15$, $p < .05$), suggesting that greater sums spent on nonleisure spending are associated with a deterioration in relationships with fathers.

Among fathers in diverse structures, interactions between nonleisure spending and family structure variables further reveal that nonleisure spending is especially consequential for biological or adoptive fathers, as opposed to other males. Nonleisure spending significantly predicts identification with the adult male in families with the biological or adoptive father ($b = .21$, $p < .01$) but not in families headed by a different male ($b = -.08$, $p > .10$). Similarly, communication to the biological or adoptive father is better with nonleisure spending ($b = .28$, $p < .01$) but not to other males ($b = .10$, $p > .10$). Thus, nonleisure spending is significantly predictive of more identification and communication with the biological or adoptive father but not with other males.

Conclusions and Discussion

This study points to differences and commonalities in the work-family nexus of urban and rural youths. In the rural setting, paid labor is associated with more sharing of advice and stable to improved emotional ties. These findings are not replicated in the urban YDS sample. Earnings are not significantly associated with identification with the parent or communication from the adolescent to the parent or from the parent to the adolescent. In conceptual terms, earnings may constitute a mechanism by which adolescent-parent relationships transform to a more adultlike association in rural but not urban settings. Our findings from the urban sample do not comport with conceptual models advanced by Linton (1942) or Greenberger and Steinberg (1986). Adolescent earnings are not associated with improvements in adolescent-parent relationships (Linton), but nor are they associated with a deterioration in these relationships (Greenberger & Steinberg).

We believe this pattern reflects ecological differences in the meaning of adolescent work. In rural settings, productive activities are more likely to be construed as adultlike behaviors because rural work functions in unique ways to the benefit of families. First, nonleisure spending is more common in rural settings: Adolescent earnings are four times more likely to be spent on the family than in the urban setting. This may follow from historical and cultural traditions, which emphasized norms of familism in a household strategy of economic adaptation.[5] And in fact, paid work is much more prevalent in the Iowa sample. Second, farm work and personal services frequently are performed within the extended family or for close associates in the rural community. In this sense, paid adolescent work can function as an integrating force, tightening social bonds in the extended family and larger community.

Nonleisure spending is associated with adolescent-mother relationships in Iowa families but with adolescent-father relationships in the urban families. The greater such spending, the more positive the relationship. The rural relationship is thought to reflect the greater involvement of mothers in the day-to-day affairs of the rural household. However, perhaps nonleisure spending is a more salient indicator of adult achievement for fathers in urban settings.

Although the interaction between nonleisure spending and earnings has a significant and positive relationship among rural youths, the relationship is actually negative among urban youths: As urban adolescents spend their earnings on more diverse types of nonleisure spending, communication with the father breaks down. We speculate that in the rural setting, with its historical emphasis on the household strategy, the constructive use of earnings is viewed as fulfilling valued norms. However, in the urban sample, which lacks a strong tradition of collective strategies within the family (at least in the 20th century), resentment may build when too much assistance is required of the adolescent. Tension between the adolescent and the father may signal a violation of the expectation that the father is largely responsible for the household economy.

Within the urban setting, family structure matters to relationships within the family. As noted, most adolescents live with their biological or adoptive mothers. In fact, the findings suggest that variations in household structure relating to the male are quite important. The presence of the biological or adoptive father (versus a single-parent household) is associated with improved relations with the mother, both in terms of identification and communication. Also, adolescents have higher levels of identification and communication with their biological or adoptive fathers. Most important in terms of work, nonleisure spending improves relationships with biological or adoptive fathers but not with other males.

The present study draws from Bronfenbrenner's (1979, 1986a) conceptual models in several respects. First, it attends to development through the use of longitudinal data and a time-sensitive analytic strategy. Second, the focus on work and family connections reflects an interest in the mesosystem, how functioning in one domain of development impacts on functioning in another domain. Finally, this research attends to the broader ecology by drawing comparisons between urban and rural settings.

At the same time, as an ecological study of human development this research is preliminary in its ability to explain both the critical aspects that differentiate the ecologies and the mechanisms underlying ecological variation. Most important, urban-rural comparisons are confounded by the economic hardships experienced by the rural sample. It may be that a less distressed rural sample would not differ from the present urban sample or that an impoverished urban sample would not differ from the present rural sample.

Despite these limitations, the results underscore that the study of adolescent work must be sensitive to differences across segments of society. Adolescent work clearly matters for development; yet how this is so varies by the broader contexts of work and family. The importance of ecology probably reflects both material and normative differences, which are based in historical circumstance as well as present patterns of everyday living. Taken seriously, these ideas suggest that research on adolescent work and its developmental implications is just beginning.

Appendix A
Descriptive Statistics of
Variables, Intact Families

(grand means and standard deviations for variables across the four waves)

Adolescent's age	17.49	(.40)
Earnings (natural log)	5.37	(1.79)
No earnings	−.68	(.49)
Current job hours	9.22	(6.89)
Nonleisure spending	.35	(.17)
Gender (1 = male, −1 = female)	−.06	(.99)
Nativity (1 = foreign, −1 = U.S.)	−.85	(.52)
Grade point average	8.45	(1.89)
Identification		
With father	2.67	(.65)
With mother	2.90	(.60)
Communication		
To father	2.53	(.69)
To mother	2.93	(.64)
From father	2.36	(.69)
From mother	2.72	(.69)

Appendix B
Hierarchical Linear Models
With Repeated Measures

Briefly, we model Y_{it}, the parent-adolescent relationship Y (e.g., the adolescent's report of identification with mother) between the 9th and 12th grades for individual i at time t. The full equation is a combination of individual and population growth curves, and an error term. The individual growth curve

$$Y_{it} = \pi_{0i} + \pi_{1i}(Age)_{it}$$

has two random-effect variables (i.e., they vary between individuals), π_{0i} and π_{1i}. Age is centered about its grand mean (17.49) so that π_{0i} represents adolescent i's expected level of identification at about 17-1/2 years old and π_{1i} represents adolescent i's expected rate of change in identification. This growth curve estimates individual-specific change over time and allows us to describe individual differences in identification's mean level and rate of change in the sample. The inclusion of the within-individual component also adjusts for the lack of independence in repeated measures of the same individual over time, permitting us to test the association between earnings and the adolescent-parent relationship with longitudinal data.

The population growth curve and error term

$$B_0 + B_1(Age)_{it} + B_2(Earnings)_{it} + B_3(Work\ Status)_{it} +$$
$$B_4(Low\ Hours)_{it} + B_5(High\ Hours)_{it} + B_6(Gender)_i +$$
$$B_7(Grade\ Point\ Average)_{it} + B_8(Nativity)_i + e_{it}$$

include all fixed-effect variables (i.e., they do not vary between individuals). The fixed intercept (B_0) represents the group mean for identification, and the fixed effect of age (B_1) represents the group mean rate of change for identification between the 9th and 12th grades. (For computational reasons, the random-effect parameters are estimated as deviations about their respective fixed-effect parameters. This is to avoid representing the mean level of these individual parameters twice in the model.) The variable of central interest, earnings, is added to this model as a fixed effect (B_2) because we are interested in how earnings and identification are associated across individuals.

Earnings could also be added to the model as a random effect. For the sake of simplicity, we estimate models with a fixed earnings effect only. The addition of a random earnings effect should not change our conclusions because fixed-effect results are robust to the specification of the random components (McLean, Sanders, & Stroup, 1991). In fact, models estimated with both a fixed and random earnings component confirm this. The random earnings covariate was not significant, and the pattern of fixed-effect results did not change substantially. Other work variables include work status (whether employed in the last year) and two categorical variables for work hours.

The model controls other factors that may be related to changes in the parent-adolescent relationship: age, gender, grade point average, and nativity; family structure was also controlled in models including both intact and nonintact families. These controls also are entered as fixed effects (e.g., gender, B_6). All continuous variables are centered about their grand means and the dichotomous variables are effect coded (e.g., girl = −1, boy = 1) to facilitate interpretation. For example, the association between earnings and identification can be interpreted as the amount of change in identification associated with an increase in earnings when age is at its grand mean of 17.49. The effect coding procedure represents the difference between the grand mean of the predicted variable and the group in the 1 category (e.g., in the case of father vs. another male, the presence of the father is 1). Because this coding provides a 2 degrees of freedom contrast, the difference between father present (= 1) and single-parent household (= −1) is twice the magnitude of the coefficient. This coding procedure is necessary when interaction terms are included in the model to ensure that a predictor's main effect represents its average effect, not its effect for a specific reference group.

The error term e_{it} represents random error for person i at time t. The design involves four measurement occasions, $t = 4$, covering 1,000 adolescents in Wave 1 and 933 by Wave 4. A case represents data for each person-year, so that the models can have a maximum of 3,854 cases (i.e., 1,000 + 964 + 957 + 933); because the equations will focus on specific subgroups (e.g., intact families), the number of possible cases is actually much smaller.

The model therefore has two types of effects. The fixed effects provide estimates of average identification (B_0), average change in identification (B_1), and how covariates like earnings relate to identification (B_2) across all subjects. In contrast, random components (π_{0i} and π_{1i}) represent effects for each individual; we include these components because we believe that age-related change and mean level of the adolescent-parent relationship vary significantly between individuals. Thus, a single regression equation is estimated which interrelates work and family variables for both the group and individual.

Other than models with additive effects, it is also plausible that more complex patterns involving interactions among the predictor variables characterize the developmental trajectories of parent-adolescent relationships. First, we test whether the model's fit improves significantly with the inclusion of a quadratic term for age; none of the quadratic terms was significant, indicating that adolescent-parent relationships change in a linear fashion and are not subject to acceleration or deceleration. This finding is consistent with conceptual arguments that personal relationships within the family are not subject to dramatic change (Laursen & Collins, 1994). Second, it is also plausible that more complex patterns involving interactions among the predictor variables characterize the developmental trajectories of parent-adolescent relationships (e.g., developmental effects, whereby the effect size of a predictor like earnings changes with age). To test these possibilities, we introduced second-order interaction terms involving earnings, hours, nonleisure spending, and age and gender—for example, B_9 (Age × Earnings). Given the large number of interactions estimated, we evaluate the significance of interactions using a Bonferroni adjustment (alpha = about .001). No significant interactions were observed, indicating that relationships between work variables and the adolescent-parent relationship are not contingent on gender or age.

The analyses were carried out using PROC MIXED in SAS. Significance levels are based on two-tailed tests.

Notes

1. The hierarchical linear models estimated with the Iowa sample include earnings, nonleisure spending, current job hours, age, gender, grade point average, pubertal status, farm context (farm or nonfarm), and family per capita income as covariates. In the present study, covariates include earnings, nonleisure spending, work status (whether employed in the previous year), current job hours, age, gender, grade point average, family structure, and nativity. The models differ in that the Iowa equations include pubertal status and family per capita income. However, per capita income did not significantly predict any of the adolescent-parent relationships in the Iowa study. Moreover, the urban sample is somewhat affluent when compared with 1980 U.S. Census data (U.S. Bureau of the Census, 1982b). Pubertal status did not significantly predict adolescent-parent relationships in any consistent manner. The models also differ in that the equations based on the St. Paul sample control nativity (whether born in the United States). However, this variable also proved to be unimportant.

2. The interpretation of the multiplicative interaction between diversity of nonleisure spending and earnings is speculative. The implicit assumption is that individuals spend the same proportion of their earnings on different types of spending regardless of their level of income. For example, people who save for college put 10% in the bank regardless of how big their paycheck is. If this assumption is true, then the interaction is a proxy for the amount spent in nonleisure ways. Unfortunately, we have no way of testing this assumption. Thus, findings with respect to the nonleisure spending-earnings interaction should be viewed as suggestive for future research.

3. Models were also estimated only for those reporting earnings in the previous year to determine if the skewness resulting from the inclusion of the 0 cases was affecting results. Findings were essentially similar to those reported in the tables.

4. The hours variable cannot be used as a continuous measure because many of the adolescents were not employed (i.e., they had 0 hours) at the time of the survey's administration, resulting in skewness. Also, it is not feasible to estimate models only among those employed at the time of the survey's administration. Issues of selection arise such that the meaning of the subsample is unclear. Thus, a dichotomous measurement strategy is used because it avoids issues of skewness and selection and makes the results readily comparable to studies concerned with work hours.

5. Household economic strategies can be found in urban settings in late 19th- and early 20th-century America (Zelizer, 1985), but the child's role seemed to involve higher levels of exploitation—at least fewer rewards—when compared with youthwork in farm settings.

5

Adolescent Work as an "Arena of Comfort" Under Conditions of Family Discomfort

KATHLEEN THIEDE CALL

The concept of an arena of comfort originates from Simmons and Blyth's (1987) study of the transition from childhood through middle adolescence. They examined the effect of age, gender, pubertal timing, and timing of school transitions on the self-image and adjustment of a sample of white, urban youths. Simmons and Blyth found that life changes do not always have negative consequences; rather, negative effects occur for some adolescents under some circumstances. Two hypotheses emerged in interpreting their findings: The first is the developmental readiness hypothesis (Peskin & Livson, 1972; Petersen & Taylor, 1980), which asserts that children can be pushed into the next developmental period earlier than they are cognitively and emotionally ready for the transition; the second is the focal theory of change hypothesis (Coleman, 1974), which maintains that it is easier to deal with one life change at a time rather than several simultaneously. Simmons and Blyth (1987) infer that underlying both hypotheses is the notion of an "arena of comfort," concluding that if change comes too suddenly or too early or if it occurs in too many areas of life at once, then individuals will experience great discomfort. They assert that "there needs to be some arena of life or some set of role-relationships with which the individual can feel relaxed and comfortable, to which he or she can withdraw and become reinvigorated" (p. 352). Although the concept of an arena of comfort was derived from these findings, it has not been directly tested.

An arena of comfort is an interpersonal context that is soothing and accepting—a place where people can relax, feel at ease with themselves, and let down their guard (Simmons, in press; Simmons & Blyth, 1987). Following the work of Thoits (1983) and Linville (1985), Simmons and Blyth (1987) hypothesize that individuals experience better mental health and use more effective coping strategies if they are involved in multiple roles and if at least one context, or set of role relationships, remains generally positive and stable. An "arena of comfort" provides a place for the person to relax and rejuvenate, so that the events and experiences that are harmful or threatening to the self-image in one context can be endured or mastered.

Although change and a certain level of discomfort are widely considered to be necessary for growth and development (Rutter, 1983; Simmons, in press), disruption in many spheres of life may be overwhelming. Simmons and Blyth (1987) suggest that people do better in terms of self-esteem and behavioral coping if at least one environment or set of role relationships remains generally positive and stable. The arena of comfort construct directs attention to contextual sources of "comfort" which enhance "readiness" to cope with, and moderate the effects of, change or discomfort in another context. Simmons (unpublished manuscript) lays out her conceptualization of "comfort" as a self-emotion. Self-comfort is described as a balanced state in which the person feels a sense of familiarity with the self, and a high degree of fit with the environment. According to Simmons, comfort occurs when the individual is at ease—when arousal is neither very high (i.e., an anxious, excited, or exhilarated state) nor very low (i.e., a bored or depressed state). A comfort arena is a context or role relationship that "provides a warm, nonjudgemental social environment, where acceptance is unconditional. Here is where one feels 'at home', where one feels at peace with oneself, where one can 'let ones hair down'" (p. 22). Thus, a comfort arena provides both experiences of self-acceptance and perceived acceptance by others.

The notion of an arena of comfort as a protective mechanism is attractive, as it directs attention to the contextual and individual features that lead to resilience. It also addresses the person's active role in the developmental process; the selection of interpersonal contexts might optimally involve balancing those that provide challenge and those that provide reassurance. By providing social support, increasing coping skills, and enhancing the self-concept, a comfort arena strengthens the person so that challenges in other life spheres can be dealt with.

The family is often characterized as a safe haven; a place where one is able to find shelter from the day's events (Lasch, 1977). However, home is not necessarily an arena of comfort for an adolescent whose family is undergoing change or when relationships with parents are fraught with discord. Adolescence is a period of disengagement from parents, when adolescents strive for greater autonomy and explore new identities (Csikszentmihalyi & Larson, 1984; Steinberg, 1990). The family context may inhibit this exploration and feel constraining to the adolescent's developing self (Simmons, unpublished manuscript); the struggle for independence often colors even routine exchanges between adolescents and parents (Csikszentmihalyi & Larson, 1984). As the home becomes less comfortable, peer, school, or work contexts may become more comfortable and concordant with this stage-specific growth and self-actualization process.

Although a certain amount of tension between adolescents and their parents is normative (Brooks-Gunn, 1991; Smetana, Yau, Restrepo, & Braeges, 1991), high levels of conflict have negative consequences. Uncomfortable or unsupportive relationships with parents influence a range of adolescent outcomes such as problem behavior (Jessor & Jessor, 1977; LeCroy, 1989), the self-concept (Gecas & Seff, 1991; Mortimer et al., 1986), psychological well-being, academic performance (Maccoby & Martin, 1983), self-reliance, and indicators of responsible independence (Steinberg & Silverberg, 1986). Evidence of the negative effects of problems with parents holds across socioeconomic and ethnic groups.

Parent-adolescent relationships characterized by a lack of communication and affection are ongoing stressors (Cohen & Wills, 1985; Wheaton, 1990). Unlike event stressors that are discrete, objective events, ongoing stressors or "daily hassles" are enduring subjective strains in the immediate environment (Cohen & Wills, 1985; Compas, Davis, Forsythe, & Wagner, 1986; Delongis, Coyne, Dakof, Folkman, & Lazarus, 1982; Rowlinson & Felner, 1988). Research on adults

(Delongis et al., 1982) and adolescents (Compas et al., 1986; Rowlinson & Felner, 1988) suggests that ongoing stressors lead to difficulties in adjustment and may be even more detrimental to individual functioning than major life events.

Studies of stress-buffering during adolescence typically examine social support (from friends and family) as moderators of the effects of life events (Windle, 1992). The results of this research are mixed (Compas, 1987; Windle, 1992). Inconsistencies in the findings may be partially attributed to the focus on distal rather than proximal stressors. Moreover, inadequate attention has been given to contextual features of the stress process; that is, support may be more effective if it comes from outside the stressor context. For example, a recent study by Lepore (1992) found evidence of cross-domain buffering effects. In a sample of college students, support from a close friend moderated the psychological distress associated with frequent conflict with a roommate. This evidence suggests that support from a friend, teacher, supervisor, or coworker could moderate the effects of stressful events or discomfort in the family.

Involvement with friends and school and work activities are particularly important for adolescents whose relationships with parents are distant and lacking in support (Savin-Williams & Berndt, 1990) or whose parents are divorcing or remarrying (Hetherington, 1989). Besides the benefits derived from social support outside the family, the skills, values, and self-knowledge developed at school and work may have an enduring effect on the adolescent's well-being and adaptation (Csikszentmihalyi & Larson, 1984). Positive experiences and accomplishments at school and work may strengthen personal coping skills (i.e., self-esteem and self-efficacy) and moderate the effects of change and discomfort at home (Bandura, 1986; Rutter, 1990). The compensating effects of experiences at work may be especially important to adolescents who are not comfortable or engaged in school (Elliott & Voss, 1974).

Experiences at work have been found to have direct effects on adolescent functioning. For example, work conditions that provide opportunities for advancement and good pay enhance adolescents' perceptions of competence, whereas work-school conflicts diminish self-efficacy (Finch, Shanahan, Mortimer, & Ryu, 1991).

Csikszentmihalyi and Larson (1984) found that adolescents' moods were enthusiastic and engaged during structured activities such as paid work, classwork, and favorite leisure activities (i.e., sports, art, music). Activities guided by structured systems of rules and regulations motivated adolescents to decipher the rules, work toward a goal within these constraints, and learn about themselves through this performance. These experiences help the adolescent develop skills and provide information about the self that fosters competence and self-worth.

Much of the research investigating intercontext effects, or "mesosystem" interrelations (Bronfenbrenner, 1979, 1986b), concerns work and family linkages and is based on adult samples (Bielby, 1992). This work typically examines how workplace stressors "spill over" into the family. Sometimes, their consequences are alleviated by spouse support (Pearlin & McCall, 1990; Weiss, 1990). Alternatively, work stress can diminish support from others at home, placing the worker at even greater risk for poor adjustment (Liem & Liem, 1990). Conversely, Piotrkowski and Crits-Christoph (1981) suggest that for some women, positive experiences at work (i.e., positive job mood, intrinsic job gratification, job security, and job satisfaction) have salutary effects on their relationships with family members and mood at home. The potential of work experiences and supports to act as moderators of family stress has been given little attention. However, some research (Kandel, Davies, & Raveis, 1985; Wheaton, 1990) indicates that being employed can moderate the effects of marital problems for women. Could similar processes occur for adolescent workers?

It is important to understand the link between work and family among adolescents because national surveys (Manning, 1990) show that the majority of adolescents work (61% of 10th graders and 90% of 11th and 12th graders). Can supportive, positive relationships with supervisors or coworkers moderate changes at home and/or strained relationships with parents? Can accomplishments and involvement in work and the satisfaction deriving therefrom diminish or offset difficulties at home and compensate for the lack of positive feedback provided by parents? Might such involvement distract the adolescent from negative rumination about relationships and events in the family?

Alternatively, if work is stressful or uncomfortable for the adolescent, will these experiences potentiate the effects of family change and discord?

In this chapter, I examine the effects of both event stressors and ongoing stressors in the family context. Although there are a number of potential arenas to which the adolescent may retreat when circumstances and relations in the family are stressful, in the analyses that follow I explore the efficacy of the work setting as an arena of comfort. Along with examining the moderating power of social support I explore the buffering effects of other experiences in the work domain.

Measures

COMFORT

Following Simmons and Blyth (1987), comfort in a context may be indicated by feelings of calmness, satisfaction, acceptance, and ease, as opposed to high arousal, challenge, disapproval, and discontent. The respondent might simply be asked whether he or she felt comfortable in a given context. In the absence of such a direct measure, a number of items were selected as indicators of comfort in the contexts of family and work. They measure the level of satisfaction and the positive or negative evaluation of interpersonal and other experiences in a particular arena or role relationship. Simmons (in press) describes comfort as a feeling of fit between self and the environment. The degree or intensity of feelings of comfort may vary from day to day, but in general, comfort is the enduring quality of the person-context interaction.

Consistent with this general definition, comfort is indicated by warm, positive, and supportive relationships and by feelings of acceptance, satisfaction, and freedom from stress at home and at work. Measures of comfort in the family are from Furstenberg's (1981) National Survey of Children; they evaluate the adolescent's relationship with parents or guardians (see Appendix A). Included are assessments of the parent-child relationship, such as perceived closeness to parents, openness of communication, and the extent to which the child can turn to the parent for support. Adolescent comfort is also indicated by the amount of time spent with parents doing enjoyable things. Thus, when I refer to comfort in the family, I am speaking of adolescents' relationships with their parents. Relationships with siblings and other family members living in the home are not assessed. However, research investigating mood states found that adolescents' expressed emotions did not vary much while at home in the company of parents versus time spent with siblings (Csikszentmihalyi & Larson, 1984).

Measures of subjective comfort in the work sphere include the adolescent's perceptions of the availability of supervisory support and support from a best friend at work. I also assess other experiences as indicators of the presence or absence of comfort at work: job satisfaction, the absence of high levels of stress, and work that is considered interesting. Work experience measures were obtained from several prior studies of adolescents and adults, including Bachman's (1970) Youth in Transition Study, Quinn and Staines's (1979) Quality of Employment Survey, Kohn and Schooler's (1974a, 1974b) Study of Occupations, and Mortimer and Lorence's (1979a, 1979b) Michigan Panel Study.

CHANGE

The family context is the change or stressor context of interest (discussed more fully later in the "Analytic Strategy" section). Within this context, the following transitions are possible: change in family composition (that may also, but not necessarily, reflect a change in the parents' marital status), change in father's employment status,[1] and a geographic change by the family and/or adolescent. The measure of change in father's employment is based on the adolescent's yearly report of whether the parent is currently working. Change in family composition is derived from an item, collected yearly, that asks the adolescent with whom they are currently living. For example, a change in family composition could reflect a transition from a two-parent intact family to a single-parent situation, from living with a single parent to a remarriage or blended family arrangement, or moving in with grandparents, friends, or others. Current addresses are obtained directly from the adolescents each year, allowing us to track and record any geographic moves. Each measure of change is expressed as a dummy variable (1 = *change*) and evaluated individually.

ADJUSTMENT

The dependent variables of interest in this study are grade point average and measures of psychological adjustment, which include global self-esteem and self-derogation (from the Rosenberg Self-Esteem Scale; Rosenberg, 1965), mastery or self-efficacy (from the Pearlin Mastery Scale; Pearlin, Menaghan, Lieberman, & Mullan, 1981), and depressive affect and well-being (from the "General Well-Being Scale" of the Current Health Insurance Study Mental Health Battery; Ware, Johnston, Davies-Avery, & Brook, 1979). Grade point average is a self-report item included annually in the child survey. Appendix A contains the full list of indicators.

Specification

MEASURING COMFORT

In this research, comfort is operationalized as a qualitative state. According to Simmons, to maintain mental health, everyone needs to have a context in which they are unconditionally accepted and do not have to worry about their presentation of self. This requires some predictability of the acceptance and support provided in that arena. If it is to be deemed an arena of comfort, people cannot feel ambiguous about whether or not they will be accepted, flaws and all, or about the level of satisfaction they experience in a context or relationship. To offer the respite and protection the arena of comfort hypothesis projects, the individual must be able to think of the setting as a "sure thing," relationships and experiences that can be counted on. In essence, this is a distinctive qualitative state; Simmons does not view the phenomenon of comfort as a continuously graded variable. In the interest of coming as close as possible to Simmons' concept of a comfort arena, I elected to risk losing the full range of variability in the comfort measures by creating dichotomous variables.

Thus, comfort is operationalized as an all-or-none phenomenon, present or absent. Dummy variables were created based on the content of each question and its response options. For example, if respondents indicate that their supervisor is "often" or "always" willing to listen to problems and help find solutions, they are considered comfortable compared to those who responded "sometimes," "rarely," or "almost never" to this item. When there are multiple indicators of an aspect of comfort in a given arena (i.e., five items measuring the level of stress at work), cutoff points were established for each item, reflecting the presence (assigned a score of 1) or absence (assigned 0) of comfort. The items were then summed to create each arena-specific "comfort" index or construct, and a cutoff point was again determined to reflect comfort in each particular arena (this method was suggested by Roberta Simmons, personal communication). This operationalization of comfort is consistent with Simmons's on/off definition of the concept; only those people who describe their contexts in quite positive terms are considered comfortable. Also, consideration of the adequacy of subgroup size for performing analyses informed decisions regarding index cutoff points (this specification strategy is described in detail in Appendix B).

As noted earlier, comfort in the family is indicated by measures of adolescents' relationships with their mothers and fathers.[2] Adolescents who responded positively to at least four of the five relevant items are described as having a comfortable relationship with each parent. With this specification (described more fully in Appendix B), approximately 59% of 10th-grade adolescents report comfortable relationships with their mothers, and 35% report comfort with their fathers. This distribution seems reasonable because relationships with mothers are typically described as warmer and more intimate than relationships with fathers (LeCroy, 1989), which appear to be more "flat" and reflect fewer activities shared with their teens (Steinberg, 1987).

The questions addressed in this research are best answered and interpreted using a single measure of comfort in the family arena. Selecting one measure of comfort in the family simplifies the analysis conceptually and empirically. The emphasis in this chapter is on the effects of discomfort in the family. Thus, adolescents who do *not* have a warm and positive relationship with either parent are defined as uncomfortable in the family arena. Although the majority of employed adolescents characterize relationships with one or both parents as close and open, 33% are described as uncomfortable with both parents. It should be noted that the measure of comfort with parents selects only adolescents who have the most positive relationships with their mothers and fathers. Such a stringent indicator may have a more pronounced effect than a continuous measure of perceived support, given the mental health outcomes of interest.

Measures of comfort at work are multidimensional; some are more interpersonal, or support related, and others are more task oriented. The emphasis in this research is on interpersonal sources of comfort; however, a fuller exploration of task-related sources of comfort is warranted. Some experiences at work may allow the adolescent to concentrate on the task at hand, diminishing self-consciousness in the process, which should be comfortable. Because of their diverse character and/or lack of applicability to all respondents, no attempt was made to form additive indices.

Two interpersonal measures of comfort at work are perceptions of supervisor support and feeling close to a friend at work. Interpersonal sources of comfort in the work setting are not available to approximately 25% of employed 10th graders. For example, some youthwork is typically performed alone, as in baby-sitting, doing yardwork, or holding a paper route. In the 10th grade, approximately 34% of working adolescents who have a supervisor report feelings of comfort in that relationship. Of those who work with peers, 46% report having a friend at work to whom they feel close.

The first task-oriented measure of work comfort is an index of work stress (i.e., involving time pressures, having too much to do, being drained of energy, and being exposed to physical discomforts). Jobs that are highly stressful (approximately 23% in the 10th grade) demand high levels of arousal; here they are defined as uncomfortable. At the opposite end of the spectrum, jobs that are perceived as boring (approximately 29%) produce uncomfortably low levels of arousal (Simmons, in press). Thus, boredom is a second task-related indicator of comfort. The third indicator, satisfaction, is a global evaluation of work experience that is indicative of general feelings of comfort (the majority of 10th-grade workers, 85%, describe their jobs as satisfying). Again, interpersonal measures of comfort are of greatest interest. However, in some analyses, the effects of both interpersonal and task-oriented measures are evaluated.

ADJUSTMENT VARIABLES

The psychological adjustment variables are self-esteem, self-derogation, mastery, depressive affect, and well-being. The item loadings for each of the adjustment constructs are derived from a series of confirmatory factor analyses (using LISREL VII). Because the study examines adolescent mental health over time, with a particular interest in gender differences, the measurement structure of each mental health construct was assessed by constraining corresponding unstandardized lambda coefficients to be equal across waves and sex. Fully constrained models were then compared to freely estimated models. The analyses revealed that the measurement structures of the adjustment constructs are similar across waves and for girls and boys. Therefore, unstandardized lambda coefficients from the fully constrained models are used as item weights. (Standardized coefficients are provided in Appendix A because of their easier interpretability.)

Analytic Strategy

The general model of adolescent stress, including the conditioning effects of an arena of comfort, is shown in Figure 5.1. In this figure, the moderating effects of the arena of comfort are highlighted (Paths C, D, and F). First, I examine the relationship between objective change and discomfort and between discomfort and adjustment (Paths A and B of Figure 5.1) in the family context (change context). Adolescents who do not perceive supportive relationships with either parent are uncomfortable in the family (33.4% of 10th-grade adolescents). I also investigate the direct effects of family change on adolescent adjustment (Path E). I initially estimate these paths (A, B, and E) without consideration of either the direct effects of the arena of comfort or the interactive effects.

Next, the moderating effects of the "presence of comfort" arena (in the work setting) are examined. The direct effects of the arena of comfort on family discomfort and adjustment are included in the moderating analysis but are not shown in Figure 5.1. The relationships are explored using regression with interaction terms to test for mod-

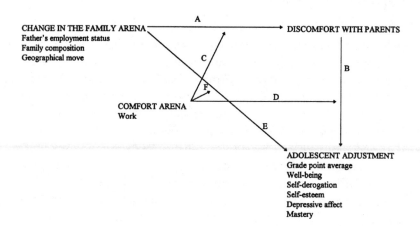

Figure 5.1. A model of adolescent stress and the moderating effects of arenas of comfort.

NOTE: All equations control socioeconomic status, race, nativity, gender, and lagged outcomes.

erating effects (Paths B, D, E, and F employ OLS regression; logistic regression is used to estimate Paths A and C because the dependent variable, discomfort in the family, is dichotomous). First, change in the family context (Path A), comfort in the work arena (path not shown), and the interaction between family change and comfort in the moderating arena (Path C) predicts discomfort in the family. Second, discomfort in the family context (Path B), comfort in the work domain (path not shown), and the interaction between family discomfort and work comfort (Path D) estimates adjustment. Third, family change (Path E), comfort at work (path not shown), and the interaction between family change and work comfort (Path F) estimates adjustment. Significant interaction terms indicate that a buffering effect exists. The analyses are performed for employed adolescents (controlling the background variables and the one-year lagged adjustment variable).[3]

The family sphere was selected as the change and/or discomfort context, first, because this is likely the arena of greatest long-term exposure and commitment for adolescents. Second, for most adoles-

cents, change and discomfort in the family should be highly consequential (Gecas & Seff, 1991; Greenberger, 1983; Hetherington,
1989; Jessor & Jessor, 1977; LeCroy, 1989; Maccoby & Martin,
1983). A variety of possible changes within the family arena between
the 9th and 10th grade are considered:[4] change in father's employment
status, change in family composition, and a geographic move by the
family or adolescent (i.e., the entire family may move, or the adolescent may move away from home).

Change in father's employment status, which occurred for 4.7% of
the adolescents) could signify a job loss, retirement, or a move back
into the workforce. Change in family composition (a self-report item
that asks the adolescent with whom they are currently living) could
reflect a transition from a two-parent intact family to a single-parent
home, or the custodial parent may remarry between the 9th and 10th
grade, or the adolescent could move away from home and live with
other relatives, friends, foster parents, or others. A change in family
composition, of some kind, was reported for 13.3% of the adolescents.
Approximately 17% of them experienced a geographic move between
the 9th and 10th grade. This experience could range from a move
within the same city (66% of moves are of this type), from the city to
a suburb or beyond (21% of all moves), out of state (about 8% of all
moves), to outside the United States (approximately 4% of those who
moved).

The measures of change do not allow an assessment of whether the
event is perceived as positive or negative by the adolescent. Some
argue (Thoits, 1983, 1991) that life events need to be categorized in
terms of the personal meaning they hold for the individual. Rutter
(1983) points out that psychiatric disorders are largely associated with
undesirable incidents. However, Luthar (1991) found that during
periods of rapid change such as adolescence, even positive events can
lead to the perception that the environment is uncertain and unstable,
increasing the adolescent's level of vulnerability.

Before discussing the results, it should be noted that the statistical
significance of an interaction effect depends on the number of adolescents for whom the modifying factor (presence of comfort) and the
stressor co-occur. Thus, it is quite possible that a strong interactive
effect will be concealed because it applies to only a small proportion

of the sample. This may be especially problematic when examining Paths C and F of Figure 5.1 given the small proportion of adolescents in this sample who experience change between the 9th and 10th grades.

Findings

DESCRIPTIVE STATISTICS

Correlations among family event stressors, the measure of proximal stress (strained parent-adolescent relations), adjustment, and moderator variables are presented in Table 5.1. As shown, the event stressors are related to several of the criterion variables. For example, a change in the father's employment status is associated with higher self-derogation, more depressive affect, and lower self-esteem. Change in family composition is associated with lower school performance. Similarly, a geographic move is related to lower grade point average. Discomfort with parents is significantly related to lower school achievement as well as diminished well-being, self-esteem, and mastery. When examining interaction effects in the context of regression models, it is recommended that moderator variables be uncorrelated with both the predictor variables and the outcome variables (Baron & Kenny, 1986; Cronbach, 1987). Table 5.1 demonstrates that several relationships between the moderators, stressors, and outcomes are significant. However, the strength of these associations is modest ($r < .19$). The displayed intercorrelations seem acceptable for investigating the moderating influence of comfort at work.

EFFECTS OF FAMILY CHANGE ON DISCOMFORT BETWEEN PARENTS AND ADOLESCENTS

I begin by examining whether family change (i.e., change in father's employment status, family composition, or geographical moves) affects adolescents' perceptions of comfort with their parents (Path A of Figure 5.1). Using logistic regression, discomfort with parents (a dichotomous construct) was regressed on each indicator of change (one at a time), the one-year lagged outcome, and background vari-

TABLE 5.1 Intercorrelations of Employed 10th-Graders Measures of Stress, Adjustment, and Moderator Variables

	1	2	3	4	5	6	7	8	9	10	11	12	13	14	15
1. Father's employment status	1.00														
2. Change in family composition	.05	1.00													
3. Change of residence	.01	.28***	1.00												
4. Discomfort with parents	-.03	.02	-.06	1.00											
5. Grade point average	-.06	-.18***	-.10*	-.17***	1.00										
6. Well-being	-.07	-.03	.02	-.19***	.13**	1.00									
7. Self-derogation	.12*	.07	-.02	.03	-.09*	-.42***	1.00								
8. Self-esteem	-.15**	-.03	-.04	-.20***	.12*	.50***	-.59***	1.00							
9. Depressive affect	.11*	.05	.03	.09	-.10*	-.39***	.50***	-.40***	1.00						
10. Mastery	-.09	-.07	.06	-.14**	.16***	.44***	-.71***	.50***	-.50***	1.00					
11. Supervisor support	-.04	.05	.05	-.14*	.02	.14**	-.11*	.09	-.08	.19***	1.00				
12. Support from coworker	.09	.02	-.01	-.05	-.03	.03	.05	.02	.10	.03	.15**	1.00			
13. Work satisfaction	-.06	.10*	.02	.09	-.09	.17***	-.15**	.10*	-.11*	.09	.11*	-.02	1.00		
14. Low work stress	-.00	-.04	-.03	-.02	.07	.10*	-.05	.12*	-.16***	.08	.13*	-.08	.08	1.00	
15. Work is interesting	.02	.01	-.02	-.03	.01	.09	-.12**	.11*	-.15**	.10*	.11*	-.07	.35***	.17***	1.00

NOTE: *n* ranges from 288 to 449.
*p < .05; **p < .01; ***p < .001.

143

ables (parents' socioeconomic status; race, coded 0 if minority, 1 if white; nativity, coded 0 if foreign born, 1 if U.S. born; and gender) that may be related to the level of comfort with parents (Baldwin, Baldwin, & Cole, 1990; Barber & Thomas, 1986; LeCroy, 1989; Lempers, Clark-Lempers, & Simons, 1989; McLoyd, 1990; Nidorf, 1985; Steinberg, 1987).

The results (not shown) indicate that the measures of family change do not significantly affect the level of comfort in adolescents' relationships with parents. These events thus appear to be unrelated to parent-adolescent relations. It should be noted, however, that inclusion of family discomfort in the prior year as a predictor makes this analysis particularly stringent. It has been argued that the effects of divorce, for example, occur over a long period of time and that the greatest difficulties stem from the conflict and discord prior to actual parental separation (Demo & Acock, 1988; Peterson & Zill, 1986). In this case, any effects of the divorce process would be registered in the lagged outcome variable and thus controlled away in the analysis. Similarly for other event stressors in the family, the stress prior to and leading up to the actual event would be captured, in part, in the lagged family discomfort variable, diminishing the effect of change. Even so, however, discomfort with parents is not significantly correlated with any of the three change measures (see Table 5.1).

EFFECTS OF FAMILY DISCOMFORT
ON ADOLESCENT OUTCOMES

Next, I examine the effects of strained relationships with both parents on adolescents' mental health and academic achievement (Path B of Figure 5.1). The six adjustment outcomes (grade point average, well-being, self-derogation, self-esteem, depressive affect, and mastery) are regressed (using OLS regression) on family discomfort, controlling background variables (parents' socioeconomic status, race, nativity, and gender) that have been found to be related to adolescent adjustment and achievement (Baldwin et al., 1990; Clark, 1983; Furstenberg, 1988; McLoyd, 1990; Spencer, Dornbusch, & Mont-Reynaud, 1990). The one-year lagged outcomes are included in all equations. It is possible that adolescents who are depressed or have a low self-image evaluate their relationships with parents less favorably than do those having higher well-being and self-esteem. By controlling the ninth-grade psychological outcomes I can account for the adolescents' stable proclivity to perceive relationships as comfortable or uncomfortable. Thus, when prior levels of psychological functioning and achievement are controlled, significant coefficients for the comfort indices may be interpreted as indicating that comfort produces change in the outcomes over time.

Discomfort with parents diminishes academic performance, well-being, self-esteem, and mastery and heightens depressive affect (see Table 5.2). Family discomfort is not related to self-derogation. As might be expected, adolescents from families of higher socioeconomic status report higher grade point averages than do those from less advantaged homes. Whites have higher grade point averages than minority adolescents. Consistent with much previous research (Allgood-Merten, Lewinsohn, & Hops, 1990; Gecas, 1989; Maccoby & Jacklin, 1974; Petersen, Sargiani, & Kennedy, 1991; Simmons & Blyth, 1987), girls report lower levels of well-being and greater self-derogation and depressive affect than boys do.

EFFECTS OF FAMILY CHANGE
ON ADOLESCENT OUTCOMES

Next, I examine the direct effects of family change on adolescent adjustment. The outcomes are regressed on each measure of change in the family (change in father's employment status, family composition, and geographical move) separately, controlling the background variables and the one-year lagged outcome variable. Change in father's employment status is negatively related to employed adolescents' self-esteem ($beta = -.113, p < .05$). These findings appear to be consistent with the work of Elder, Caspi, and Van Nguyen (1986), who found that fathers became more punitive and inconsistent under the strain of financial loss, which had deleterious effects on children's psychological adjustment (the measure used in the present study, however, includes reemployment as well as job loss). Change in father's employment status is not related to academic performance, well-being, self-derogation, depressive affect, or perceived competence.

Change in family composition between the 9th and 10th grade is negatively related to academic achievement ($beta = -.157, p < .001$).

TABLE 5.2 Effects of Family Discomfort on Employed Adolescents' 10th-Grade Academic Achievement and Mental Health (unstandardized OLS regression coefficients)

	Grade Point	Well-Being	Self-Derogation	Self-Esteem	Depressive Affect	Mastery
Family discomfort						
B	-.208***	-1.086***	.364	-.687***	1.170*	-1.000***
Beta	-.136	-.175	.068	-.138	.105	-.190
Socioeconomic status						
B	.053**	-.002	.004	-.016	-.071	.071
Beta	.121	-.001	.003	-.011	-.022	.046
Race (0 = minority, 1 = white)						
B	.191*	.187	.351	-.378	.181	-.227
Beta	.105	.024	.053	-.062	.013	-.035
Nativity (0 = foreign, 1 = U.S. born)						
B	-.052	-.098	-.683	.377	-.643	.138
Beta	-.015	-.007	-.056	.034	-.025	.012
Gender (0 = boys, 1 = girls)						
B	.004	-.604*	.490*	-.350	1.076*	-.225
Beta	.003	-.099	.092	-.072	.098	-.043
Lagged outcome (9th grade)						
B	.533***	.328***	.520***	.480***	.346***	.423***
Beta	.543	.317	.511	.465	.367	.435
R^2	.400***	.165***	.303***	.293***	.172***	.260***
n cases	401	399	395	402	401	397

NOTE: The background variables are measured in the 9th grade.
*$p < .05$; **$p < .01$; ***$p < .001$.

Change in family composition has no significant impact on the five psychological adjustment variables. A geographical move between the 9th and 10th grade is not significantly related to employed adolescents' adjustment. Again, this analysis is quite rigorous given that the influence of an impending change may occur prior to the change event and be reflected in the lagged outcome.

DIRECT EFFECTS OF COMFORT AT WORK ON FAMILY DISCOMFORT

Before examining whether an arena of comfort moderates the effects of change on family discomfort or family discomfort on adolescent outcomes, we first examine whether comfort at work affects adolescents' perceptions of comfort with parents (path not shown). Family discomfort is regressed (using logistic regression) on each indicator of work comfort one at a time, family discomfort one year prior, and the background variables. None of the work moderators has a direct effect on relationships with parents.

DIRECT EFFECTS OF COMFORT AT WORK ON ADOLESCENT OUTCOMES

I now examine whether relationships and experiences at work influence adolescents' academic achievement and mental health (path not shown). The outcomes are regressed on each measure of comfort at work separately, controlling the background variables and the one-year lagged outcome variable.

Table 5.3 shows that support from a supervisor decreases employed adolescents' depressive affect and increases mastery; support from a best friend at work is not significantly related to adolescents' grade point average or the mental health outcomes. Job satisfaction strengthens feelings of well-being and decreases self-derogation and depressive affect. Low levels of stress at work, which signify comfort, enhance adolescents' well-being and self-esteem and reduce depressive affect. When work is considered interesting, depressive affect is diminished.

TABLE 5.3 Effects of Work Comfort on Employed Adolescents' 10th-Grade Academic Achievement and Mental Health (unstandardized OLS regression coefficients)

Comfort at Work	Grade Point	Well-Being	Self-Derogation	Self-Esteem	Depressive Affect	Mastery
Supervisor support	—	—	—	—	-1.356*	.874**
Coworker support	—	1.457***	—	—	—	—
Work is satisfying	—	—	-.718*	—	-1.735*	—
Low work stress	—	.851*	—	.906**	-2.41**	—
Work is interesting (lack of boredom)	—	—	—	—	-1.609**	—

NOTE: All equations control socioeconomic status, race, and nativity, which are measured in the 9th grade, and the one-year lagged outcome. — = nonsignificant results.

*$p < .05$; **$p < .01$; ***$p < .001$.

DOES THE ARENA OF COMFORT
CONDITION EFFECTS OF FAMILY
CHANGE ON FAMILY DISCOMFORT?

Here I examine whether an arena of comfort moderates the effects of family change on adolescents' perceptions of discomfort with parents (Path C of Figure 5.1). Family discomfort is regressed (using logistic regression) on the background variables, each measure of change one at a time, one work moderator, and the product of the same change and moderator variable. None of the interaction terms is significant. As discussed earlier, the three measures of change in the family are not directly related to discomfort with parents, nor are they conditionally related to discomfort.

DOES THE ARENA OF COMFORT
CONDITION THE EFFECTS OF FAMILY
DISCOMFORT ON ADJUSTMENT?

Can supportive and positive experiences at work moderate the effects of family discomfort on adolescents' adjustment (Path D of Figure 5.1)? To address this question, interaction analyses of the buffering effects of work comfort are performed. Each adjustment construct (grade point average, well-being, self-derogation, self-esteem, depressive affect, and mastery) is regressed on the one-year lagged adjustment measure, family discomfort, the background variables, one work moderator (supervisor support, support from a friend at work, satisfaction, low levels of stress and boredom at work, entered one at a time), and the product of family discomfort and the same moderator.[5] Significant coefficients for the product terms indicate that moderating effects exist; that is, family discomfort has different effects on the outcomes, depending on the level of comfort at work.

Three interaction terms are significant.[6] The interaction of family discomfort and support from a supervisor is significantly related to well-being ($beta = .160, p < .05$), self-esteem ($beta = .161, p < .05$), and mastery ($beta = .163, p < .05$). Because beta coefficients for interaction terms are not easily interpretable, regressions are performed separately for each condition (i.e., the presence or absence of comfort) of the significant work moderator. For example, as shown in Table 5.4, Panel A, well-being in the 10th grade is regressed on

9th-grade well-being, discomfort with parents, and the background variables, separately for employed adolescents who have comfortable, supportive relationships with their supervisors and for those who do not. (Employed teens who have no supervisors are excluded from the analysis.)

Table 5.4 (Panels A through C) show that the effect of family discomfort on adjustment is present only when employed adolescents do not have comfortable relationships with supervisors at work.[7] That is, when supervisor support is low, family discomfort decreases employed adolescents' well-being, self-esteem, and mastery. Discomfort with parents is not significantly related to these outcomes when employed adolescents feel comfortable at work. It should be noted that these effects are significant even when the adjustment indicators, one year prior, are controlled.

DOES THE ARENA OF COMFORT CONDITION THE EFFECTS OF FAMILY CHANGE ON ADJUSTMENT?

In the final set of analyses, I examine whether relationships and experiences at work moderate the effects of family change on adolescent academic performance and mental health (Path F of Figure 5.1). Interaction analyses are performed with the work moderators, regressing each adjustment construct (grade point average, well-being, self-derogation, self-esteem, depressive affect, and mastery) on the one-year lagged adjustment measure, the background variables, each measure of family change one at a time, one work moderator (supervisor support, support from a friend at work, satisfaction, and low levels of stress and boredom at work), and the product of the same family change and work moderator.[8] Significant coefficients for the product terms indicate that moderating effects exist; that is, family change has different effects on the outcomes, depending on the level of comfort at work.

Eight interaction terms are significant.[9] The interaction of a change in father's employment status and work stress is related to self-esteem (*beta* = .399, $p < .01$), of a change of residence and work stress to self-derogation (*beta* = −.262, $p < .05$), of a change in family composition and support from a best friend at work to well-being (*beta* =

TABLE 5.4 The Moderating Effects of Work Comfort on the Relationship Between Family Discomfort and 10th-Grade Mental Health

	Supervisor Support Absent		Supervisor Support Present	
	B	Beta	B	Beta
A. Well-being				
Family discomfort	-1.375	-.213**	.034	.005
Socioeconomic status	-.127	-.059	.033	.020
Race	.175	.023	.436	.063
Nativity	1.177	.093	-.745	-.076
Gender	-1.063	-.169*	.421	.073
Well-being (9th grade)	.368	.361***	.264	.291**
R^2	.258***		.097	
n cases	184		94	
B. Self-esteem				
Family discomfort	-.849	-.157*	.456	.084
Socioeconomic status	.002	.001	-.041	-.029
Race	-.474	-.073	-1.215	-.202
Nativity	1.329	.134*	-.381	-.045
Gender	-.299	-.057	.477	.097
Self-esteem (9th grade)	.515	.458***	.498	.429***
R^2	.336***		.214*	
n cases	183		94	
C. Mastery				
Family discomfort	-.962	-.178**	.527	.086
Socioeconomic status	.037	.020	.166	.105
Race	-.820	-.125	.660	.099
Nativity	.837	.085	-.712	-.076
Gender	-.256	-.048	-.099	-.018
Mastery (9th grade)	.542	.472***	.430	.378***
R^2	.297***		.161*	
n cases	180		92	

NOTE: The background variables are measured in the 9th grade.
*$p < .05$; **$p < .01$; ***$p < .001$.

.266, $p < .001$), of moving and support from a friend at work to mastery (*beta* $= -.158, p < .05$), of moving and work satisfaction to self-esteem (*beta* $= .276, p < .05$), and the interaction of moving with whether or not work is interesting is significantly related ($p < .05$) to well-being, self-esteem, and mastery (*beta* $= .196, .176,$ and $.183,$ respectively).

Regressions were then performed separately for each condition of work comfort. For example, as shown in Table 5.5, Panel A, self-esteem is regressed on change in father's employment status, the background variables, and the lagged outcomes separately for employed adolescents who report high and low levels of stress at work. In four conditional analyses, findings are not robust; therefore, they are not presented in table form.[10]

As presented in Table 5.5, Panel A, change in the father's employment status diminishes self-esteem only when work stress is high. When work stress is low (comfortable), change in fathers' employment status has no significant effect on employed adolescents' self-esteem. Change in family composition decreases well-being for employed adolescents who are not comfortable with a friend at work (see Table 5.5, Panel B). In contrast, a change in family composition is associated with increased well-being for workers who have a supportive friend at work. Panel C shows that a geographical move increases perceptions of mastery when workers do not have a comfortable relationship with a coworker; this result is difficult to comprehend. When support from a coworker is high, moving has no significant impact on competence. Panel D demonstrates that moving has no impact on mastery when work is boring; however, when work is described as interesting, moving increases adolescents' sense of mastery. Thus, relationships and experiences at work appear to buffer the effects of change on employed adolescents' mental health.

Summary and Discussion

The concept of an arena of comfort is useful in that it draws attention to events within particular contexts or role sets and the interface between these different arenas—a growing focus of concern in developmental research (Bronfenbrenner, 1986b) and the stress

TABLE 5.5 The Moderating Effects of Work Comfort on the Relationship Between Family Change and 10th-Grade Mental Health

	High Work Stress		Low Work Stress	
	B	Beta	B	Beta
A. Self-esteem				
Change of father's employment status	−5.932	−.493***	−.685	−.054
Socioeconomic status	.074	.047	.022	.013
Race	.906	.165	−1.059	−.148**
Nativity	−.670	−.067	1.563	.144*
Gender	−.391	−.075	−.283	−.054
Self-esteem (9th grade)	.596	.461**	.432	.393***
R^2	.381**		.206***	
n cases	44		309	

	Coworker Support Absent		Coworker Support Present	
	B	Beta	B	Beta
B. Well-being				
Change of family composition	−1.745	−.189*	1.628	.192*
Socioeconomic status	−.077	−.041	.019	.010
Race	.129	.017	.292	.039
Nativity	.310	.024	−.861	−.072
Gender	−.698	−.116	−.701	−.122
Well-being (9th grade)	.280	.245***	.341	.401***
R^2	.113**		.235***	
n cases	172		137	
C. Mastery				
Change of residence	1.219	.165*	−.595	−.075
Socioeconomic status	.153	.097	.064	.039
Race	−.469	−.072	.599	.092
Nativity	.968	.095	.011	.001
Gender	−.278	−.055	−.029	−.006
Mastery (9th grade)	.521	.456***	.461	.402***
R^2	.266***		.166***	
n cases	171		133	

(continued)

TABLE 5.5 Continued

	Work Is Boring		Work Is Interesting	
	B	Beta	B	Beta
D. Mastery				
Change of residence	-.671	-.090	.966	.124*
Socioeconomic status	.167	.098	.017	.012
Race	-.497	-.071	.163	.025
Nativity	1.249	.119	.079	.007
Gender	-.510	-.097	-.076	-.015
Mastery (9th grade)	.475	.415***	.511	.478***
R^2		.218***		.244***
n cases		120		286

NOTE: The background variables are measured in the 9th grade.
*$p < .05$; **$p < .01$; ***$p < .001$.

field (Eckenrode & Gore, 1990). This research contributes to our knowledge of cross-domain buffering effects and the interface between family and work during adolescence.

In accord with prior research, I find that experiences of objective change in the family and discomfort with parents have adverse consequences for adolescents. Ongoing strain (i.e., discomfort with parents) appears to have more negative consequences for adolescent adjustment, as compared to the life event stressors examined, consistent with the contention that chronic stressors may be more predictive of adjustment than major life events (Delongis et al., 1982; Rowlinson & Felner, 1988). That is, strained or uncomfortable relationships with parents affect five of the six outcomes, diminishing adolescents' academic performance, their sense of well-being, self-esteem and self-efficacy, and increasing depressive affect.[11] In contrast, change in the father's employment status only decreases self-esteem, and depressive affect. Change in family composition is associated only with lower academic achievement, and a geographical move has no effect on employed adolescents' adjustment.

Surprisingly, events such as a change in father's employment status, change in family composition, and a geographic move had no significant impact on adolescents' relationships with their parents. Perhaps the circumstances preceding the event have greater impacts on perceptions of comfort with parents. However, these effects may be rather transient. Alternatively, they may be persistent and reflected in the lagged outcomes that I control. In addition, the arena of comfort did not moderate the effects of change in the family on discomfort with parents.

The results indicate that supportive relationships with supervisors moderate the effects of family discomfort on employed adolescents' adjustment. That is, strained relationships with parents diminish employed adolescents' well-being, self-esteem, and mastery only when relationships with supervisors are uncomfortable. In addition, support from supervisors decreases employed adolescents' depressive affect and boosts their feelings of competence. None of the task-related measures of comfort at work moderates the relationship between family discomfort and the outcomes. However, comfortable experiences at work may strengthen or build coping skills. I found that job satisfaction directly enhances well-being and decreases self-derogation and depressive affect. In addition, low levels of stress at work heighten well-being and self-esteem and reduce depressed mood. When work is described as interesting, depressive affect is diminished.

Comfort in the work arena also moderates the effects of family change on employed adolescents' adjustment. That is, change in the father's employment status has no effect on self-esteem when work stress is low (comfort is present). However, when work stress is high, this change diminishes employed adolescents' self-esteem. Change in family composition only reduces well-being when adolescents do not have a comfortable relationship with a friend at work. When support from a friend at work is perceived as available, change in family composition increases well-being. Inexplicably, moving increases feelings of competence when coworker support is absent and has no significant effect on mastery when coworker support is present. Moving boosts adolescents' feelings of competence when work is considered interesting but has no influence on mastery when work is described as boring.

In conclusion, not all measures of work comfort were equally efficacious. However, it appears that having supportive relationships at work may help adolescents deal with stress at home. Adolescents' coping capacities may be strengthened first of all because of an arena of comfort's impact on mental health. Work also moderates the effects of discomfort with parents on adolescents' adjustment. Furthermore, supportive and positive experiences at work moderate the effects of family change on adolescent achievement and mental health.

The results of this study suggest that investigators look beyond social support to other contextual features that promote individual coping and mental health. Paid work that is satisfying and highly engaging may be especially beneficial, offering distraction from strains at home or in other domains and opportunities to build skills and strengthen the self-concept. By providing social support, increasing coping skills, and enhancing the self-concept, a comfort arena strengthens the individual so that challenges in other life spheres can be dealt with.

It is interesting that work emerged as an important moderator of stress within the family, given the controversy surrounding the implications of work during adolescence (Greenberger & Steinberg, 1986). Further research is needed to see whether the workplace serves as an arena of comfort for older adolescents. By the 11th and 12th grade, more adolescents are working (90%), they are more likely to work in formal job settings, and their work becomes increasingly complex (Mortimer et al., 1994). These changes have the potential to offer greater individual and interpersonal rewards and to enhance adolescents' ability to cope with family stress.

Appendix A
Measures

Comfort in the Family Context

Parent-child relationship (The same set of question is asked for both mother and father.)

How close do you feel to him/her?

Extremely close (4) to Not close at all (1)

When you are faced with personal concerns and decisions, do you talk them over with him/her?

How often does he/she talk over important decisions that he/she has to make with you?

How often does he/she listen to your side of an argument?

How often do you do things with him/her that you enjoy?

Never (1) to Often (4)

Comfort with mother: Cronbach's alpha $W1^a$ = .829, W2 = .842.
Comfort with father: Cronbach's alpha W1 = .832, W2 = .853.

Comfort and Involvement in the Work Context

Comfort with supervisor (Cronbach's alpha W1 = .560, W2 = .659):

How often is your supervisor willing to listen to your problems and help find solutions?

Never (1) to Almost always (5)

How close do you feel to your supervisor?

Not close at all (1) to Extremely close (4)

Comfort with friend at work

How close do you feel to your best friend at work?

Not close at all (1) to Extremely close (4)

Work stressors (Cronbach's alpha W1 = .640, W2 = .696):

How often is there time pressure on your job?

How often are you exposed to excessive heat, cold, or noise at work?

Almost always (1) to Never (5)

I have too much work to do everything well.

My job requires that I work very hard.

I feel drained of my energy when I get off work.

   Very true (1) to Not at all true (4)

Work satisfaction

How satisfied are you with your job as a whole?

   Extremely dissatisfied (1) to Extremely satisfied (6)

Boredom

   How often do you feel bored at work, or that time is dragging?

   Always (1) to Almost never (5)

Involvement (Cronbach's alpha W1 = .743, W2 = .750)

   Most of my interests are centered around my job.

   The most important things that happen to me involve my job.

   I am very much involved personally in my job.

      Not at all true (1) to Very true (4)

   How often are you interested enough in your job to do more work than your job requires?

   How often do you feel that your work is meaningful and important?

      Almost never (1) to Always (5)

Adjustment Measures[b]

Well-being

During the past month, how much of the time:

   Have you felt that the future looks hopeful and promising? (.434, .481)

   Have you generally enjoyed the things you do? (.511, .566)

   Have you felt calm and peaceful? (.584, .646)

   Have you felt cheerful, lighthearted? (.519, .575)

      None of the time (1) to All of the time (5)

Self-derogation

   I certainly feel useless at times. (.499, .543)

   I feel I do not have much to be proud of. (.423, .461)

   I wish I could have more respect for myself. (.522, .568)

   At times I think I am no good at all. (.608, .662)

      Strongly disagree (1) to Strongly agree (4)

Self-esteem

    I feel I have a number of good qualities. (.278, .312)

    I take a positive attitude toward myself. (.506, .567)

    On the whole, I am satisfied with myself. (.469, .526)

        Strongly disagree (1) to Strongly agree (4)

Depressive affect

During the past month, how much of the time:

    Have you been under any strain, stress, or pressure? (.470, .488)

    Have you felt downhearted or blue? (.700, .726)

    Have you been moody or brooded about things? (.616, .640)

    Have you felt depressed? (.826, .857)

    Have you been in low or very low spirits? (.788, .818)

        None of the time (1) to All of the time (5)

Mastery

    There is really no way I can solve some of the problems I have.
(.501, .503)

    Sometimes I feel that I'm being pushed around in life. (.356, .357)

    I have little control over the things that happen to me. (.430, .431)

    I can do just about anything I really set my mind to do. (.212, .212)

    What happens to me in the future mostly depends on me. (.106, .106)

    I mostly feel helpless in dealing with the problems of life. (.487, .488)

    There is little I can do to change many of the important things in my life.
(.405, .406)

        Strongly disagree (1) to Strongly agree (4)

Grade point average

    What is your grade point *average* so far this year (Circle ONE LETTER)

      A A- B+ B B- C+ C C- D+ D D- F

---

a. Reliability scores are reported for Waves 1 (W1) and 2 (W2).

b. Standardized coefficients are reported for Waves 1 and 2, respectively.

Appendix B
Dichotomous Specification of
Comfort Measures and 10th-Grade Frequencies

Perceived Comfort With Mother

How close do you feel to her?

			%	
Discomfort	(0)	Not close at all	6.2	
		Fairly close	19.9	= 26.1
Comfort	(1)	Quite close	34.9	
		Extremely close	39.0	= 73.9

When you are faced with personal concerns and decisions, do you talk them over with her?

Discomfort	(0)	Never	12.5	
		Rarely	24.0	= 36.5
Comfort	(1)	Sometimes	40.0	
		Often	23.4	= 63.4

How often does she talk over important decisions that she has to make with you?

Discomfort	(0)	Never	10.1	
		Rarely	27.5	= 37.6
Comfort	(1)	Sometimes	41.4	
		Often	21.1	= 62.4

How often does she listen to your side of an argument?

Discomfort	(0)	Never	8.1	
		Rarely	20.7	= 28.8
Comfort	(1)	Sometimes	40.5	
		Often	30.6	= 71.1

How often do you do things with her that you enjoy?

Discomfort	(0)	Never	4.3	
		Rarely	22.5	= 26.8
Comfort	(1)	Sometimes	51.2	
		Often	22.0	= 73.2

The above items are summed and cutoffs established to specify presence or absence of comfort. The additive construct is recoded to follow a fairly strict definition of comfort: The adolescent must be comfortable on at least four of five items to be considered comfortable.

Comfort with mother:

		Value	f	%	
Discomfort	(0)	0	79	8.6	
		1	79	8.6	
		2	97	10.6	
		3	121	13.2	= 41.0
Comfort	(1)	4	182	19.9	
		5	358	39.1	= 59.0
		Total	916	100.0	

Perceived Comfort With Father

How close do you feel to him?

			%	
Discomfort	(0)	Not close at all	7.0	
		Fairly close	31.1	= 48.1
Comfort	(1)	Quite close	29.5	
		Extremely close	22.4	= 51.9

When you are faced with personal concerns and decisions, do you talk them over with him?

Discomfort	(0)	Never	27.9	
		Rarely	34.5	= 62.4
Comfort	(1)	Sometimes	29.3	
		Often	8.2	= 37.5

How often does he talk over important decisions that he has to make with you?

Discomfort	(0)	Never	24.2	
		Rarely	33.4	= 57.6
Comfort	(1)	Sometimes	32.2	
		Often	10.2	= 42.4

How often does he listen to your side of an argument?

Discomfort	(0)	Never	17.1	
		Rarely	23.1	= 40.2
Comfort	(1)	Sometimes	33.9	
		Often	25.8	= 59.7

How often do you do things with him that you enjoy?

Discomfort	(0)	Never	11.7	
		Rarely	25.9	= 37.6
Comfort	(1)	Sometimes	44.0	
		Often	18.4	= 62.4

Comfort with father:

		Value	f	%	
Discomfort	(0)	0	160	18.5	
		1	130	15.1	
		2	128	14.8	
		3	145	16.8	= 65.2
Comfort	(1)	4	131	15.2	
		5	169	19.6	= 34.8
		Total	863	100.0	

NOTE: The measure of comfort with father considers adolescents' relation with fathers who currently live with them and fathers who do not but are in contact with their child.

Family Discomfort

A single indicator was created that combines the adolescent's relationships with both mother and father. That is, adolescents who have distant or noncommunicative relationships with one or both parents are considered uncomfortable.

			f	%
Comfortable	(1)		550	66.6
Uncomfortable	(0)		276	33.4
		Total	826	100.0

Work Comfort

Work stress

How often are you under time pressure?

			%	
Comfort	(1)	Never	17.6	
		Rarely	28.1	
		Sometimes	27.4	= 73.1
Discomfort	(0)	Often	18.0	
		Almost always	8.9	= 26.9
		$n = 449$		

How often are you exposed to excessive heat, cold or noise at work?

Comfort	(1)	Never	20.3	
		Rarely	18.9	
		Sometimes	19.6	= 58.8
Discomfort	(0)	Often	19.8	
		Almost always	21.4	= 41.2
		$n = 449$		

I have too much work to do everything well.

Comfort	(1)	Not true	47.5	
		Little true	33.3	= 80.8
Discomfort	(0)	Somewhat true	14.5	
		Very true	4.8	= 19.3
		$n = 442$		

My job requires that I work very hard.

Comfort	(1)	Not true	18.9	
		Little true	32.6	= 51.5
Discomfort	(0)	Somewhat true	29.2	
		Very true	19.3	= 48.5
		$n = 445$		

I feel drained of my energy when I get off work.

Comfort	(1)	Not true	25.4	
		Little true	33.0	= 58.4
Discomfort	(0)	Somewhat true	26.3	
		Very true	15.3	= 41.6
		$n = 445$		

Work stress items are summed and cutoffs established to specify presence or absence of comfort. The construct was recoded so that only those adolescents reporting high levels of stress (i.e., uncomfortable on four or more items) are considered uncomfortable on the indicator of stress at work.

Work stress construct:

		Value	f	%	
Discomfort	(0)	0	22	5.0	
		1	37	8.5	= 13.5
		2	73	16.7	
		3	96	21.9	
		4	108	24.6	
Comfort	(1)	5	102	23.3	= 86.5
		$n = 438$			

Supervisor support

How often is your supervisor willing to listen to your problems and help
find solutions?

			%	
Discomfort (0)	Almost never	3.9	
	Rarely	10.7	
	Sometimes	18.8	= 33.4
Comfort (1)	Often	32.1	
	Always	34.5	= 66.6
	n = 336		

How close do you feel to your supervisor?

		%	
Discomfort (0)	Not close at all	21.1	
	Fairly close	40.2	= 61.3
Comfort (1)	Quite close	25.6	
	Extremely close	13.1	= 38.7
	n = 336		

Supervisor support construct:

	Value	*f*	%	
Discomfort (0)	0	97	28.9	
	1	124	36.9	= 65.8
Comfort (1)	2	115	34.2	= 34.2
	n = 336			

Friend support

How close do you feel to your *best* friend at work?

		%	
Discomfort (0)	Not close at all	13.4	
	Fairly close	40.7	= 54.0
Comfort (1)	Quite close	27.9	
	Extremely close	18.1	= 46.0
	n = 337		

Job satisfaction

How satisfied are you with your job as a whole?

		%	
Discomfort (0)	Extremely dissatisfied	2.3	
	Very dissatisfied	3.6	
	Somewhat dissatisfied	8.8	= 14.7
Comfort (1)	Somewhat satisfied	45.0	
	Very satisfied	29.7	
	Extremely satisfied	10.6	= 85.3
	n = 444		

Boredom at work

How often do you feel bored at work, or that time is dragging?

Comfort	(1)	Never	6.0	
		Rarely	23.4	
		Sometimes	41.6	= 71.0
Discomfort	(0)	Often	21.4	= 29.0
		Almost always	7.6	
		$n = 449$		

Notes

1. Change in mother's employment status was also assessed. However, because in preliminary analyses this type of change was not significantly related to any of the measures of adolescent adjustment nor to adolescents' perceptions of comfort with their mothers, it was dropped from further consideration.

2. In the event that parents are separated or divorced, adolescents are asked whether or not they have contact with the noncustodial parent. If so, the adolescent completes the same items assessing the level of comfort with that parent.

3. Interaction analyses were performed to investigate whether the effects of family change on family discomfort (Path A of Figure 5.1), family change on adolescent adjustment (Path E), and family discomfort on adolescent adjustment (Path B) vary for girls and boys. In addition, three-way interactions were tested to examine whether the moderator effects (Paths C, D, and F) are different for girls and boys. Few interaction terms were significant; therefore, the results for the total panel are presented.

4. The analyses focus on Grades 9 and 10 for several reasons: first, due to the greater frequency of change during this period than occurred between the 10th and 11th grade; and second, for the benefit of a larger sample during this two-year period. Furthermore, it is possible that adolescents who are least comfortable are more likely to leave the study during later waves.

5. The distribution of two of the five interaction terms are quite skewed. Only 8.1% of employed adolescents report both discomfort with parents and comfort with a supervisor, and 12.7% of employed adolescents report discomfort with parents and comfort with a best friend at work. Therefore, it is possible that significant interactions are obscured.

6. Of the 36 interaction terms examined, three were significant (8.3%), which is slightly more likely than chance expectation.

7. The interactions can also be interpreted in another way. That is, using the same procedure, comfort in the family moderates the effects of work discomfort on employed adolescents' adjustment. I investigated the effects of work discomfort within each condition of comfort at home (present or absent) and found that, for the most part, the effects of the stressors at work on adolescents' mental health were only present when they were uncomfortable with their parents. When relationships with parents were comfortable and positive, discomfort with supervisors had no effect on workers' adjustment.

8. Given the small proportion of adolescents experiencing family change and that only half of the adolescents worked in the 10th grade, the interaction terms for family change and work comfort (i.e., supervisor support, support from a best friend at work, work satisfaction, low work stress, and work that is interesting) are very skewed. The proportion of adolescents whose fathers changed employment status and who were comfortable at work was less than 4% for each of the five product terms. Less than 12% experienced both a change in family composition and were comfortable at work. And 11% or less moved and reported being comfortable at work (on each of the five measures). The analysis is conservative, and it is possible that significant interactions are obscured.

9. Eight of the 90 interaction terms (8.9%) examined were significant (i.e., five measures of work comfort multiplied by three measures of change, multiplied by six outcome variables), which is slightly better than chance.

10. The effect of moving on self-derogation was not significant for employed adolescents with high or low work stress, had no significant effect on adolescent self-esteem for either condition of work satisfaction, and had no effect on well-being or self-esteem whether work was considered boring or interesting.

11. That discomfort with parents increases depressed mood contradicts the work of Shanahan, Finch, Mortimer, and Ryu (1991), who found that parental support was a better predictor of depressive affect for nonemployed than employed adolescents. They suggest that work may allow adolescents to become more emotionally independent of their parents. This discrepancy may be due to differences in measurement: Shanahan et al. use continuous measures of perceived support from mothers and fathers. The measure used in the present analysis combines adolescents' evaluations of relationships with both mother and father. Because this measure distinguishes the one third of employed boys and girls who are most uncomfortable with their parents, it may be more sensitive to the kinds of relational problems that have deleterious emotional implications.

6

The "Occupational Linkage Hypothesis" Applied to Occupational Value Formation in Adolescence

SEONGRYEOL RYU

JEYLAN T. MORTIMER

Social psychologists have paid much attention to occupational re- ward values because of their relevance to occupational attainment processes. Work values have been found to be important determinants of occupational choice (Mortimer, 1974; Rosenberg, 1957). When people enter the labor force, they try to choose occupations and select work experiences that are consistent with their values so that they can maximize the rewards they deem the most important (Mortimer & Kumka, 1982; Mortimer & Lorence, 1979a; Mortimer et al., 1986). Some researchers also find that work values are related to job and career changes. That is, if there is incongruence between reward values and work experiences, workers are likely to be dissatisfied with their jobs (Mortimer & Lorence, 1995) and to want to change jobs to realize a better fit (Holland, 1976). Also, when work experiences are incon-

This study was supported by a grant, "Work Experience and Mental Health: A Panel Study of Youth," from the National Institute of Mental Health (MH 42843). An earlier version of this chapter was presented at the annual meeting of the American Sociological Association in Los Angeles, 1994.

sistent with the individual's values, value orientations may change in a direction that fosters congruence (Kumka, 1984).

Occupational reward values are assessments of the importance of the various rewards offered by work. Two distinct, but interrelated dimensions of work values have been established: extrinsic and intrinsic (Mortimer & Lorence, 1995; Rosenberg, 1957). Extrinsic values concern rewards that are derived from the job but are external to the work itself, such as income, prestige, opportunities for advancement, and security. Intrinsic rewards are inherent in work experiences: gratifications derived from being able to express one's interests and abilities, to be creative, to exercise self-direction and responsibility, to work with people, and to be helpful to others.

There is evidence that the socioeconomic position of the family, particularly the father's occupation, influences the formation of work values among young people (Lindsay & Knox, 1984; Mortimer, 1974, 1976; Mortimer & Kumka, 1982). However, the processes through which parental values are transmitted to adolescent high school students, who will shortly enter the labor force or be preparing themselves by postsecondary education for labor force entry, have, with few exceptions (Lueptow, McClendon, & McKeon, 1979; Super, 1957; Vondracek, Lerner, & Schulenberg, 1986), been neglected. The purpose of this chapter is to examine the effects of parental work on adolescent value socialization.

The formation of work values occurs through the interaction of the developing person with the environment. The environment may either directly impinge on the developing person, as does the family, or it may exert its influence indirectly and more distally, as does the broader cultural context. Bronfenbrenner (1979) sees the linkages of work and family as part of the broad contextual system of interconnections that influence the developing child. According to Vondracek et al. (1986), the parental workplace is one of the most important environments influencing the vocational development of children; it is thus pertinent to examine the characteristics of parental occupations. Research by Kohn and his colleagues (Kohn, 1969, 1977; Kohn & Schooler, 1973, 1983) and other assessments of the "occupational linkage hypothesis" (Lueptow et al., 1979; Mortimer & Kumka, 1982) are consistent with this ecological approach to the development of work values.

The occupational linkage hypothesis presumes that the task characteristics of parental work establish certain behavioral demands (and rewards that are relevant to the enactment of those occupational role demands). These influence major dimensions of parental personality, including values. Such personal characteristics may induce certain socialization orientations and practices that, in turn, affect the adolescent child's psychological attributes.

Kohn and his colleagues' work provides a key exposition of this conceptualization. Kohn's theoretical approach established three basic linkages between parental work characteristics and socialization outcomes: first, from parental occupational experiences of self-direction to parental values; second, from parental values to parental behaviors; and third, from parental values and behaviors to the values and behaviors of children (Kohn, 1969, 1981; Mortimer et al., 1986). Kohn and his colleagues (Kohn, 1969; Kohn & Schooler, 1973) have focused mainly on the first path in this chain, the effects of occupational conditions on parental psychological functioning. These effects come about through processes of "learning-generalization" (Kohn, 1969). The personality traits which are important to the father's occupational success are generalized and come to influence values concerning the most desirable qualities for children. For Kohn and his collaborators, the most important factor among parental work conditions is the degree of occupational self-direction (Kohn, 1969; Kohn & Schooler, 1983; Pearlin & Kohn, 1966), which fosters self-directed values for oneself as well as for one's children. That is, middle-class parents who have more self-directed work and place a higher valuation on self-direction put more emphasis on self-directed qualities relating to the inner psychological development of children, whereas working-class parents focus more on conformity to external standards of behavior (Kohn, 1969). Kohn and Schooler (1983) concluded that occupational experiences that facilitate or deter the exercise of self-direction come to permeate men's views, not only of work and of their role in work, but also of the world and of self. Consistently, Mortimer and Lorence (1979) also found that work autonomy exerted significant influence on men's intrinsic work values.

With respect to the second linkage, the causal chain from parental values to parental behaviors that affect socialization, differences in parental values may be expressed in parental discipline (Gecas & Nye,

1974; Kohn, 1969). According to Kohn (1969), "Working class parents are more likely to punish or refrain from punishing on the basis of the direct and immediate consequences of children's actions, middle class parents [punish] on the basis of their interpretation of children's intent in acting as they do" (p. 104). That is, parents punish their children for transgressing the values which they deem most important (Kohn, 1969).

The third path posits that differences in parental values and behavior influence children's socialization outcomes. Kohn and his colleagues (1986) found that parents' valuation of self-direction promoted a high valuation of self-direction in their children. Studies of the status attainment process also provide support for this final linkage. The encouragement of significant others, including parents, influences adolescents' educational and occupational aspirations, and subsequently, their actual attainments (Hauser, Tsai, & Sewell, 1983; Sewell & Hauser, 1976). Also, the degree of supportiveness in the parent-child relationship has been found to influence various child attitudes and behaviors which facilitate socioeconomic attainment (Mortimer et al., 1986). For example, sons who reported more close and communicative relationships with their fathers are more self-confident.

Mortimer and Kumka (1982) examined the occupational linkage hypothesis by studying the effects of fathers' occupations on sons' work values and career outcomes. They focused on two groups of fathers: professionals and businessmen. In professional families, they reasoned, intrinsic and people-oriented values would be emphasized in accord with the professional's training, ethical codes, and occupational subculture. In contrast, in business families, extrinsic orientations to work would be the more salient as a result of institutionalized reward structures and paths to success in profit-oriented organizations. Mortimer and Kumka hypothesized that close and supportive relationships between father and son, which facilitate identification and attitude transmission, would mediate the transfer of intrinsic values in professional families and extrinsic values in the business sector.

Using data from a longitudinal study of college men, they found that among professional families, as the relationship between father and son became more positive, sons' intrinsic and people-oriented values intensified. In contrast, in the business families, paternal support fostered sons' extrinsic values. These findings clearly supported the occupational linkage hypothesis. They concluded that the actual socialization experiences of children, including the quality of their relationships with their parents, must be taken into account in studying the effects of parental work on the child's psychological outcomes.

Furthermore, the distinctive occupational values, fostered in professional and business families, predicted sons' occupational attainments 10 years after completing college. For example, the young men who reported stronger people-oriented values, as adolescents, were more likely to have found work that placed a premium on interpersonal relations. Those who had earlier expressed stronger extrinsic values had higher earnings than other young men.

Although there is considerable support for the hypothesized theoretical framework, there are several deficiencies in prior investigations of the occupational linkage model, particularly with respect to vocational development. First, even though Kohn proposed a three-stage process of socialization, in actual research the model has been examined piecemeal. Initially, Kohn and his colleagues (Kohn, 1969; Kohn & Schooler, 1983) focused on the relationship between parental occupations and parental psychological functioning and found that occupational self-direction was related to several psychological dimensions including parental values, work values, self-confidence, self-deprecation, and intellectual flexibility. In their subsequent study of value transmission from parent to child, Kohn et al. (1986) examined the relationship between the parent's and the child's valuation of self-direction without considering the parent's behavior, though it is a critical factor in the theoretical model (Kohn, 1981). Second, children's valuation of self-direction was the only child outcome considered in the intergenerational study by Kohn and his colleagues (Kohn, 1969; Kohn et al., 1986). The transmission of occupational reward values was not subject to empirical test.

Third, only a limited aspect of parental work was studied in Mortimer and Kumka's (1982) assessment of the occupational linkage hypothesis. They distinguished between the business versus professional sector, based on sons' reports of their fathers' occupations.

Because they lacked relevant data, they were unable to examine the implications of fathers' self-direction, the occupational condition that has been found to be so pervasively linked to adult psychological functioning, for children's occupational values. Furthermore, because they collected no data from parents, they merely assumed that intrinsic values would be regarded as more important in the professional families and extrinsic values as most important in the business sector. Whereas their study provided support for the importance of the parent-child relationship in fostering presumed paternal values that were linked, theoretically, to paternal occupational positions, a study in which both parents' and children's work values were measured directly would be far more convincing.

Fourth, given Mortimer and Kumka's (1982) focus on families with fathers who were professionals and businessmen, they did not apply the occupational linkage model to working-class families. Because the present study is based on a random sample of youths (for more information, see Chapter 1, this volume, and Finch et al., 1991), the findings are not limited to particular levels of the socioeconomic status hierarchy.

Finally, prior research has a pronounced male bias. For example, Mortimer and Kumka's (1982) research focused on the father's occupational experiences and the development of sons' work values, and Kohn and his colleagues' studies were also mainly concerned with fathers' work conditions and their influence on fathers' psychological functioning. Little is known about the occupational linkage model with respect to the influence of mothers' work on children of both genders or about the influence of fathers' work on girls. Gender-specific effects are certainly to be expected; status attainment researchers have repeatedly found that the same-sex parent has a greater effect on adolescent expectations and attainments than the opposite-sex parent (Chase, 1975; Rosen & Aneshensel, 1978; Treiman & Terrell, 1975). For example, with respect to educational attainment, mothers are more important role models for daughters than sons (Marini, 1978). Given these several limitations of prior studies, it is useful to reexamine the occupational linkage hypothesis with respect to the process of intergenerational work value transmission.

The Hypothetical Model

Consistent with the "occupational linkage" model, Vondracek et al. (1986) claim that in order to demonstrate that distal factors, such as parental work conditions, influence the vocational development of the child, it is necessary to establish causal sequences connecting those external factors to proximal processes within the family. Furthermore, the investigator must connect these microsystem processes to changes in the developing person.

The main exogenous factor in the occupational linkage model is the parent's work conditions. The degree of occupational self-direction exercised in work, because of its pervasive influence on parental psychological functioning, is an important determinant of class-linked socialization (Kohn, 1969; Kohn & Schooler, 1983). Accordingly, we examine the extent to which parental occupational self-direction influences parental work values. Conceptually, intrinsic reward values are quite compatible with self-directed values more generally. That is, adults who have greater occupational self-direction, that is, those who have more decision-making capacity, who do more complex work, and those who are not closely supervised, would attach greater value to individual responsibility and self-reliance. Consistently, they might also be expected to emphasize the intrinsic qualities of jobs, such as autonomy, the opportunities to use their own abilities at work, and to be creative, all of which would enable them to be self-directed at work (Mortimer & Lorence, 1979a; Mortimer et al., 1986). Given that persons in higher social class positions also have the more self-directed jobs (Spaeth, 1976), it is not surprising to find that as socioeconomic status increases, concern with intrinsic values also rises (Kohn, 1969). Therefore, we hypothesize that parents with higher levels of occupational self-direction at work will have stronger intrinsic occupational reward values. We find no theoretical justification in the literature for an association between occupational self-direction and extrinsic values, although empirically a positive association has been observed (Kohn, 1969; Kohn & Schooler, 1983).

Second, there is likely to be a direct effect of parental values on adolescent work values. It is plausible to assume that adolescents will learn work values directly from their parents by simply observing their behaviors and listening to them talk about their jobs. Moreover, through broader processes of identification and role modeling, adolescents will be motivated to internalize the kinds of values that their parents consider to be important. Thus, we hypothesize that adolescents whose parents have higher levels of intrinsic and/or extrinsic values will have similar work values themselves.

However, as Kohn (1981) has noted, similarity in parents' and adolescents' work values does not necessarily mean that parental values are transmitted to adolescents, as both parents and children could be responding to the same external environmental influences. To establish a parent-to-child transmission process, it is necessary to examine the mechanism responsible for the similarity of work values between parents and adolescents. Mortimer and Kumka's (1982) findings suggest that features of the socialization process must be included in studies of the effects of occupational origins on vocational development.

To understand the *process* of value transmission, we focus on the degree of supportiveness in the parent-adolescent relationship. Warmth and communication between parents and children, central components of parental support, are crucial factors affecting identification with parents and the transference of parental values (Coleman, 1988; Mortimer, 1976; Mortimer & Kumka, 1982; Parcel & Menaghan, 1994; Vondracek et al., 1986). Paralleling Mortimer and Kumka's (1982) research, we believe that the parent-child relationship is the conduit through which vocational socialization occurs. The particular values that are transmitted through this relationship will depend on the character of the parents' own values that are critically determined by key features of parental work.

Accordingly, we assess whether parental self-direction at work moderates the effect of supportive parent-child relationships on children's values. We estimate the interaction between parental work conditions and parental support in the process of vocational development.[1] We posit that the more supportive the relationship between a parent and a child, the more likely the child will internalize parental values and thus have values that are compatible with parental occupational experiences. Specifically, we hypothesize that when the parent has a highly self-directed job, parental support will foster intrinsic values.

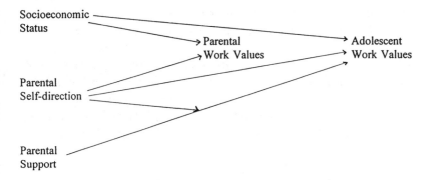

Figure 6.1. Hypothetical model of parental and adolescent work values.

Unlike prior studies that focused mainly on the relation between fathers and sons, we test the occupational linkage hypothesis with data from father-son, father-daughter, mother-son, and mother-daughter pairs. It has been well documented that the process of status attainment is different for boys and girls, in that parents not only provide gender-specific role models but also treat male and female children differently (Marini & Brinton, 1984). With respect to the transmission of work values, it is not known whether boys and girls are influenced by parental work conditions, parental values, and parental support in the same fashion.

It is necessary to control relevant exogenous factors in examining the process of vocational development. Kohn and his colleagues (Kohn, 1969; Kohn, 1977; Schooler, 1983) found that besides occupational self-direction, education was a powerful determinant of parental values. That is, those with higher levels of educational attainment had stronger intrinsic occupational reward values. Family income is also an important factor in this process. Mortimer and Lorence (1979a) found that young men from higher-income families had higher levels of extrinsic values. Therefore, in this chapter, the father's and mother's education and family income are assumed to be correlated with parental work conditions and parental support and to influence both parental and adolescent work values. The hypothetical model for this study is shown in Figure 6.1.[2]

As noted earlier, this study has several advantages over previous work on occupational value transmission. First, unlike other studies, the entire chain of linked causal processes, set forth in the "occupational linkage model," is subject to empirical scrutiny. All relevant factors in the occupational linkage model are measured directly: parental work conditions, parental values, the quality of the parent-child relationship, and adolescent values. Second, by examining the interactions between parental support and work experiences, the process of intergenerational value transmission is clarified. Finally, by including mothers and girls in the analysis, the scope of investigation is extended well beyond previous work.

Data Source

In this chapter, we use data from the Youth Development Study (YDS) panel, collected when the students were seniors, and from their parents, collected at the same time. The senior year in high school is an important period in the process of vocational development and status attainment. It is the time when students typically decide whether to pursue postsecondary education, consider various kinds of postsecondary schooling, and begin to explore career options. Thus, the occupational reward values that senior high school students have can play a critical role in determining their eventual work careers.

As described in Chapter 1, in the fourth year, 928 of the initial 1,000 respondents were retained; data were also obtained from 690 mothers and 440 fathers who were living with the child at the time of the fourth-year data collection. For 385 of the high school seniors, both fathers and mothers completed surveys; at least one parent of 738 children responded. The parents who were employed at the time of survey (403 fathers and 598 mothers) provided detailed information on their work values and their current socioeconomic characteristics and work experiences. Because the information regarding work experiences and work values are only obtained from those who were employed at the time of survey, we do not have the data for nonworking parents. The children provided data about family relationships and their own work values.

Measures

All the variables are measured with multiple items (see appendix), except parental education and family income. Confirmatory factor analysis (using LISREL Version 7.16; Jöreskog & Sörbom, 1989) provides empirical verification that adolescent boys' and girls' work values and those of their fathers and mothers have two distinct dimensions: extrinsic and intrinsic. Ten items (six presumably of an intrinsic character and four extrinsic, see Appendix) were subject to a confirmatory factor analysis. A two-factor model fits the data reasonably well for four groups defined by gender and generation. The standardized lambdas (analogous to factor loadings) are shown in the appendix. Comparison of the factor structures between adolescent boys and girls shows that a freely estimated model, in which lambdas may be unequal in the two groups, does not show a significantly better fit than a model in which the corresponding lambdas are constrained to be equal across gender. Based on this result, we form indices for the boys and girls using the unstandardized lambda coefficients from the constrained measurement model. Likewise, comparison of the factor structures of fathers' and mothers' work values reveals no significant difference in goodness-of-fit measures. Thus, the indices of fathers' and mothers' work values were created using the unstandardized lambda coefficients from the constrained model.

With respect to occupational self-direction, Kohn and Schooler (1983) suggested three main components: closeness of supervision, substantive complexity of work, and the complexity of organization of work. According to them, insofar as men are free of close supervision, do complex work with data or with people, and work at complexly organized tasks, their work is necessarily self-directed. Consistent with this approach, five items from the parents' survey are employed to represent parental occupational self-direction: the degree of control over the way they spend time at work, freedom in decision-making, the extent to which the job requires innovative thinking, the degree of repetitiveness of work, and how closely they are supervised on their jobs. Because information about the substantive complexity of work is not available in the data, this component is not represented in our measure of occupational self-direction.

Confirmatory factor analysis shows that a one-factor model with these five indicators fits the data well both for fathers and for mothers. However, comparison of the factor structures of fathers' and mothers' occupational self-direction shows that a freely estimated model fits the data better than a constrained model with equal lambdas across the two groups. Visual inspection indicates that the lambda coefficients for the corresponding items for mothers and fathers are quite similar. One difference between the two measurement structures is that the degree of routinization of work for mothers had a weaker relationship to the self-direction construct than among fathers. Because work routinization has weaker correlations with other indicators of self-direction for mothers than for fathers, only 5% of the variance of this item is explained by mothers' occupational self-direction, compared to 15% for fathers. Accordingly, distinct indices of occupational self-direction for fathers and mothers are formed using the freely estimated, unstandardized lambda coefficients. (Standardized coefficients for mothers and fathers, given in the appendix, show that routine work, characterized by a high degree of repetition, is less important in defining the construct for mothers than for fathers.)

Parental support, indicating closeness and communication between each parent and the adolescent child, was also measured with five indicators obtained from the adolescents. A one-factor model fits the data well with respect to the relationships with both fathers and mothers. Factor structures for both father and mother support constructs were compared across four dyads (i.e., father-son, father-daughter, mother-son, and mother-daughter). That is, a model in which lambda coefficients were freely estimated in the four groups was compared to a model in which the lambdas were constrained to be equal. The analyses show that the factor structure of perceived parent-child support is invariant across groups. Therefore, the unstandardized lambda coefficients from the constrained models, in which corresponding lambda coefficients are set to be equal in all four groups, are used to form indices of the father's and the mother's support of the child.

Information regarding parental education and family income is based on single items obtained from the parents' survey. Parents reported their educational attainment ranging from "less than high school graduation" to "Ph.D. or professional degree." As for the measure of family income, when both parents reported their total household income, the father's report was used as the indicator. Otherwise, information from either parent was employed. (Individual earnings of each parent are not available.)

Findings

Our application of the occupational linkage model is tested with a series of ordinary least squares regressions.[3] Because different parts of the hypothetical model should be tested in different subgroups, we do not estimate it in its entirety as in the typical path-analytic framework. That is, although we are interested in four dyads, defined by the gender of parent and child, it is appropriate to estimate the effects of work on values for all mothers and all fathers (irrespective of the gender of their children).

First, we investigate the relationship between parental work and parental values separately for fathers and mothers. Specifically, we assess the effects of parental occupational self-direction on parental intrinsic and extrinsic values, controlling parental education and family income. Second, we examine the determinants of adolescent work values. We examine the additive effects of parental occupational self-direction, parental work values, and the degree of supportiveness of the parent-child relationship on adolescent work values, with parental education and family income controlled. This investigation is done separately for father-son, father-daughter, mother-son, and mother-daughter dyads.

We used the following strategy to examine whether parental support fosters different work values in adolescents, depending on parental work conditions. First, an interaction term, the product of parental occupational self-direction and parental support, is introduced. Second, when the coefficient representing this interaction is significant in a dyad, then the effect of parental support is examined separately for parents with higher and lower levels of self-direction. In these two subgroups, adolescent work values are then regressed on parental support, along with parental work values, parental education, and family income.

TABLE 6.1 OLS Estimates of the Effects of Occupational Self-Direction, Education, and Family Income on Fathers' and Mothers' Work Values (standardized regression coefficients in parentheses)

	Fathers		Mothers	
	Intrinsic Values	Extrinsic Values	Intrinsic Values	Extrinsic Values
Occupational self-direction	.276***	.086	.260***	.098[†]
	(.276)	(.091)	(.231)	(.081)
Education	.470***	−.060	.492***	−.201[†]
	(.263)	(−.036)	(.233)	(−.088)
Family income	.042	−.003	−.015	−.237**
	(.025)	(−.002)	(−.010)	(−.153)
R^2	.204***	.007[a]	.129***	.039***
n	342	343	510	513

a. Equation is not significant at .10 level.
[†]$p < .10$; *$p < .05$; **$p < .01$; ***$p < .001$.

Consistent with Kohn and his colleagues' work (Kohn, 1983, Chap. 1), we find that the degree of occupational self-direction exercised by parents in their work influences their intrinsic values. The coefficients expressing the effects of occupational self-direction on parental intrinsic values are statistically significant and substantial in size for both fathers and mothers (see Table 6.1). Whereas mothers who exercise higher levels of self-direction at work also tended to place more emphasis on extrinsic values, this relationship is only marginally significant.

Consistent with prior work (Kohn, 1969; Kohn & Schooler, 1983), educational attainment is also a significant predictor of both the father's and the mother's intrinsic values. That is, those who have higher levels of educational achievement evaluate intrinsic features more positively. Although fathers' extrinsic values are not affected by educational attainment, mothers' extrinsic values are negatively influenced; again, however, this effect is only marginal. Unlike fathers, employed mothers with higher family income showed less interest in the extrinsic aspects of occupational rewards. It is interesting to note

TABLE 6.2 OLS Estimates of the Effects of Fathers' Occupational
Self-Direction, Work Values, and Paternal Support on Adolescent
Work Values (standardized regression coefficients in parentheses)

	Boys		Girls	
Fathers	Intrinsic Values	Extrinsic Values	Intrinsic Values	Extrinsic Values
Occupational self-direction	.043	.158*	.072	–.072
	(.053)	(.198)	(.088)	(–.090)
Education	–.092	–.174	.174	–.155
	(–.059)	(–.115)	(.124)	(–.111)
Family income	.212	–.034	–.048	.116
	(.146)	(–.024)	(–.037)	(.089)
Intrinsic values	.162†	.044	.130	.063
	(.197)	(.055)	(.160)	(.078)
Extrinsic values	–.022	.080	–.095	–.112
	(–.024)	(.089)	(–.119)	(–.141)
Paternal support	.223**	.116	.044	–.014
	(.223)	(.120)	(.052)	(–.017)
n	150	149	166	166
R^2	.148***	.074†	.068†	.030[a]

a. Equation is not significant at .10 level.
†$p < .10$; *$p < .05$; **$p < .01$; ***$p < .001$.

how much better we are able to predict intrinsic values with the
independent variables at hand for both fathers and mothers.

We now examine the additive effects of parental occupational self-
direction and parental work values on adolescent work values, controlling the parent's educational attainment, family income, and the
degree of supportiveness of the parent-child relationship. This analysis
was done separately for father-son, father-daughter, mother-son, and
mother-daughter dyads. The results are reported in Table 6.2 for
fathers and 6.3 for mothers. It is striking that of the eight equations,
only three are statistically significant: for father-son dyads predicting
boys' intrinsic values, for mother-son dyads predicting boys' intrinsic

TABLE 6.3   OLS Estimates of the Effects of Mothers' Occupational Self-
Direction, Work Values, and Maternal Support on Adolescent
Work Values (standardized regression coefficients in parentheses)

	Boys		Girls	
Mothers	Intrinsic Values	Extrinsic Values	Intrinsic Values	Extrinsic Values
Occupational self-direction	-.040	.049	-.023	-.026
	(-.037)	(.048)	(-.026)	(-.027)
Education	-.001	-.340*	.089	-.232[†]
	(-.001)	(-.174)	(.052)	(-.123)
Family income	.214*	.135	.218*	.324***
	(.154)	(.103)	(.186)	(.251)
Intrinsic values	.136[†]	.082	.026	-.155*
	(.131)	(.084)	(.033)	(-.182)
Extrinsic values	-.033	.023	.063	.277***
	(-.038)	(.028)	(.083)	(.337)
Maternal support	.264***	.149*	.003	-.016
	(.227)	(.136)	(.004)	(-.018)
R^2	.097**	.051[†]	.045[a]	.118***
n	222	222	238	238

a. Equation is not significant at .10 level.
[†]$p < .10$; *$p < .05$; **$p < .01$; ***$p < .001$.

values, and for mother-daughter dyads predicting girls' extrinsic
values.

It is especially noteworthy that parental occupational self-direction
itself has no direct influence on adolescent intrinsic values in any of
the four dyads. (The father's occupational self-direction has an unexpected positive effect on the son's extrinsic values—see Table 6.2—
although the equation is only marginally significant.)

Fathers' and mothers' intrinsic values have some direct influence
on boys' intrinsic values, though the coefficients in both the father-son
and mother-son dyads are only marginally significant (see Tables 6.2
and 6.3). Girls' intrinsic values are not affected at all by parental

intrinsic values. With respect to adolescent extrinsic values, fathers' extrinsic values do not seem to be important for either boys or girls. Mothers' extrinsic values are also unrelated to the extrinsic values of their sons. However, the significant effect of mothers' extrinsic values on those of their daughters is particularly noteworthy. The positive relationship between mothers' and girls' extrinsic values suggests that girls acquire their extrinsic values at least partly by observing their mothers. Interestingly, mothers' intrinsic values have a negative effect on girls' extrinsic values. The father, in contrast, is apparently not an important source of adolescent girls' work values. Neither the father's work conditions nor his work values are related to girls' intrinsic and extrinsic values.

Although the mother's educational attainment does not have a significant effect on adolescent intrinsic values, boys whose mothers have higher levels of educational attainment tend to place less emphasis on extrinsic features of occupational rewards. The father's educational attainment does not seem to be important in explaining adolescent work values, and family income is not a predictor of adolescent values in father-son and father-daughter dyads. However, rather inexplicably, family income has a significant positive influence on adolescent intrinsic values in mother-son and mother-daughter dyads (although the latter equation is not significant). Family income also has a positive influence on girls' extrinsic values in the mother-daughter analysis.

Supportiveness of the parent-child relationship seems to be an important factor in explaining the development of boys' values. Supportive father-son and mother-son relationships positively influence boys' intrinsic values (Tables 6.2 and 6.3). Besides, a supportive mother-son relationship also has significant positive influence on boys' extrinsic values (see Table 6.3). It is noteworthy that the quality of the parent-daughter relationship has no influence on daughters' values.

We have found that parental support has a direct positive influence on boys' values. But we have not yet assessed whether parental support has different effects, depending on the character of parental work. As discussed earlier, prior studies have found that parental support is the conduit through which value socialization occurs (Mortimer & Kumka, 1982; Vondracek et al., 1986). This finding suggests that the content of values that is transmitted to adolescents through parental support will not be the same for all parents. To test the possibility of interaction between parental occupational self-direction and parental support, we create a dummy variable reflecting parental work conditions. Parents at or above the median on occupational self-direction are coded 1 and those below the median coded 0. An interaction term, reflecting the combination of parental occupational self-direction and parental support, is created by multiplying this dummy variable and parental support. Then, all three variables—the dummy variable for parental occupational self-direction, parental support, and the interaction between them—are included in the equations predicting adolescent values (along with parental education, family income, and parental work values).

The coefficient representing this interaction term was found to be statistically significant only in the equation predicting intrinsic values in the father-son model. A statistical test of increments to the proportions of explained variance revealed that the addition of an interaction term significantly increased the proportion of explained variance only in this analysis. This finding suggests that supportiveness in the father-son relationship has different influence on the son's intrinsic values, depending on the levels of occupational self-direction exercised by fathers. However, this pattern is not observed in any other dyads. Because coefficients for interaction terms are not readily interpretable, the model shown in Table 6.2 is reestimated for the father-son dyad in two groups defined by the fathers' self-direction: high (at or above the median) and low (below the median); therefore, occupational self-direction is omitted from the equation (see Table 6.4).[4]

Consistent with the pattern shown in Mortimer and Kumka's (1982) research, paternal support had a significant influence on sons' intrinsic values when fathers had higher levels of occupational self-direction (see Table 6.4); the difference in the regression coefficients between the two groups is statistically significant ($p < .05$). Given the fact that fathers with high self-direction have stronger intrinsic values, the strong influence of paternal support on sons' intrinsic values suggests that supportiveness in the parent-child relationship reinforces the transmission of fathers' intrinsic values to sons. It is especially noteworthy that fathers' intrinsic values have no significant influence, among the fathers with higher self-direction, when paternal support

TABLE 6.4 OLS Estimates of the Effects of Fathers' Work Values and Paternal Support on Boys' Intrinsic Values in Groups Defined by the Fathers' Occupational Self-Direction (standardized regression coefficients in parentheses)

	Low Occupational Self-Direction	High Occupational Self-Direction
Education	−.099	−.154
	(−.051)	(−.107)
Family income	.147	.190
	(.076)	(.148)
Intrinsic values	.249†	.088
	(.278)	(.100)
Extrinsic values	−.057	.034
	(−.059)	(.039)
Paternal support	.082	.429***
	(.085)	(.423)
R^2	.075[a]	.233***
n	81	69

a. Equation is not significant at .10 level.
†$p < .10$; *$p < .05$; **$p < .01$; ***$p < .001$

is controlled. This pattern confirms that the content of socialization (i.e., what is transmitted through close and communicative father-son relations) is different, depending on the fathers' occupational experiences. Because the equation for the low self-direction group was not statistically significant, we cannot address processes of father-son value transmission in that group. Given that the interaction of parental occupational self-direction and parental support was not significant in father-daughter, mother-son, and mother-daughter dyads, we do no further analysis of these groups.

Discussion

The results clearly confirm that parental occupational self-direction influences parental intrinsic values. This relationship is observed for both fathers and mothers. Regardless of the gender of a job-holder, intrinsic values are directly affected by the degree of occupational self-direction in work. It seems that parents who have considerable self-direction come to realize the importance of the possibilities the job affords for self-expression, responsibility, and individual accomplishment (Kohn & Schooler, 1983).

Mortimer and Lorence (1979a) reported that men with higher income tend to place higher value on the extrinsic aspects of occupational reward. However, our analysis does not confirm this pattern for fathers and shows a negative relationship between family income and extrinsic values among mothers. It may be that mothers with higher family income are more likely to work by choice than by necessity. That is, if a mother with low family income works in order to meet the financial needs of her family, she may put more emphasis on the monetary reward her job offers. However, a mother with higher family income is more likely to work because she wants to. In this case, monetary and other extrinsic rewards may not be as salient.

Our analysis suggests that parental work conditions operate as a moderator of the effect of paternal support in the process of father-son occupational value transmission. Paternal support reinforces the transmission of intrinsic values to sons only when fathers exercise a relatively high degree of self-direction in their jobs. That is, the effect of the quality of the father-child relationship on value transmission is contingent on the nature of the father's occupation (Mortimer & Kumka, 1982). This finding supports Vondracek et al.'s (1986) claim that the connection between parental work conditions and adolescent developmental outcomes should be made through study of the microsystem processes within a family setting. Adolescents whose fathers have higher occupational self-direction learn the importance of intrinsic work values through their close and supportive relationships with their fathers. The fathers' occupational self-direction also had a direct positive influence on sons' extrinsic values.

With respect to mother-son value transmission, mothers' intrinsic values have only marginal influence on boys' intrinsic values. As for explaining sons' extrinsic values, mothers' extrinsic values are not important at all. Moreover, mothers' self-direction did not moderate the effects of maternal support on sons' values.

Girls' intrinsic and extrinsic work values were not influenced by any variable in the father-daughter model. However, mothers' intrinsic and extrinsic values significantly influenced girls' extrinsic values. Given the more frequent visits of adolescent girls to their mothers' workplaces and listening to their mothers talk about jobs,[5] this pattern suggests that adolescent girls may be more attentive to their mothers' work values than their fathers'. However, the self-directed character of mothers' jobs did not moderate the effects of maternal support on daughters.

In conclusion, this study demonstrates that parents' work conditions influence their work values. Mothers and fathers who experience more self-direction in their work have more pronounced intrinsic values. Furthermore, we find that parental support, the warmth and communication between fathers and sons, fosters intrinsic values in sons when fathers have higher self-direction in their jobs. The results also suggest that the occupational linkage hypothesis is more adequate for explaining the development of work values among boys than girls. Moreover, in the process of vocational development, adolescents tend to acquire their occupational values more from the same-sex parent than from the opposite-sex parent. Future research on the occupational linkage hypothesis should give further attention to the manner in which girls develop their work values.

Appendix
Measures

1. Parental Occupational Self-Direction

   How much control do you have over the way you spend your time at work—over when and how long you work on the various parts of your job?

   (1 = almost no control at all to 5 = complete control) (.818[a], .912[b])

   Overall, how much freedom do you have to make important decisions about what you do at work and how you do it?

   (1 = almost none at all to 5 = complete freedom) (.922, .996)

   Do you have to think of new ways of doing things or solving problems on your job?

   (1 = never to 5 = almost always) (.644, .563)

   Does your work involve doing: 1 = the same thing in the same way repeatedly to 3 = a number of different kinds of things? (.582, .349)

   The next question is about the person who has the most control over your own work. How closely does he/she supervise you?

   (1 = He/she decides what I do and how I do it, to
   4 = I am my own boss within the general policies of the firm, organization, or department) (.642, .583)

---

a. Standardized lambda coefficients for fathers.
b. Standardized lambda coefficients for mothers.
Fit index for fathers: χ^2/df = 12.57/4; GFI (Goodness of Fit Index) = .99; for mothers: χ^2/df = 21.14/4; GFI = .98.

2. Parental and Adolescent Work Values

   Intrinsic values (1= not at all important to 4 = extremely important)
   Job that uses my skills and abilities (.461[c], .538[d])
   Chance to learn a lot of new things at work (.525, .597)
   Chance to make my own decisions at work (.534, .576)
   Job where I have a lot of responsibility (.572, .592)
   Chance to be helpful to others or useful to society (.483, .510)
   Chance to work with people rather than things (.460, .525)

Extrinsic values (1 = not at all important to 4 = extremely important)

Good pay (.251, .285)

Good chances of getting ahead (.594, .319)

Steady job, with little chance of being laid off (.258, .547)

Job that people regard highly (.460, .525)

---

c. Even though the unstandardized factor loadings are invariant for fathers and mothers, the standardized lambda coefficients are not the same for fathers and mothers. But because they are quite similar, the standardized lambda coefficients only for fathers are presented.
d. Likewise, the unstandardized factor loadings are invariant for boys and girls. However, the standardized lambda coefficients only for boys are presented.
Fit index for fathers: χ^2/df = 124.28/32; GFI = .94. For mothers: χ^2/df = 206.02/32; GFI = .93. For boys: χ^2/df = 141.65/32; GFI = .94. For mothers: χ^2/df = 118.49/32; GFI = .95.

3. Parental Support (father and mother)

How close do you feel to him (her)?

(1 = not at all close to 4 = extremely close) (.697[e])

How often do you do things with him (her) that you enjoy?

(1 = never to 4 = often) (.575)

When you are faced with personal concerns and decisions, do you talk them over with him (her)?

(1 = never to 4 = often) (.737)

How often does (s)he talk over important decisions that (s)he has to make with you?

(1 = never to 4 = often) (.656)

How often does (s)he listen to your side of an argument?

(1 = never to 4 = often) (.616)

---

e. The factor loadings are invariant across four dyads (father-son, father-daughter, mother-son, and mother-daughter). The standardized lambda coefficients are also very similar across the four dyads; those for father-son dyad are reported here.
Fit index for father-son dyad: χ^2/df = 11.42/5; GFI = .98. For father-daughter dyad: χ^2/df = 19.76/5; GFI = .98. For mother-son dyad: χ^2/df = 21.69/5; GFI = .98. For mother-daughter dyad: χ^2/df = 16.65/5; GFI = .99.

4. Parental Education

How much schooling did you complete?

(1 = less than high school to 8 = PhD or professional degree)

5. Family Income

What was your total household income in 1990 before taxes?

(1 = under $5,000 to 13 = $100,000 or more)

Notes

1. Other factors, such as the typical mode of parental control, may also influence identification processes and value transmission. Kathleen Call's Chapter 3 shows how parental assignment of housework influences adolescent competence. However, we do not have measures of more general features of parental control.

2. It should be noted that we depart from the occupational linkage model as formulated by Kohn and his colleagues in one essential respect. Whereas they posited a linkage between parental psychological characteristics fostered by work and parental socialization practices, we posit no connection between parental work values and parental support.

3. One of the important assumptions in ordinary least square regression analysis is the absence of multicollinearity among explanatory variables. Considering correlations among all predictors, the highest occurred between father's education and family income ($r = .5447$). Thus, we conclude that there is no serious problem of multicollinearity.

4. Even though there are some statistical problems related to this procedure, such as inflated Type I error rates, it is a widely used conservative exploratory strategy that allows one to examine the nature of interaction effects (Jaccard, Turrisi, & Wan, 1990; Pedhazur, 1982).

5. Seventy-one percent of adolescent girls in the sample ever visited their mothers' workplaces, compared to 64.1% who visited their fathers'. Also, mothers tended to talk more often about their jobs to daughters than fathers did (84% vs. 55%). Boys were more likely to visit fathers' workplaces than mothers' (69% vs. 62%). However, mothers talked more often about their work to boys than fathers did (74% vs. 60%). It seems that girls tend to be more familiar with their mothers' work through visiting her workplace and listening to her talk about work.

7

Effects of Adolescent Achievement and Family Goals on the Early Adult Transition

ELLEN EFRON PIMENTEL

The young adult years, more than any other period in the life course, are characterized by multiple transitions; they are "demographically dense" (Rindfuss, 1991). The different transitions and the life spheres in which they occur are not separate from each other but overlap. Events in one area can affect events in others, influencing the life course in complex ways. For example, becoming pregnant can lead to early school leaving, or involvement in postsecondary schooling might delay marriage. The sequencing and interrelations of various activities may also differ by gender and other important social attributes (Marini, Shin, & Raymond, 1989).

In addition, the experience of becoming an adult may vary for different generations of young adults, depending on the sociopolitical context and economic opportunities of the historical period (Modell, 1989). The processes of family formation, timing and completed level of schooling, and entry into the labor force are strongly affected by historical events and contexts. Therefore, the study of role transitions and statuses during the transition to adulthood is of great interest.

Although there is a great deal of research on the life course in the social sciences, the interplay between "subjective" and "objective" factors (i.e., plans and their outcomes) has been subject to very little empirical scrutiny (Buchmann, 1989). Justifying this neglect, it has been argued recently that plans are not predictive of outcomes, given the character of the life course in modern society. Modern society, it is argued, has seen a "destandardization" of the life course, characterized by an increasing diversity in potential outcomes (Buchmann, 1989; Rindfuss, Swicegood, & Rosenfeld, 1987). Rindfuss et al. (1987), for example, found it difficult to categorize occupational trajectories because they were so numerous. Marini (1984) noted that many people experience what were once thought of as atypical patterns, such as entering full-time work while still in school. This destandardization, sometimes called disorder, is supported and encouraged by an increasing range of choices and paths from which to choose, such that the quest for identity becomes an ongoing project rather than something that is established relatively early in life.

Earlier research suggested that the transition from adolescence to adulthood involved events that are ordered in a normative manner: leaving formal schooling, becoming employed full-time, and marrying (Hogan, 1978). Deviation from the normative pattern resulted in negative outcomes because social institutions had been arranged primarily to accommodate the "natural" pattern. In the case of Hogan's (1978) research, life course "disorder" led to higher rates of marital disruption for men.

However, Buchmann (1989) argues that the educational, work, and family spheres are all changing in advanced industrial societies so as to encourage greater diversity among individuals and expansion of a given individual's choices in life. She links the process to an expansion of time in the bureaucratically defined educational system with its "ideology of individual achievement," which "fosters the development of highly individualized identity patterns" (p. 67). At the same time, work demands greater flexibility of individuals and greater adaptability to changing tasks and professional qualifications. The traditional family, it is argued, is also dissolving, further encouraging individual independence and exploration.

Change in all these spheres of life therefore creates and reinforces greater individualization and flexibility of life course trajectories, what Lerner (1984) calls "human plasticity." Arnett's (1994) research on college students' conceptions of adulthood demonstrates that role transitions, such as leaving school or entering marriage or parenthood, are infrequently identified as necessary for the assumption of adult status. Arnett labels all these transitions "emerging adulthood," as the process has become increasingly lengthy and individualized over time. This lengthening and variable occurrence and ordering of role transitions in modern Western society results in ambiguity in the transition to adulthood. Nearly two thirds of the college students Arnett (1994) studied were uncertain about their adult status.

With increased opportunities to change at every juncture of the life course, early experiences may have little role in determining adult outcomes. Buchmann (1989) states that

> the increased dispersion of actual trajectories diminishes the likelihood of more or less identical career paths among individuals endowed with similar social attributes (i.e., social class, sex, age). As a consequence, the objective possibility of comparing various life trajectories declines. (p. 76)

In other words, pathways to adulthood become less based on social backgrounds and attributes as choices grow for individuals of all backgrounds. Thus, destandardization implies greater difficulties for the researcher in predicting trajectories.

Because of the greater number of choices and possible pathways throughout the life course, predictability becomes more difficult for the person as well. According to Buchmann (1989),

> increased discontinuity/flexibility in the configuration and sequencing of positions and roles tends . . . to undermine the chances for anticipating and predicting the various trajectories and thus tends to reduce the likelihood of building up long-term, stable expectations. In this sense, it is considerably more difficult for the individual to induce his or her future from his or her present circumstances. (p. 77)

Thus, expectations about future plans and pathways may have diminishing salience, as persons become more able to change earlier choices at a later date as new situations or information become available to them. People may also come to invest less thought in making predictions about their futures, if they feel that new possibilities are always likely to arise. This absence of careful deliberation, or lack of "planfulness," would also diminish the predictive power of plans for the future. Adolescents especially may be more likely to live for the moment, with no particular plans in mind for the future.

Given the density of transitions individuals face during the young adult years, it is not surprising that adolescent expectations for adulthood are in fact unstable (Jacobs, 1991; Rindfuss, 1991). As ability, educational attainment, job skills, family pressures, and unpredictable period shocks intervene in young adult lives, plans are likely to change.

Does the inherent instability of plans for the future, and the increasing number of options and opportunities (i.e., destandardization of the life course), mean that it is useless to examine the impacts of plans and aspirations on later outcomes? Actually, there is good reason to believe that, notwithstanding these considerations, plans are still useful predictors of later actions.

Although those who make a strong case for destandardization of the life course tend to focus on the continual possibilities for change throughout life, there is another, overlooked aspect of an individual's "life career" (Sweeting & West, 1994). The notion of a "life career" implies that certain events set up a chain of future events or life changes. Thus, despite the multitude of pathways available to young people today, early choices still narrow the field of later choices to some extent, and therefore, early plans can importantly define later outcomes. For example, the complexities of the occupational system often require an early commitment (if you want to be a physician, you would not take a vocational-technical curriculum in high school). Early plans may constrict the range of future opportunities available to the young person by determining the scope of actions taken in the present.

In addition, gatekeepers, such as college admissions officers and employers, may use their knowledge of a young person's life history (e.g., the record of academic investment and types of coursework pursued in secondary schools or early termination of schooling) in making critically important decisions, thereby perpetuating a trajectory based on earlier choices (Heinz, 1992). This gatekeeping process may happen during schooling, with the tracking of students into various types of academic coursework (Hallinan, 1994).

High school seniors are an optimal group to consider in studying personal preferences; because they soon will face a number of major life course decisions, they have presumably thought about their future lives and may be able to articulate the reasons behind their desires (Crimmins, Easterlin, & Saito, 1991). However, as few have yet embarked on those life course transitions, their desires are less likely (than among older people) to be conditioned by resource constraints.

Because the transition to adulthood involves the major adult roles, anticipations about family (leaving home, marriage, and children) and achievement (education and work) are likely to be especially salient. Tentative ideas and goals regarding these arenas almost certainly begin to be formulated before they are actually confronted. Given the pronounced differentiation of adult roles by sex, there are likely to be gender differences in these expectations. For example, girls' orientation toward boys and dating in high school may prompt them to think more seriously and at an earlier life stage than boys do about issues of marriage and parenthood (Eder, 1985). Although young adults might further explore and change their preferences when they actually face the implications of those plans, early plans should not be discounted.

Additionally, outcomes of the transition to adulthood depend to a large extent on resources differentially available to young people from an early age. Timing of transition events, or even the opportunity to experience some events at all, may be constricted by socioeconomic circumstances. In this regard, the family of origin is extremely important in determining the level of resources available to successfully complete the adult transition and in setting the context that influences the pathways young adults find most attractive.

Family-Related Plans

LEAVING HOME

Leaving home is often framed as a part of the transition to adulthood along with movement out of school and into full-time work and family formation. However, researchers who focus on adult transition rarely use leaving home as an indicator to measure that transition (see Goldscheider & Goldscheider, 1993, for an exception). In addition, while parents and their children may see this move as an important marker of adulthood, what constitutes "leaving home" appears to mean different things to different people—from going away to school to moving to a separate residence to getting married (Harkins, 1978). We need to know more about the role of coresidence in the transition to adulthood.

Methodologically, defining the point when a child has indeed "left" home permanently is ambiguous: Should one count the first time of leaving home or the last time? Is moving away from parents to live in a college dorm, only to return to parents in the summer, independent living? Most would argue that the latter situation is really a case of "semiautonomy," in which young adults have left the control and supervision of their parents but are still under the supervision of other agencies, such as college or the military (Goldscheider & Goldscheider, 1993; White, 1994).

Race, gender, and class differences have been noted in the timing and propensity to leave home, with blacks and Hispanics more likely than whites to stay, women more likely to leave earlier, and upper-class youths more likely to be able to finance (or have their parents finance) independent living (White, 1994). Family structure also has an impact on adult child residence—children from nonintact families reside with parents for a shorter time than do children from intact families (Aquilino, 1990). Thus, issues of family background and resources along with intergenerational transmission of values appear to play important roles in young people's own family transitions.

Although the popular press has portrayed the current generation of young adults as particularly slow to leave the nest and establish independence, there is no empirical evidence that this is the case. There has indeed been an increase in the number of young people staying (or returning) home within the total population, but the trend is the result of an increase in the "pool" of young people traditionally available to reside at home, namely, the unmarried (White, 1994). In fact, looking only among *unmarried* young people, White (1994) argues that residence with parents has been declining steadily since 1940.

One recent study showed that young adults desired to live at their parents' standard of living and were willing to forgo some independence and tolerate some restrictions so as to continue in that environment (Crimmins et al., 1991). Crimmins et al. (1991) called this phenomenon an "intergenerational taste effect," whereby the luxuries of one generation become the necessities of the next one.

Thus, the minimum level of earnings necessary to leave home increases over time. However, as noted above, White (1994) indicates that there has actually been a decline in young adults residing at home since 1940. She speculates that parents' desires for independence from their children may have increased even more rapidly than their children's desire for goods, so that parents will more heavily subsidize children to live apart from them.

My study contributes to this debate by examining the behavior of a recent cohort of young adults. How does this cohort plan to live following high school? What are its actual circumstances in the two years following high school graduation? Are substantial proportions of this sample continuing to live with parents during these two years?

MARRIAGE AND FERTILITY

The United States has seen a trend toward later marriage over time, which has coincided with the emergence of premarital residential autonomy (Goldscheider & Goldscheider, 1993). This trend may be exacerbated by what Bachman, Johnson, and O'Malley (1983) called "premature affluence," caused by employed adolescents' relatively great discretionary income. Research on the predictive impact of marriage plans on actual marital outcomes is sparse. However, Goldscheider and Goldscheider (1993) do find evidence that expected age at marriage more accurately coincides with actual outcomes than do expectations for timing of leaving the parental home.

Because we look at young people through the two years following high school only, we cannot predict marital outcomes for a fully representative group. However, we can make some tentative conclusions about differences between those who are already married or cohabiting during this period and those who are not. Did the former group have younger expected ages at marriage, for example, when the respondents were still in high school?

Much of the work on the predictive ability of plans is in the area of fertility research and is characterized by great disagreement (Hendershot & Placek, 1981). Some contend that expectations data are better for predicting completed fertility of real cohorts than data on actual fertility gathered in a single period and extrapolated to the lifetime of a real cohort (Long & Wetrogan, 1981). Others argue that expectations data can in fact be as sensitive to circumstances, and therefore, as inaccurate, as any other period measure, especially during times when conditions are changing (Westoff, 1981). That is, expectations appear to reflect rather than anticipate changes in conditions that lead to changes in fertility rates. It is also argued that such questions appear to address the number of children that women *want*, irrespective of limiting conditions, rather than the number they *expect* (Hendershot & Placek, 1981).

Although completed fertility behavior certainly cannot be assessed in the two years following high school, one can examine differences in postsecondary parental status by earlier fertility expectations in this panel. Any differences might be suggestive of the impact, if any, of expectations in this area on subsequent behavior.

Educational and Occupational Aspirations and Achievements

There is a sizable body of research on achievement aspirations and their effects on later attainment (Kerckhoff, 1995; Sewell, 1975; Sewell & Hauser, 1972). This literature argues that social background influences attainment by leading children in different circumstances to plan for, or to move toward, different goals (Sewell & Hauser, 1972). Looking at high school students, Dennehy and Mortimer (1992) find that parental education strongly influences the educational and occupational plans of both boys and girls, as does high school achievement (measured by grade point average, or GPA). For girls, family income also significantly impacts achievement plans.

Alternatively, social allocation could be the cause of the background-attainment link, in that gatekeepers actively channel children in certain directions, conditional on their socioeconomic status (Jacobs, 1991). The children themselves may recognize their barriers to a successful future and act accordingly.

The educational and occupational aspirations of teenagers may be quite unstable, and in fact, may have their own trajectories (see Dennehy & Mortimer, 1992). Because American society is characterized by overambition (Jacobs, 1991), aspirations *must* change over time if they are to conform successfully to available opportunities.

Otherwise, the individual may experience considerable role strain or cognitive dissonance between ambitious expectations and the kinds of choices available in reality. Jacobs (1991) reports a steady decline between the ages of 15 and 27 in the highest occupational aspirations (i.e., to be a professional), although managerial expectations do increase (probably because acquisition of positions in management, and realistic aspirations of achieving them, are based more on actual work experience). In addition, the documents differ in aspirations by race that increase over time.

Rindfuss, Cooksey, and Sutterlin (1990) examine the links between expectations and attainments using the National Longitudinal Study of the Class of 1972. The data were analyzed separately by gender, given males' and females' very different occupational opportunity structures. Agreement between expected occupation and actual job at age 30 is not high, although it increases as the date the expectation is measured moves closer to age 30. The agreement is stronger for men than women, probably because the uncertainties caused by family events are greater for women than for men. When there is no match between expectations and achievements, men's outcomes tend to move up relative to their expectations, whereas women's move down. Interestingly, Rindfuss et al. (1990) found little effect of background variables on the relationships between achievement-related expectations and outcomes, although higher grades in school did predict a better match.

The role of achievement-related plans and orientations in actual attainment is examined in a variety of ways. Often, questions about general aspirations and plans for educational attainment are used to predict attainment outcomes. However, because these kinds of questions may simply measure an idealized desire, the impacts of more concrete, short-term plans and steps taken to actualize those plans are also examined. Not only might the latter type of question elicit more accurate reflections on the short-term future, but the effects of immediate plans and actions may extend over a longer time period, given the constraints imposed by early choices on later pathways and outcomes.

Studying plans in a variety of life domains helps researchers better understand the social psychological processes underlying the transition to adulthood and the psychological mechanisms through which background variables affect outcomes. For example, family background—characterized by family income or parental education—may differentially constrain or facilitate achievement plans. Children are importantly influenced by the family environment as they grow up and by the values, beliefs, and social locations of their parents. Parents both consciously and unconsciously influence the plans their children make and consider realistic and the behaviors children pursue in order to achieve their goals (Mortimer et al., 1986). Moreover, family resources may be seen as limiting realistic opportunities for advanced education, and they may restrict aspirations from the start. Higher parental education may foster higher achievement aspirations among children, thereby leading to more effective or persistent attempts to realize those goals. Social background is also likely to affect family plans, thereby influencing outcomes. Children of intact families may be more likely to want to marry; women whose mothers work may expect the same for themselves and plan to marry later than others.

Families may also have an impact on the linkage between plans and outcomes through the development of feelings of efficacy or competence in children. A number of studies indicate the importance of efficacy or a planning orientation for later successful outcomes (Clausen, 1993; Coleman et al., 1966; Finch et al., 1991; Mainquist & Eichorn, 1989). In discussing the dynamics of stability and change over the life course, Mortimer et al. (1986) found that people construct social or environmental contexts that are consistent with prior psychological states. That is, "the impact of earlier upon later life experiences occurs through the influence of relatively stable personality attributes, developed in adolescence, that foster the acquisition of consonant roles and experiences" (Mortimer et al., 1986, p. 193). The family of origin influences achievement, they argue, through the development of these achievement-related personality traits, such as competence or efficacy.

Similarly, Clausen (1993) argues that what he calls "adolescent planful competence" is predictive of a number of adult achievements. Using longitudinal data from the Berkeley Growth and Guidance Studies and the Oakland Growth Study, Clausen found that those who are initially competent tend to set goals and make decisions that mesh with their abilities. The life experiences they thus create for themselves foster realization of their capabilities and achievement of their goals, thereby further enhancing their competence and success. These reciprocal processes of personal selection and environmental influence give rise to increasing advantages, or disadvantages, over time, consonant with Elder's accentuation principle (Elder & O'Rand, 1995).

It is therefore important to examine differences between those adolescents in the Youth Development Study (YDS) who are able to realize their plans and those who are not. Key differences in efficacy among adolescents may influence whether or not they are able to achieve their goals, with very long-term consequences for achievement and further psychological development (Call, Mortimer, Dennehy, & Lee, 1993).

The analysis here is simple and preliminary. Further waves of data will enable an examination of the predictive ability of plans, aspirations, and goals with respect to future outcomes over a longer time period. However, it is important to examine even the short-term consequences of plans for the future; if there is little predictive power after a relatively short time span, there will likely be even less over longer periods of time.

Data and Methods

Data for this analysis come from the first six waves of the YDS. The sample used in this analysis reflects attrition through the six years of the study from the initial panel of 1,000 students. Respondents were selected based on available data from Wave 5 (1992) and/or Wave 6 (1993), with $N = 884$.[1]

In examining the effects of plans and aspirations on outcomes, it is important to assess the determinants of the aspirations themselves. Previous work (Dennehy & Mortimer, 1992; Stevens, Puchtell, Ryu, & Mortimer, 1992) indicates several background variables, which are included in these analyses, that may affect both aspirations and outcomes: race (white, black, other), family type (two-parent versus other), GPA measured in the senior year of high school, parental education, and family income.[2]

In terms of family and living arrangement plans, this chapter first looks at whether adolescents in the senior year of high school plan to live with their parents the following fall. Their plans in this regard are then used to predict whether they actually live (or do not live) with their parents that fall (Wave 5) and then extended to see whether senior-year plans predict continued residence with parents at the end of Wave 6.

The marriage and childbearing plans of the panel as seniors in high school are examined, including plans to marry eventually, estimated age at marriage, and estimated number of children they would like to have. It is too early in the lives of these young people to meaningfully analyze marriage and childbearing because those who have already completed these transitions are, on average, early marriers and young parents and therefore not representative of the entire cohort. Because of the small number of respondents who are currently married, marriage-related plans are used to predict a combination of cohabitation and marital outcomes (as well as cohabitation separately), as greater numbers of the panel experience cohabitation, which is often preliminary to marriage, than enter the married state in the years following high school.

The link between prior expectations about children and actual childbearing is then assessed. However, the results should be interpreted with much caution, not only because the childbearing group is so selective but also because even those who have had one or more children at this point have by no means completed their childbearing.

To measure achievement goals and the plans made to facilitate that achievement, several measures of educational aspirations and plans are used as are concrete actions taken to reach those goals. For a measure of school aspirations, students were asked how far they would *like* to go in school (less than high school, high school, community college, university, master's degree, and doctorate). Then, as an indication of more realistic plans, students were asked about how far they really felt they would get in school (same categories). These two questions have been widely used in prior attainment studies.

Also considered are more immediate actions and goals for the future. For example, students were asked what steps they had taken to pursue a higher education, with their scores representing the most active step taken. Responses progressed from doing nothing, only talking about it, taking some kind of entrance examination, writing for college applications, and actually submitting college applications. Finally, students indicated their immediate educational plans for Fall

1991 (Wave 5) after graduating from high school (none, continue high school, vocational technical school, 2-year college, 4-year college).

In terms of achievement-related outcomes, both school attainment and work experience are analyzed in a variety of forms. Educational achievement in Waves 5 and 6, measured as the highest level of schooling attended through the respective year, was predicted in the following order: high school, job training, vocational-technical, community college, and 4-year college/university. Also examined is a more long-range but also more inclusive schooling outcome—full-time student status in Waves 5 and 6 (measured as being in any form of postsecondary schooling at least 8 months out of the year). In other words, do aspirations and plans while still in high school continue to affect schooling beyond the time frame of the original question?

Besides educational outcomes, achievement aspirations and plans were related to work experience in Wave 6. Are adolescents who had higher educational goals while still in high school *less* likely to work full-time throughout the year than those aiming lower on the educational ladder? First examined is the simple outcome of whether or not the respondent is currently working at all by the end of Wave 6. Then, respondents were divided into categories according to their work experience during that year (those who never worked, those who worked mostly or completely part-time, and those who worked mostly or completely full-time) so as to assess the relation of these outcomes to earlier achievement orientations.

Finally, in examining the question of efficacy with regard to the ability to achieve plans, the effects of domain-specific efficacy on agreement between plans and outcomes are analyzed. In other words, are those with higher efficacy with respect to particular arenas of life more likely to carry out their plans? For family-related areas, a single indicator of family efficacy is used: How do you see your future? What are the chances that you will have a happy family life? Answers are coded from 1 (*very low*) to 5 (*very high*). Achievement plans and outcomes are rated on a scale of economic efficacy, the sum of weighted lambda factor scores of three questions: What are the chances that (1) you will have a job that pays well? (1.000), (2) you will be able to own your own home? (1.195), and (3) you will have a job that you enjoy doing (0.860)?[3] Again, higher scores indicate higher efficacy.

In the analysis, differences in plans are assessed by examining distributions of senior year plans by various individual and family background characteristics. Then, the relations between plans and outcomes are assessed by displaying distributions of behavioral outcomes by the corresponding initial plans. Next, a series of logistic regressions is estimated for dichotomous outcomes, including background characteristics and the most relevant of plans for the future to predict the related outcome statuses. For interval level variables—number of children and school achievement in Waves 5 and 6—OLS regressions are performed. Finally, another series of logistic regressions is estimated, using background characteristics and the appropriate measure of efficacy to predict agreement between initial plans and later outcomes.

Findings

SOCIAL BACKGROUND AND PLANS FOR THE FUTURE

How does social background influence family-related plans during the senior year of high school? Parents with below median education are more likely to have children who plan to live with them after high school (Table 7.1). Other family characteristics do not significantly differentiate plans about living with parents, however. For boys, lower GPA is also associated with greater likelihood of coresidence with parents. Girls from intact families are significantly more likely to plan to marry; black girls are less likely to have these plans. For boys, these relationships are weak at best, although in similar directions. Black boys have exceptionally low expectations of marriage—only 58% plan to marry—but their number is small (see appendix).

There are few significant differences in mean expected marriage age by background characteristics for either females or males in Table 7.1.[4] Among girls, blacks report the highest expected age at marriage, followed by whites, and those of other races. Higher GPA, family income, and parental education are all associated with somewhat higher expected marriage ages for girls. What is particularly interesting here is how most young people cluster around the same expected

TABLE 7.1 Distribution of Living Arrangement and Marriage Plans[a], by Social Background Characteristics

	Plan to Live With Parents in Wave 5		Plan to Marry		Mean Expected Age at Marriage	
	Female	Male	Female	Male	Female	Male
Race						
White	38.1	34.9	88.5	78.5	24.5	25.5
Black	25.6	29.2	72.1	58.3	25.4	25.8
Other	22.2[†]	28.6	79.0**	81.1[†]	23.8*	26.3
Family type						
Two-parent	37.3	36.2	89.7	82.0	24.5	25.5
Other	32.8	30.4	82.3*	73.9[†]	24.4	25.7
Grade point average[b]						
Median+	32.1	28.4	88.8	81.4	24.8	25.8
< Median	38.3*	40.6***	85.0	75.3	24.0*	25.3[†]
Parental education[c]						
Median+	31.5	28.2	87.1	80.0	24.8	25.9
< Median	38.1	37.3***	83.1[†]	76.1	23.1*	25.5
Family income[d]						
Median+	33.9	33.1	89.0	82.5	24.9	26.0
Median	33.7	36.9	85.4	74.1[†]	24.2*	25.5
Total[e]	35.1	33.6	86.0	78.3	—	—
n[f]	387	308	464	387	391	299

a. Plans were measured in the spring of the senior year of high school (Wave 4). Respondents were selected for whom Wave 5 and/or Wave 6 data on outcomes are available.
b. Median grade point average = 3.00 (equivalent to a "B").
c. Median parental education = 2.50 (between high school graduate and some college).
d. Median family income = 7.00 ($40,000-$49,000).
e. Percentage who plan to live with parent or marry (virtually all respondents who plan to marry gave an expected marriage age).
f. Total number who answered the question.
†$p < .10$; *$p < .05$; **$p < .01$; ***$p < .001$; χ^2 test.

marriage ages (24-25 for females and 25-26 for males).[5] As in other research, questions about family expectations elicited answers clustering around the modal ages at which these events actually occur in American society (McLaughlin et al., 1988; Modell, 1980).

TABLE 7.2 Educational Aspirations, Plans, and Steps Taken[a] by Social Background Characteristics

	Aspirations for College		Plans for College		Submit College Applications		Plan to Attend 2-, 4-Year College Fall of Wave 5	
	Female	Male	Female	Male	Female	Male	Female	Male
Race								
White	70.8	65.8	58.1	54.7	47.1	40.9	62.9	58.0
Black	76.8	70.8	54.8	49.9	30.2	29.2	69.8	33.3
Other	72.6	84.0	53.3	65.4	38.1**	30.4**	54.0	60.7
Family type								
Two-parent	76.4	68.6	64.6	53.6	55.6	46.4	67.1	60.9
Other	66.4	68.5	49.3**	58.3†	32.8***	28.7*	57.7***	50.9*
Grade point average[b]								
Median+	84.1	87.7	73.8	82.8	62.4	59.9	75.6	77.7
< Median	58.7***	54.8***	39.8***	36.6***	25.9***	22.8***	49.2***	41.2***
Parental education[c]								
Median+	78.0	81.1	66.8	71.2	52.3	51.5	72.4	65.0
< Median	61.9***	54.3***	43.7***	38.3***	33.9***	24.0***	47.0***	46.3***
Family income[d]								
Median+	82.5	77.5	71.0	65.0	62.3	49.4	75.4	66.9
< Median	66.8**	60.0**	50.5***	48.9*	29.8***	31.9**	57.9***	48.2**
Total[e]	71.4	68.4	57.1	55.7	44.2	38.2	62.5	56.4
n[f]	465	390	463	389	466	390	466	390

a. Aspirations and plans were measured in the spring of the senior year of high school (Wave 4). Respondents were selected for whom Wave 5 and/or Wave 6 data on outcomes are available.
b. Median grade point average = 3.00 (equivalent to a "B").
c. Median parental education = 2.50 (between high school graduate and some college).
d. Median family income = 7.00 ($40,000-$49,000).
e. Percentage who aspire to or plan to attend college, who submit college applications, or have college plans for Fall 1991.
f. Total number who answered the question.
†$p < .10$; *$p < .05$; **$p < .01$; ***$p < .001$; χ^2 test.

Table 7.2 indicates the relationship between social background and educational aspirations, plans, and early pursuit of those plans. First, it should be noted that aspirations are generally fairly high, ranging from 54% to 88% of students who aspire to a college degree or postgraduate education. Although the question about educational plans prompts a more realistic consideration of future attainment, the majority of students in most cases still believe they will complete a college-level education. Second, the characteristics that significantly predict aspirations and plans are high school GPA, parental education, and family income; family structure is only significantly associated with educational plans. Children from families where parents are more highly educated, have higher income, and are themselves higher than the median in terms of academic achievement are more likely to have aspirations and plans of college-level attainment. Girls from two-parent families are also significantly more likely to plan to graduate from college.

Examining the relationship between social background and steps taken to actualize more concrete, short-term plans yields a number of significant relationships. Students with higher GPAs, children from intact families, and those with more highly educated parents and higher income are more likely to have submitted college applications in their senior year of high school and to plan to attend a 2- or 4-year college in the fall.

RELATIONSHIP OF PLANS TO OUTCOMES

It is not surprising that young people who planned to live with their parents in the fall after their senior year (on average, about 6 months after the Wave 4 survey administration) are significantly more likely to do so than are respondents who did not have such plans (Figure 7.1). Moreover, they continue to be much more likely to live with their parents in the following year as well. Although the percentage declines somewhat, among those who had had short-terms plans to live with parents, two thirds of girls and over three quarters of boys continue to live with their parents in Wave 6. For both waves of data, larger percentages of boys than girls continue to live with parents, consistent with other research on young adult living arrangements (Goldscheider & Goldscheider, 1993).

Boys and girls who planned to marry (at some time in the future) are not significantly more often in cohabiting or married arrangements in Wave 6 than are those who did not plan to marry (not shown). However, expected age at marriage is significantly predictive of co-

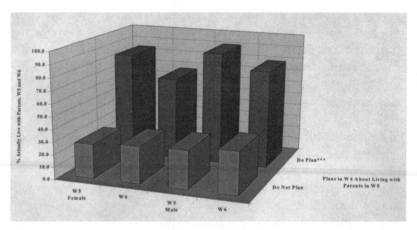

Figure 7.1. Coresidence outcomes in Waves 5 and 6, by plans[a] to live with parents in fall of Wave 5.

a. Plans were measured in the spring of the senior year of high school (Wave 4). Respondents were selected for whom Wave 5 and/or Wave 6 data on outcomes were available.

habitation (girls only) and marriage (both genders) by Wave 6. Girls and boys in these kinds of family arrangements had significantly lower expected marriage ages in their senior year.[6]

There are no significant differences in parental status by mean expected number of children at Wave 6 (not shown), which might be expected given the small numbers of respondents who have become parents by this point and their probable unrepresentativeness.

Turning to achievement outcomes shortly after the completion of high school, those who had concrete college plans for the fall or who had submitted college applications are most likely to be attending a college or university in both Waves 5 and 6 and are also more likely to continue as full-time students in both years (not shown). These relationships are strongly significant (all $p < .001$) and hold for both young men and women. Likewise, both higher educational aspirations and plans are associated with greater percentages of boys and girls attaining either some college or university education by Wave 6 or having full-time-student status ($p < .001$, not shown).

Relationships between educational aspirations and plans, on the one hand, and work status and involvement, on the other, are less consistent than for educational outcomes themselves. However, for both genders, higher educational aspirations and plans are associated with *less* involvement in full-time work (as measured by self-reports of full-time involvement in a job for the full year) in Wave 6 ($p < .01$ and $< .001$ for aspirations and plans, respectively, not shown). At this early stage, higher aspirations are linked to continued education, which tends to preclude full-time work.

REGRESSION RESULTS

Multivariate regression models, including both background characteristics and the relevant plan, are used to predict behavioral outcomes in Waves 5 and 6. These enable an assessment of the independent effects of plans. Do they have significant impacts on early post-high-school outcomes, independent of the social background variables with which they are associated?

Living arrangement plans, as expected, strongly influence actual living arrangements measured the following fall even with the background variables controlled (Table 7.3). Girls who planned to live with their parents are over four times as likely to actually do so in the fall, whereas boys with the same plans are over five times as likely. Residential arrangements are also directly affected by various background characteristics, particularly for young women. Consistent with other research (Aquilino, 1990; White, 1994), black women, women from two-parent homes, and those with lower GPAs are likely to live at home following high school. For boys, however, blacks are significantly less likely to live with parents (however, the number of black males in the sample is small); GPA has a near significant effect.

By the end of Wave 6, the effects of most of these variables are somewhat attenuated. Plans made in Wave 4, regarding Wave 5 living arrangements, continue to significantly affect actual living arrangements, but the magnitudes of these effects are smaller than in the previous wave (boys and girls are about 2-1/2 times as likely to live with parents if they planned to do so two years prior). Of the background variables, only GPA remains near significant and then only for males.

There is little of note in the multivariate models for cohabitation/marriage, predicted by marriage plans, most likely due to the relatively small numbers engaged in these behaviors and the selective nature of

TABLE 7.3 Logistic Regression Models Predicting Coresidence With Parents[a]

| | Live With Parents Fall of Wave 5 | | Live With Parents End of Wave 6 | |
	Female	Male	Female	Male
Plan to live with parents	4.88***	5.66***	2.49***	2.32***
Black[b]	7.22*	0.09*	2.71	.065
Other race[b]	1.26	0.37	0.63	0.51
Two parents	2.86*	1.73	0.95	0.84
Grade point average	0.41**	0.58†	0.85	0.63†
Parental education	0.80	0.83	1.08	0.85
Family income	0.93	0.94	1.11	0.91
$-2\log L$	198.74	154.30	250.11	187.92
Model χ^2	106.83	91.86	40.08	45.94
(df)	(7)***	(7)***	(7)***	(7)***
n	222	183	210	172

a. Exp (B) is presented for ease of interpretation.
b. Reference category for race is white.
†$p < .10$; *$p < .05$; **$p < .01$; ***$p < .001$.

this group (results not shown). Expected age at marriage, however, has a predictable effect on girls' likelihood of cohabiting or marriage in Wave 6, with those planning to marry at later ages also less likely to be engaged in either behavior (Table 7.4). The gender difference in the effect of expected age at marriage is probably due to the relatively young age of the sample and the propensity of girls to engage in these behaviors sooner than boys.

The effect of expected number of children on parental status by Wave 6 can only be estimated for females, as there is little variation in the dependent variable for males (only 8 males have one or more children at this point). Plans for children do not have a significant effect on parental status; the only significant predictor in this model is race—black women are almost seven times more likely to have a child than are whites (results not shown).

Turning to achievement outcomes, first examined is the short-term predictive power of planful behaviors taken in Wave 4 in order to pursue a postsecondary education. Taking concrete actions to apply

TABLE 7.4 Logistic Regression Models Predicting Wave 6 Cohabitation/
Marriage, by Expected Age at Marriage[a]

	Cohabit		Cohabit or Married	
	Female	Male	Female	Male
Expected age at marriage	0.66**	1.13	0.63**	1.07
Black[b]	1.02	1.01	3.42	0.01
Other race[b]	1.02	2.54	2.88	1.88
Two parents	0.62	1.07	0.99	0.71
Grade point average	0.80	1.37	0.71	1.12
Parental education	0.49*	0.64	0.81	0.70
Family income	0.92	1.06	0.95	0.97
$-2\log L$	99.03	75.83	137.18	86.30
Model χ^2	27.48	5.53	35.47	4.73
(df)	(7)**	(7)	(7)**	(7)
n	184	137	191	140

a. Exp (B) is presented for ease of interpretation.
b. Reference category for race is white.
*$p < .05$; **$p < .001$.

to college (the most concrete being submitting college applications)
leads to higher educational attainment—in the form of enrollment in
higher levels of education (e.g., high school vs. community college vs.
university)—in the following year for both males and females (Table
7.5). Higher GPA and parental education (males only) also facilitate
higher attainment in Wave 5. Students' plans for school the fall after
high school graduation likewise are positively associated with attainment that following year. Again, GPA and parental education are also
positively related to attainment (although the latter is not a significant
predictor for girls). Higher income has a small positive effect on girls'
educational attainment.

Although longer-term school aspirations and plans are still tied to
level of educational achievement by Wave 6, the effects are inconsistent (Table 7.6). There are probably two reasons for this. The first is
measuring this cohort of young people at too early a time to see
completed attainment. The second is that the respondents had somewhat unrealistically high aspirations, and even their more "realistic"

TABLE 7.5 OLS Regression Models of Educational Attainment in Wave 5, Predicted by Planful Application Behavior and Fall School Plans

	Educational Attainment[b]			
	Female	Male	Female	Male
College applications	0.42***	0.40***	—	—
Fall school plans	—	—	0.50***	0.49***
Black[a]	−0.38	0.19	−0.62†	0.29
Other race[a]	0.18	−0.10	0.15	−0.04
Two parents	0.10	−0.18	0.19	−0.13
Grade point average	0.49***	0.53***	0.56***	0.52***
Parental education	0.06	0.15**	0.01	0.17**
Family income	0.07*	0.05	0.10***	0.03
Constant	0.30	0.23	−0.41	−0.11
F test	35.85***	35.51***	35.28***	37.97***
R^2	0.54	0.59	0.54	0.60
n	221	182	221	182

a. Reference category for race is white.
b: Unstandardized coefficients.
†$p < .10$; *$p < .05$; **$p < .01$; ***$p < .001$.

estimation of their future attainment appears higher than is probable. In fact, cross-tabular data show that anywhere from 25% to 40% of students who aspired to or thought they would at least reach a community college education still had only a high school or less than high school education by Wave 6 (not shown).

If one looks simply at whether the respondent was a full-time student in Wave 6, as opposed to level of schooling, both educational aspirations and plans positively influence full-time status—those with higher aspirations and plans are anywhere from 44% to 83% more likely to be full-time students in Wave 6 (although plans have no significant effect for boys). For girls, higher GPA positively affects full-time status in Wave 6; for boys, higher GPA, parental education, and family income are associated with full-time status.

Although educational aspirations and plans undoubtedly influence occupational attainment later in life, there is little effect two years after high school, for either gender, on either the probability of simply

TABLE 7.6 Educational Attainment (OLS) and Status (logistic) in Wave 6, Predicted by Educational Aspirations and Plans[a]

	Educational Attainment (OLS unstandardized coefficients)		Full-Time Student (logistic, exp (B))	
	Female	Male	Female	Male
Educational aspirations	0.14*	0.05	1.66***	1.44*
Black[b]	0.70†	−0.75	1.59	0.37
Other race[b]	0.18	0.03	0.81	1.36
Two parents	0.10	−0.13	1.91	0.83
Grade point average	0.68***	0.84***	3.22***	2.29**
Parental education	0.08	0.19**	1.18	1.28†
Family income	0.11***	0.04	1.11	1.30**
Constant	−0.02	0.25	—	—
F test	17.73***	21.56***		
R^2	0.37	0.47		
−2logL			288.94	175.78
Model χ^2			68.65	67.39
(df)			(7)***	(7)***
n	215	175	216	176
Educational plans	0.11*	0.03	1.83***	1.12
Black[b]	0.69†	−.67	1.75	0.62
Other race[b]	0.27	0.05	1.09	1.53
Two parents	0.06	−0.13	1.74	0.81
Grade point average	0.69***	0.84***	3.15***	2.45**
Parental education	0.08†	0.20**	1.18	1.35*
Family income	0.11***	0.04	1.11	1.29**
Constant	0.14	0.35	—	—
F test	17.63***	21.41***		
R^2	0.37	0.47		
−2logL			222.16	181.98
Model χ^2			76.63	61.19
(df)			(7)***	(7)***
n	216	175	217	176

a. Exp (B) is presented for ease of interpretation in logistic models.
b. Reference category for race is white.
†$p < .10$; *$p < .05$; **$p < .01$; ***$p < .001$.

TABLE 7.7 Logistic Regression Results[a], Using Efficacy to Predict Agreement Between Aspirations/Plans and Outcomes[b, c]

Dependent Variables[d]	Effect of Economic Efficacy	
	Female	Male
Educational aspirations		
Aspire to college degree and in college, Wave 5	—	1.21[†]
Aspire to college degree and is full-time student, Wave 5	1.22*	—
Aspire to college degree and is full-time student, Wave 6	1.20[†]	—
Educational plans		
Plan to attain college degree and is full-time student, Wave 5	1.29*	—
Plan to attain college degree and is full-time student, Wave 6	1.24*	—

a. Exp (B) is presented for ease of interpretation.
b. Plans were measured in the spring of the senior year of high school (Wave 4). All models include background characteristics: race (black, other vs. white), family structure (two-parent vs. other), grade point average, parental education, and family income.
c. Nonsignificant coefficients are not displayed.
d. Dependent variables are coded so that 1 indicates that the aspiration or plan for college education and the outcome are in agreement; 0 is to have the same high aspirations but not a matching outcome.
$†p < .10$; $*p < .05$; $**p < .01$; $***p < .001$.

working versus not or part- versus full-time commitment to the workforce (results not shown).

EFFICACY AND LINKS BETWEEN
PLANS AND OUTCOMES

Finally, are there differences in efficacy between those who are able to realize their plans and those who are not? Table 7.7 presents effects of efficacy on agreement between plans and outcomes, based on logistic regression models including the background characteristics as controls. Only significant differences are noted in the table.

First, it is noteworthy that the achievement of family-related plans, at least within the first two years after high school, is not significantly linked to family efficacy. None of the coefficients for family efficacy is significant in any of the models (results not shown).[7] That family efficacy does not predict achievement of family-related plans is possibly the result of the early life course position of this cohort, relative to family-related behaviors.

Economic efficacy has a more consistently significant relationship to educational outcomes. In general, with respect to educational aspirations and plans, young people with higher efficacy in Wave 4 are more likely to follow through with their plans and goals. Among those who were initially high-aiming, it is girls and, to a lesser extent, boys with higher efficacy who actually managed to attend college or achieve full-time student status, thus capitalizing on the earlier steps they took. The results are not as consistent when one looks at young people with lower educational plans and aspirations. There is some tendency for those with higher initial efficacy to more likely achieve in the educational sphere *despite* their initial plans, but the pattern is not consistent, and the results are generally marginally significant (not shown).[8]

Conclusions

Despite the limitations of this analysis—particularly the short period of post-high-school follow-up at this time—it shows that the plans that adolescents make in high school do continue to affect them for at least two years after high school. Although conclusions about marriage and childbearing at such an early point cannot be drawn, it is clear that adolescents follow through on plans involving living arrangements with parents (vs. independent living). Even though respondents were asked only to say what they planned for the fall following high school (an average of 6 months in the future), these plans continued to significantly impact their living arrangements two years later.

Expected age at marriage was also significantly related to cohabitation for young women, such that those in cohabiting arrangements after high school had previously expected to marry at significantly younger ages than others. This result may be an indicator of rapid movement into adult family roles for some young women, with important implications for adult socioeconomic attainment.

Likewise, concrete plans and actions regarding continued schooling did significantly affect educational achievement in the following year. On the other hand, asking young people general questions about their educational aspirations and plans (how far would you like to go, or think you will go?) was less successful in predicting level of subsequent educational attainment, perhaps because of the restricted time frame here. However, these variables do predict full-time student status. Higher aspirations and goals do affect level of involvement in school.

Although young adults in contemporary society may have an increasing number of pathways from which to choose, using their plans for the future to predict actual outcomes is not a hopeless goal. Those who argue the case for destandardization most strongly might have one think that it is a futile project to link plans for the future to actual trajectories. It is clear from this analysis that predictive power does decline as time elapses between the stated goal and the actual outcome, as events intervene and plans and goals perhaps change. However, early plans do appear to set the stage for later behaviors.

Likewise, social background attributes continue to have an impact on plans for the future for this cohort. In terms of family-related plans, both boys and girls whose parents have lower than the median level of education are more likely to plan to reside with parents. White girls and girls from intact families are somewhat more likely than others to plan to eventually marry. Girls from higher-income families and those who have higher grades themselves plan to marry at older ages.

Achievement-related aspirations and plans are strongly influenced by a variety of background characteristics. Educational aspirations and plans are particularly strongly associated with level of parental education, family income, and school performance. In all cases, having parents with higher education and income and having a higher GPA are associated with aspirations and plans for a 4-year college education. Boys and girls who are white, from two-parent families, have higher GPAs, and whose parents' education and income are above the median are all more likely to submit college applications; with the exception of the race differential, all these differences hold as well for plans to attend college in the fall following high school. Thus, the effect of social background on these particular aspirations, plans, and achievement-related actions is also not eliminated by the increasing disorder and individualization of the life course.

Finally, do adolescents differ in their success in realizing their early plans? Family efficacy had no significant effect on the match between plans and outcomes in residential and marital relations. However, it is possible that any real effects are eliminated by the unrealistically short time frame within which we examine these behaviors. Perhaps in the longer run, as more members of this cohort have time to experience these behaviors, measures of prior efficacy will more clearly predict differential success.

Unlike family efficacy, economic efficacy did differentiate between young people who realized their educational goals from those who did not. Adolescents with higher efficacy in the senior year of high school went on to actualize their plans more effectively in terms of full-time school attendance. As feelings of efficacy are developed within a supportive family environment, these findings suggest that family background, family relationships, plans, and later outcomes do indeed continue to be tied together in close and important ways.

These data indicate that rather than giving up on questions about plans and expectations, researchers should perhaps reconsider the kind of questions that best elicit intentions predictive of later outcomes. For example, questions about short-term, more concrete plans with respect to residential arrangements and schooling were not only predictive in the short term in this analysis but carried through into the longer time frame. Moreover, age at marriage—a more specific and temporally relevant measure of marriage expectations—was a more powerful predictor of cohabitation, a status that is often preliminary to marriage, than the more general intention to marry.

It may seem obvious that asking people what they plan to do in a few months' time will successfully predict what they actually do in a few months. However, it is less obvious, and more interesting, that such short-term goals and plans will continue to successfully predict behavior over a longer time period. This finding supports the notion of the "life career" discussed earlier, that choices made early on serve to constrict to some degree choices available later in the life course. Even with the increasing range of options available to adolescents today, if the right questions are asked, their life trajectories are not entirely unpredictable.

Further waves of this study may hopefully shed further light on the power of plans to predict outcomes that are increasingly distant in time.

Appendix
Frequencies of Independent Variables, by Gender

	Female	Male
Race		
White	357	306
Black	44	26
Other	66	61
Family type		
Two-parent	234	207
Other	232	181
Grade point average		
Median+	234	162
< Median	243	245
Parental education		
Median+	283	209
< Median	174	184
Family income		
Median+	186	161
< Median	180	164
Living arrangement plans for Fall 1991		
Definitely/probably not live with parents	224	177
Definitely/probably live with parents	163	131
Marriage plans		
Definitely/probably will not marry	65	84
Definitely/probably will marry	399	303
Educational aspirations		
Less than high school	1	1
High school graduate	14	18
Community college degree	94	66
4-year college degree	116	116
Master's degree	103	74
PhD or professional degree	113	77

Educational plans

Less than high school	7	4
High school graduate	30	43
Community college degree	136	92
4-year college degree	142	130
Master's degree	68	53
PhD or professional degree	54	34

Highest step taken to attend college

Nothing	106	132
Only talked about it	80	46
Took entrance exams	28	25
Wrote away for applications	46	38
Submitted applications	206	149

School plans for Fall 1991

None	69	87
High school	16	23
Vocational/technical	90	60
2-year college	86	64
4-year college	205	156

Notes

1. Respondents must have responded to *at least* one of the two post-high-school waves of the survey (1992 or 1993), if not both, to be included in this analysis.

2. A variable indicating whether or not the mother worked outside the home was originally included in all analyses. However, because it had little significant influence and because a large number of cases were missing this information, it was subsequently dropped from the analysis.

3. Weightings derived from confirmatory factor analysis were used to form the index of economic self-efficacy. No significant difference in measurement structures was found by gender, so weights are the same for males and females.

4. There are almost no significant differences by social background in mean expected number of children (not shown). The only significant finding was that boys with nonworking mothers expected more children than those whose mothers worked (2.56 vs. 2.03).

5. Most respondents also clustered around the same expected number of children —about two.

6. Cohabiting girls' mean expected marriage age in high school was 22.93, as compared to 24.67 for noncohabitors in Wave 6 ($p < .001$). For married girls in Wave 6, the expected marriage age was 21.92, compared to 24.48 for the nonmarried ($p < .05$). For married versus nonmarried boys in Wave 6, the corresponding age expectations were 23.19 and 25.75 ($p < .05$).

7. Only one family efficacy coefficient is even marginally significant ($p < .10$), indicating a somewhat greater tendency for girls with higher efficacy who plan to live with parents to continue to live with them into Wave 6.

8. In some models of educational plans and outcomes, respondents with low-aiming plans (i.e., less than college) who did not continue in school were those with higher efficacy. In other models, higher efficacy predicted higher achievement *despite* lower initial plans. Overall, the patterns were weak and inconsistent.

8

Future Directions for Research on Adolescents, Work, and Family

MICHAEL D. FINCH

JEYLAN T. MORTIMER

Through their intergenerational, developmental perspectives, the preceding chapters illuminate our understanding of the interrelations of work, family, and adolescence. Considered in tandem, they raise fundamental questions about the changing character of adolescent socialization in contemporary American society. In doing so, they challenge prominent theoretical paradigms about the preparation of youths for adulthood that almost completely neglect the contributions of early work experience.

Developmental psychologists emphasize the quality of parent-child relationships in childhood and adolescence as sources of emotional stability, security, competence, and resilience, all of which, in turn, enhance adaptation to school, promote achievement, and facilitate coping with life's adversities (Bronfenbrenner, 1979; Steinberg, 1990). Whereas much of the developmental literature is focused on quite contemporaneous experiences and outcomes, if early experiences are, in fact, highly formative, and if personality is increasingly stable over time, then such experiences will have enduring implications (Alwin, 1994; Mortimer, Finch, & Kumka, 1982; Mortimer et al., 1986). A life course perspective draws attention to these connections between earlier and subsequent life experiences (Clausen, 1993; Elder & O'Rand, 1995).

Sociologists, in their studies of status attainment, have placed major emphasis on the family's socioeconomic position as a determinant of parents' educational and occupational aspirations for the child (significant others' influence), as an index of economic resources available for the attainments of the next generation, and as an indicator of many other familial resources—cultural and social—that may facilitate the child's mobility or maintenance of status position (Coleman, 1994; Sewell & Hauser, 1976). Educational attainment is seen as the key intervening variable, mediating the effects of the family of origin on adult occupational attainment, human capital accumulation, and earnings potential.

Coleman (1990) makes an important distinction between human capital and social capital. Human capital is created by the acquisition of skills and capabilities that increase the individual's productivity and hence earnings capacity. Social capital arises from social structure, from relations of trust and authority, and from norms that facilitate individual goals that could not be achieved in the absence of the structure or relational bonds or could only be attained at greater cost. It is much to the advantage of the person to be connected to relationships involving mutual aid and information exchange, as Granovetter (1974) and Lin, Ensel, and Vaughn (1981) have so aptly shown with respect to occupational attainment. Such connections, especially those of an intimate, confiding nature, can also be of great assistance in buffering (and perhaps compensating for) the effects of stressors and fostering resilience (Thoits, 1995).

Vast literatures in psychology and in sociology have been generated by these perspectives—focused on personality development; status attainment; the accumulation of human capital through education, work, and job training; and the acquisition of social capital through informal and formal social ties. However, they have almost entirely overlooked the potential implications of adolescents' work experiences in the home or in the paid labor market. In the relatively few extant studies that have considered adolescent work, it is construed rather narrowly. For example, studies of adolescent participation in housework have examined total hours of work, differences in contributions by gender, differences in the meaning of responsibility in families and more formal settings, and monetary compensation in the form of an allowance or other special payments (see Goodnow, 1995; Miller & Young, 1990; Mortimer, Dennehy, Lee, & Finch, 1994).

In prior studies of paid work in high school, only a very restricted set of long-term consequences has typically been examined—for example, its effects on unemployment and income in the years immediately after leaving school (Meyer & Wise, 1982; Steel, 1991). As discussed in Chapter 1, adolescent paid work is often viewed as something that detracts from personality development, educational achievement, and future attainment (Greenberger & Steinberg, 1986).

Does the increase in adolescent involvement in the paid labor force in fact signal a breakdown of developmental processes and human capital investment? It is reasonable to question whether human capital can be heightened through work that requires little training, features simple tasks, and involves frequent movements in and out of the labor force. Alternatively, the increasing prevalence of adolescent paid work could point to new forms of acquisition of personal and social resources in a changing economic and social context. Adolescent work could foster competence, resilience, and the actualization of the adolescent's desired adult "possible self." Social capital, or the adolescent's capacity to acquire it, could also be enhanced by paid work. Contrary to much of the "accepted wisdom," the analyses presented in this volume, as well as prior findings of the Youth Development Study (YDS), point to the potential utility of early work experiences— in the family and in the paid workforce—to develop capacities that enhance status attainment, foster the acquisition of efficacy and self-competence, and contribute to the development of other forms of human and social capital.

Adolescent Work
and Parent-Child Relations

We have seen that contemporary adolescents perform considerable housework, that their allocation of time to housework is responsive to family need, and that this helping behavior, under favorable circumstances, evokes a sense of competence—a key component of psychological resilience. But what costs might be entailed? Some adolescents might do too much housework, such that their school-work is compromised. Moreover, gender-stereotyped household tasks might only prepare young girls for the gender-typed division of labor in their future workplaces and families of procreation.

With respect to paid work, is this an experience that is harmful or beneficial? Does it interfere with, or increase, resilience, the development of human capital, or the acquisition of social capital? Our prior analyses have shown that paid work experience, under favorable circumstances, has the potential to enhance the adolescent's sense of competence (Finch et al., 1991), to promote adolescent well-being (Shanahan et al., 1991), and to clarify work values (Mortimer, Pimentel, Ryu, Dennehy, & Lee, in press). We might ask how paid work influences relationships with parents, key precursors of competence and other dimensions of mental health and a major component of the adolescent's social capital. Thus far, we have found no indication that working during high school diminishes the quality of relationships with parents and some evidence that adolescent work can strengthen these relations—for example, when adolescents have high-quality jobs in which they gain useful skills (see Mortimer & Shanahan, 1994). Furthermore, Shanahan and his colleagues (this volume) demonstrate that such strengthening is particularly likely to occur in the rural setting where adolescent earnings are more frequently applied to familial needs (Shanahan, Elder, Burchinal, & Conger, in press). We have seen from Aronson and her colleagues' analysis that the parents of the YDS participants also frequently used their earnings to assist their own parents. Again, the experience of helping is intricately tied to the experience of paid work.

We know from Elder's research (Elder, 1974; Elder, Nguyen, & Caspi, 1985; Elder & O'Rand, 1995; Elder & Rockwell, 1979) how important the ability to help the family at a time of adversity is for the development of competence and subsequent attainment. Employed rural youths might then have some advantages. They might grow up faster than urban youths, using their earnings in more adultlike, collectivistic ways rather than in a more "adolescent" fashion, promoting their own, individualistic, leisure-time pursuits. This experience of contributing to their families could promote their feelings of responsibility for others and hence their capacity to care for others and to participate in adultlike family roles.

A Historical, Intergenerational
Perspective on Adolescent Work

Aronson et al.'s chapter shows that parents themselves believe that working enabled them to develop aspects of human capital that are rarely considered in sociologists' and economists' more narrowly defined operationalizations. That is, work in adolescence enabled them to develop a greater sense of responsibility, instilled the "work ethic," and fostered money management skills, confidence, and self-esteem. Working also helped them understand their own work preferences, to identify their job-related skills, and to prepare for their adult careers in other ways. Many also said that they acquired abilities to get along with other people and made friendships on the job, key elements in the development of social capital.

Aronson and her collaborators find that parents of adolescents in the YDS and their children report similar benefits (and costs) of employment and that the advantages of working far outweigh any drawbacks in both parents' and children's reports. All of these data, of course, are perceptions tapping the subjective, not the objective reality. One might ask, have parents who worked for longer or shorter periods of time during their own adolescence, or who worked more or less intensively, or who had different kinds of jobs, actually experienced differing levels of success in their careers? Has their early work experience, while in high school, contributed to their own occupational attainment in middle adulthood? Whereas in status attainment studies sociologists generally consider the first job after leaving school and economists have studied the consequences of jobs while still in school on short-term employment stability and income, the long-term implications of working early on in the life course are not known. What are the consequences of different kinds of work in adolescence on adult vocational development and peak occupational attainment? As noted at the end of this chapter, we will begin to address this question in examining the early transition to adulthood among the adolescents, but such analyses do not illuminate the experience of the parental cohort.

Moreover, one wonders whether the YDS adolescents, as they grow older, will come to have similar sanguine judgments about their own early work in adolescence. How does the historical experience of a cohort in the labor force influence retrospective assessments of their early work? Given the generally favorable occupational conditions that prevailed when the parents entered the workforce at a time of general economic expansion and prosperity, it may be that they would perceive their early jobs, and their occupational careers more generally, rather favorably. Their children will likely encounter a much more difficult job market in early adulthood, and it is likely that many of them will never attain the same standard of living as that enjoyed by their parents. If they come to experience harder times, would this make them less sanguine later in life when looking back on their early work experiences?

Adolescent Participation in the Family Economy and Paid Work: Implications for Development

The three chapters by Aronson, Call, and Shanahan and their colleagues, considered in tandem, raise important questions about the child's role in the family economy. Zelizer (1985), in her historical analysis of family change, emphasizes the historical decline in the economic contribution of children. In fact, in her view, contemporary children are more economic liabilities than assets and come to have mainly "sentimental" value to their parents. Although this may be correct, the findings presented in this book, based on the St. Paul and the Iowa data, show that contemporary adolescents as well as those in the prior generation contributed to the family economy in many ways —through their chores, contributions of earnings, and spending patterns. Although not often contributing to the family directly, large proportions of working adolescents buy their own clothes, use their earnings for school-related expenses, and save their earnings for college. These data point to the importance of children in the family division of labor and in the functioning of the family as an economic unit (Waite & Goldscheider, 1991). Thus, children's contributions of labor in the family setting may be seen as resources that increase their parents' ability to pursue their occupations while at the same time maintaining their households, thus enhancing their parents' social capital.

As noted earlier, we have discovered considerable amounts of gender stereotyping in adolescent household labor in terms of both the time spent working in the household and in the types of housework and caring tasks that are performed. Moreover, Call finds that sex typing in household work becomes increasingly pronounced over time. Boys substantially diminish the amount of housework they perform in the latter period of high school, whereas girls' efforts remain relatively constant. We need to know more about the internal dynamics in the family that precipitate this change. Are adolescents being pressured by parents to take on a more stereotyped division of labor? Are boys given more "time off" with respect to household responsibilities as they grow older because their performance in school or their paid work is considered more consequential for their later attainments?

What are adolescents' motivations and feelings regarding this change? Do they recognize the increasing gender inequality in household labor? Are girls comfortable with this change? Call finds that girls report more opportunities to be helpful at work, and because of their gendered socialization experiences, it may be more congenial for them to help others more in the home as well. Examination of these family dynamics and both parental and adolescent reactions to them requires a more qualitative, intensive study.

Finally, we need to know more about the implications of the gender-stereotyped division of labor for the future development and attainment of boys and girls. How does it affect attitudes toward gender roles, or the various expectations, aspirations, and plans for the future that were found by Pimentel to be useful in predicting short-term (over a two-year period) behavioral outcomes and attainments?

This issue might usefully be subsumed under a consideration of adolescent time use more generally. Much attention has been directed by social scientists to the relative contributions of husbands and wives to breadwinning and homemaking and to their decision making with respect to the allocation of time to paid and unpaid work (Becker, 1981; Tilly & Scott, 1978). The outcomes of these decisions have widely recognized implications for gender inequalities in the household and in the workplace (Giele, 1988; Miller & Garrison, 1982).

It should be noted that, although less studied, adolescent children are also making important decisions regarding their allocations of time that may have major consequences for their eventual attainment. The chapters by Aronson et al., Call, and Shanahan et al. raise questions about the total allocation of adolescent time. To a large extent, teenagers can decide how much time to devote to school (even though the school day is fixed, many adolescents arrange their schedules so as to leave school early) and how much time to spend on homework and extracurricular activities in the school setting; the degree of investment in household chores, caring for younger siblings, and caring for grandparents; time spent in both paid work and volunteer work outside of the home; and time devoted to socializing with peers.

Call determined that adolescents, throughout high school, spend more time doing household chores when their families are larger and when they have smaller incomes. What is sacrificed? Paid work? School work? Time just "hanging out" with friends?

Although sociologists have studied the implications of school achievement for future educational and occupational attainment (Rosenbaum & Kariya, 1991; Sewell & Hauser, 1976) and thus address the issue of school investment on subsequent outcomes, these studies address just a small piece of the overall puzzle. We know little about the implications of different mixes of these activities in adolescence for development and attainment. A typology of adolescent time use could possibly be constructed, based on the relative proportions of time spent in these various activities. It would be interesting to know whether the various "types" of adolescents, so identified, have different levels of long-term "success" with respect to their capacity, in adulthood, to cope with problems in important spheres of adult life (work, family, friendship, etc.). What are the implications of one pattern of time use versus another—for the development of personality characteristics, like competence and self-esteem that promote attainment; for the acquisition of skills and abilities and other forms of human capital that will enhance productivity in the labor market; and finally, for the potential to develop social ties and obtain organizational memberships that will increase youths' social capital as they make the transition to adulthood? To our knowledge, the adolescent's total pattern of time use, considering these various trade-offs and including both the more collective and individualistic uses of time, have not been subject to systematic scrutiny.

As we have seen from Aronson et al.'s and Call's analyses, gender differences in the allocation of housework and caring activities in the home are striking. How might these activities enhance or compromise the development of personality resilience, human capital, and social capital? Girls could be learning a pattern of adaptation in adolescence —having to pay more attention than boys to the coordination of their housework and extrafamilial roles—that will serve them well as they take on paid jobs and the "second shift" in adulthood. They could acquire, in adolescence, a greater sense of competence at being able to contribute in the family sphere in addition to their schoolwork and possibly paid work, that will be paralleled by their more extensive involvement in household maintenance and parenting in future years. Alternatively, they may be learning patterns that perpetuate women's inequality in the workplace and that could hinder their own socio-economic attainment. We plan to devote considerable attention to this set of issues in future work with the YDS data.

Adolescent Work in
Urban and Rural Contexts

Chapter 4, by Shanahan et al., raises important questions about the differences in the experience of adolescence in urban and rural settings. Further study of differences in the effects of working in urban and rural contexts is clearly warranted, such as its effects on personality dimensions such as self-efficacy, self-esteem, and depressive affect, on school achievement, substance use, and the other outcomes that have up to this point only been studied in urban settings. Juxtaposition of the St. Paul and Iowa data with respect to the effects of earnings on parent-child relations yielded positive effects in the rural setting and essentially null findings in the urban setting. These are explained by the collective versus individualistic uses of adolescent earnings. It is interesting to speculate whether a similar pattern might emerge with respect to psychological development. That is, we have found (Mortimer, Finch, et al., in press) that employment status and hours of work have no significant impact in the urban setting on several dimensions of adolescent mental health, including self-esteem, self-efficacy, well-being, and depressive affect. But if adolescent work takes on a more positive, collective meaning in the rural setting, it may have more generally salutary implications for mental health. We hope to conduct further analyses to explore this possibility in the future.

Shanahan et al. depict rural adolescents as using their earnings largely to promote family welfare, whereas urban adolescents are more self-oriented in this regard. What leads to different uses of earnings within the urban and rural settings? Call, in Chapter 3, in analyzing the urban data, was not successful in predicting earnings use from background variables. It has become a truism that working helps youths learn how to "handle money," there is evidently considerable diversity in spending patterns, and it would be useful to know how attitudes toward money and its use develop in the contexts of work and family life. Surely, effectiveness in money management is an important life skill that would likely have major implications for subsequent adjustment and attainment. Moreover, earning and spending patterns and the family's response to them may be reflected in adolescents' developing self-concepts (Shanahan, Elder, & Burchinal, 1995). Shanahan et al. acknowledge that both the consequences of investment in paid work and various spending patterns may differ within urban and rural settings as a function of the degree of economic stress experienced in the context. That is, it is possible that families in very depressed urban areas would look more like the rural families studied in Iowa. Clearly, there needs to be more study of differences in adolescent participation in family economic strategies in diverse community environments. Adolescent work, both legal and otherwise, may be quite important for family adaptation in the inner city (Sullivan, 1989).

Adolescent Work as an "Arena of Comfort"

In Chapter 5, Call examines the extent to which work acts as an arena of comfort with respect to family stressors during the first two years of high school. Thus, at the level of Bronfenbrenner's (1979) "meso-system," there are complex developmental dynamics with important implications for mental health and adjustment. Her analysis raises the possibility that work may have an increasing function in buffering adverse circumstances as students mature and move into more highly involving and responsible occupational activities. She speculates that there may be increasing interpersonal as well as task-related rewards of work as youths take on more complex tasks and move into more congenial settings.

The changing effects of work, as an arena of comfort, can be examined with the YDS data that have already been collected. Yet unexplored are the implications of work as an arena of comfort with respect to reactions to stressors in other contexts (e.g., in school and the peer group). Do adolescents who are doing more poorly in school seek "comfort" and a source of self-esteem and mastery in work? If they do, they could be protected from the otherwise adverse consequences that failure in school might have. Conversely, familial or educational "comfort" might typically buffer the effects of adolescent workplace stressors.

Socialization to Work
in the Family Setting

In Chapter 6, Ryu and Mortimer draw attention to patterns of occupational value socialization related to the self-directed work experiences of parents. Whereas self-direction is a significant determinant of both mothers' and fathers' occupational values, it only moderates the effect of parental support on adolescent value socialization in the father-son dyad. As is noted in Chapter 6, we need to know more about the vocational development of girls as well as the influence of working mothers.

Ryu and Mortimer's analysis also raises some general issues about the study of vocational socialization processes. For example, it is evident from their findings that the transference of occupational reward values does not occur automatically but only via a conduit of close, communicative parent-child relationships (and only in one of four parent-child dyads). But even though mothers tend to have closer relationships with both daughters and sons, as reported by the children, we find little evidence that working mothers' values concerning occupational rewards are transferred to children of either gender.

Like Call's analyses of adolescent housework in Chapter 3, Ryu and Mortimer's chapter paints a rather traditional portrait of family life. Despite the great prevalence of maternal employment, boys seem to acquire work values from their fathers. If the crystallization of occupational values can be considered a form of human capital, promoting career decision making and the mobilization of effort to achieve career goals, girls could be disadvantaged by the lack of influence from their fathers. How do boys and girls perceive their working mothers? Does the mother's occupation matter? If the mother works merely to supplement the family income, and if she has had a somewhat erratic career, moving in and out of the labor force, her influence on children's developing vocational preferences could be diminished. Moreover, if the mother is a successful professional or manager, making a substantial contribution to the family's economic welfare, her efficacy in transferring her work values to her children could be enhanced. The particular times of the child's life during which the mother was employed could also be important. These and other questions, concerning the dynamics of occupational value socialization and their implications for gender differences in occupational attainment, remain to be addressed.

Adolescents Planning for Their Future Work and Family Lives: Implications for Early Attainments

In Chapter 7, Pimentel shows that despite the increasing "destandardization" and "disorder" in the early life course, adolescents' aspirations and plans clearly matter for early attainments. Surely, as she points out, the full force of the constellation of future orientations she examines (regarding residential arrangements, preferred age of marriage, fertility plans, and educational plans and aspirations) cannot be discerned until the adolescents grow older—as they complete their schooling and move into early adult familial and occupational roles. We will need to continue to follow the panel to further understand the linkages between subjective orientations to the future and actual behavior and the characteristics of those who are more or less successful in achieving their goals.

It must be emphasized that the person is the unit of analysis in Pimentel's study and in the rest of the analyses presented in this book. However, the person does not always have full control over the phenomena at issue. That is, all of the "outcomes" or achievements that Pimentel examines—including living with parents, cohabitation, marriage, fertility, educational attainment, and work—require actions or cooperation from other actors, be they parents (who may permit or prevent the adolescent from moving back into the parental home), intimate partners, school admissions officers, or employers. These actors, in turn, may be heavily influenced by other actors or circumstances (e.g., the demand for employers' products in the broader society). Thus, the individual person may have greater or lesser ability to fulfill early aspirations and plans.

Although our individualistic purview may be seen as a drawback, it might also function to make these analyses rather conservative. The power of earlier subjective orientations to predict subsequent subjective outcomes, despite all such external contingencies that may be completely outside the individual's control, testifies to the force of individual agency in the determination of the life course trajectories of family, education, and work.

In fact, there may be more room for choice when the individual is less tightly constrained by prior circumstances. For example, given the loose coupling between education and work in the United States (particularly in comparison to countries like Germany and Japan), it may be that adolescents' orientations and values with respect to the work sphere, and the direction (or lack thereof) that is provided by parents or other adult role models, are especially important determinants of occupational attainment (Kerckhoff, 1995; Mortimer, 1996).

It will be important to observe whether the relationship between plans and outcomes is more tenuous for young women than for young men, as women may face greater constraints from family demands, employer bias, and so on, thus weakening the plans-outcomes connection more for them as they move through the early life course. Are girls factoring these potential obstacles into their early expectations? That is, they could possibly be just as successful in realizing their plans as boys, if they recognize greater barriers to begin with and effectively compensate for them. They could compensate by lowering their aspirations to what they deem more realistic or by holding high aspirations and putting in greater effort. Either path would have real personal costs. As more long-term outcomes are observed, it will be interesting to discover whether the link between efficacy and achievement of aspirations and plans differs for girls and boys.

Of course, we need to know much more about the reciprocal influences of person and environment, as individuals continually change their conceptions of themselves, their value preferences, aspirations, and plans in light of their actual circumstances, and as those circumstances change in response to individual selection and "role making." We know something about these dynamics in adulthood from prior studies of occupational experience, work values (Mortimer & Lorence, 1979a, 1995), and psychological functioning (Kohn & Schooler, 1983). And the YDS has begun to address these dynamics in the context of adolescent work. The kinds of orientations that we have found (in our earlier work reviewed in Chapter 1) to be responsive to adolescent work experiences—changes in occupational values (Mortimer, Pimentel, et al., in press), self-competence (Finch et al., 1991), and depressive affect (Shanahan et al., 1991)—may be especially important in the early attainment process (Mortimer et al., 1986). We need to know more about the reciprocal interrelations of person and environment with respect to other life domains (e.g., educational plans, marital aspirations, and fertility goals) as young people make their way into early adult roles.

The Youth Development Study:
Looking Ahead

In future years, we will continue to examine the process of movement into adulthood by studying the effects of adolescent work in high school on the patterning and timing of markers of transition. Bachman and Schulenberg (1993) have suggested that adolescents who work "grow up faster"; as they gain economic independence, they may come to think of themselves as more like adults, taking on adult styles of leisure time use. Accordingly, we find (Mortimer, Finch, et al., in press) that adolescents who work more intensively engage in more alcohol use. This could merely be a sign that they are indeed "growing up faster," spending their leisure time in social activities in a manner that fosters social relationships in adulthood but viewed with concern when engaged in by younger people. Alternatively, it could be a harbinger of later drinking problems, which would certainly interfere with socioeconomic attainment and jeopardize mental health.

It would be consistent with the "growing up faster" thesis to find that adolescents who have worked more during high school also move into adult familylike roles more quickly—into cohabitation, marriage, and childbearing. They may also have different styles and patterns of combination of work and educational roles. That is, working in adolescence could set the stage for continued simultaneity of work and educational involvement, such that adolescents who work in high school continue to combine the two roles effectively as they go through college and other institutions of postsecondary education. This pattern could help or hinder their eventual educational attainment. Does the investment in, or quality of, employment during high school have any long-term implications for adolescent economic and/or emotional independence from parents, or for other dimensions of parent-child relationships during the transition to adulthood?

It is reasonable to suppose that working during high school would lead to better coping with the demands of early adult work roles or with the pressures of combining education, work, and family. Working adolescents could learn to cope with occupational stressors so that they respond to stress in more mature and effective ways in their early adult jobs. These speculations imply developmentally beneficial instead of detrimental lagged effects of early work on adaptation to the combinations of early adult roles that adolescents experience. Do adolescent workers, in fact, become better time managers so as to be able to cope with the multiple demands and overloaded schedules typical of adult urban life?

Two plausible contrasting hypotheses can be applied to these dynamics. According to the "developmental readiness" hypothesis, espoused by Greenberger and Steinberg (1986), adolescents are not yet ready for the stressors they encounter in the workplace, having not yet acquired adequate coping skills. If adolescents are indeed not yet "ready" in this sense, we might expect continuing long-term deficits, particularly among those who were exposed earlier to the most intensive, stressful work experiences. According to this hypothesis, such work experiences would have negative contemporaneous impacts on dimensions of psychological functioning that have a relatively high degree of stability over time. Relatedly, the "accentuation" hypothesis (Elder et al., 1984; Elder & O'Rand, 1995) posits that initial personal problems become magnified in adverse circumstances.

The second hypothesis points to the development of work-related "stress resistance" or "steeling." It argues that whereas initial encounters with the workplace may be contemporaneously stressful, having immediate negative consequences for mental health and behavioral adjustment, the long-term lagged effects may be quite different. Just as Depression-era stressors in adolescence were found to have long-term benefits (Elder, 1974), it is plausible to argue that work experience in adolescence may lead to the development of long-term styles of cognitive appraisal and behavioral coping, particularly relevant to the workplace, that facilitate subsequent adjustment in work settings. Through work experience trial and error, adolescents may learn which coping mechanisms are most efficacious. Moreover, earlier work experiences may trigger attribution processes that lead to later feelings of mastery and control, increasing the threshold of stress that would have to be reached before psychological problems (e.g., depressive feelings) arise (Shanahan & Mortimer, in press).

It should be pointed out that those features of the adolescent labor market that have been viewed as most deleterious—for example, the high degree of movement in and out of the labor force and between jobs—may be considered increasingly characteristic of the economy as a whole. That is, the link between employing organizations and employees is becoming increasingly tenuous with more use of contract and other temporary workers, and the ever-increasing pace of technological change makes it necessary to change careers as well as jobs several times in the course of a career (Kalleberg, 1996). Are employed adolescents acquiring orientations toward work that will enable them to cope with this increasingly precarious labor market? Are they acquiring interpersonal skills that will enable them to find jobs and deal with the changing constellation of employers and coworkers that they may be expected to encounter in the course of their work careers?

These are the questions that will occupy us and hopefully attract the attention of other researchers in our continued attempts to understand the long-term effects of early work experiences—on personality development and on the acquisition of the many forms of human and social capital—as young people make the transition to adulthood.

References

Allgood-Merten, B., Lewinsohn, P. M., & Hops, H. (1990). Sex differences and depression. *Journal of Abnormal Psychology, 99,* 55-63.

Alwin, D. E. (1994). Aging, personality, and social change: The stability of individual differences over the life span. In D. L. Featherman, R. M. Lerner, & M. Perlmutter (Eds.), *Life span development and behavior* (Vol. 12, pp. 135-185). Hillsdale, NJ: Lawrence Erlbaum.

Aquilino, W. S. (1990). The likelihood of parent-adult child coresidence: Effects of family structure and parental characteristics. *Journal of Marriage and the Family, 52*(2), 405-419.

Arnett, J. J. (1994). Are college students adults? Their conceptions of the transition to adulthood. *Journal of Adult Development, 1,* 213-224.

Bachman, J. G. (1970). *Youth in transition: Vol. 2. The impact of family background and intelligence on tenth-grade boys.* Ann Arbor: University of Michigan, Survey Research Center, Institute for Social Research.

Bachman, J. G. (1983). Premature affluence: "Do high school students earn too much?" *Economic Outlook USA, Vol. 10, No. 3.* Ann Arbor: University of Michigan, Survey Research Center, Institute for Social Research.

Bachman, J. G., Bare, D. E., & Frankie, E. I. (1986). *Correlates of employment among high school seniors.* Ann Arbor: University of Michigan, Institute for Social Research.

Bachman, J. G., Johnston, L. D., & O'Malley, P. M. (1983). *Monitoring the future: Questionnaire responses from the nation's high school seniors.* Ann Arbor: University of Michigan, Survey Research Center, Institute for Social Research.

Bachman, J. G., & Schulenberg, J. (1993). How part-time work intensity relates to drug use, problem behavior, time use, and satisfaction among high school seniors: Are these consequences or merely correlates? *Developmental Psychology, 29,* 220-235.

Baker, F., & Green, G. M. (1991). Work, health, and productivity: Overview. In G. M. Green & F. Baker (Eds.), *Work, health, and productivity* (pp. 3-29). New York: Oxford University Press.

237

Baldwin, A. L., Baldwin, C., & Cole, R. E. (1990). Stress-resistant families and stress-resistant children. In J. Rolf, A. S. Masten, D. Cicchetti, K. H. Nuechterlein, & S. Weintraub (Eds.), *Risk and protective factors in the development of psychopathology* (pp. 257-280). New York: Cambridge University Press.

Bandura, A. (1977). Self-efficacy: Toward a unifying theory of behavioral change. *Psychological Review, 84,* 191-215.

Bandura, A. (1986). *Social foundations of thought and action: A social cognitive theory.* Englewood Cliffs, NJ: Prentice Hall.

Barber, B. K., & Thomas, D. L. (1986). Dimensions of fathers' and mothers' supportive behavior: The case for physical affection. *Journal of Marriage and the Family, 48,* 783-794.

Baron, R. M., & Kenny, D. A. (1986). The moderator-mediator variable distinction in social psychological research: Conceptual, strategic, and statistical considerations. *Journal of Personality and Social Psychology, 51,* 1173-1182.

Baumrind, D. (1975). Early socialization and adolescent competence. In S. E. Dragastin & G. Elder, Jr. (Eds.), *Adolescence in the life-cycle* (pp. 117-143). Washington, DC: Hemisphere.

Becker, G. S. (1981). *A treatise on the family.* Cambridge, MA: Harvard University Press.

Berk, S. F. (1985). *The gender factory: The apportionment of work in American households.* New York: Plenum.

Bielby, D. D. (1992). Commitment to work and family. *Annual Review of Sociology, 18,* 281-302.

Blair, S. L. (1992a). The sex-typing of children's household labor: Parental influence on daughters'and sons' housework. *Youth & Society, 24,* 178-203.

Blair, S. L. (1992b). Children's participation in household labor: Child socialization versus the need for household labor. *Journal of Youth and Adolescence, 21,* 241-258.

Boocock, S. (1976). Children in contemporary society. In A. Skolnick (Ed.), *Rethinking childhood* (pp. 414-436). Boston: Houghton Mifflin.

Bronfenbrenner, U. (1979). *The ecology of human development: Experiments by nature and design.* Cambridge, MA: Harvard University Press.

Bronfenbrenner, U. (1986a). Ecology of the family as a context for human development: Research perspectives. *Developmental Psychology, 22,* 723-742.

Bronfenbrenner, U. (1986b). Recent advances in research on the ecology of human development. In R. K. Silbereisen, K. Eyferth, & G. Rudinger (Eds.), *Development as action in context* (pp. 287-310). Berlin: Springer-Verlag.

Brooks-Gunn, J. (1991). How stressful is the transition to adolescence for girls? In M. E. Colten & S. Gore (Eds.), *Adolescent stress: Causes and consequences* (pp. 131-149). Hawthorne, NY: Aldine de Gruyter.

Bryk, A. S., & Raudenbush, S. W. (1992). *Hierarchical linear models: Applications and data analysis.* Newbury Park, CA: Sage.

Buchmann, M. (1989). *The script of life in modern society.* Chicago: University of Chicago Press.

Burchinal, M. R., Bailey, D. B., Jr., & Snyder, P. (1994). Using growth curve analysis to evaluate child change in longitudinal investigations. *Journal of Early Interventions, 18,* 422-442.

Call, K. T., Mortimer, J. T., Dennehy, K., & Lee, C. (1993, August). *High risk youth and the attainment process.* Paper presented at the annual meeting of the American Sociological Association, Miami.

Call, K. T., Mortimer, J. T., & Shanahan, M. J. (1995). Helpfulness and the development of competence in adolescence. *Child Development, 66,* 129-138.

Campbell, E. O. (1969). Adolescent socialization. In D. A. Goslin (Ed.), *Handbook of socialization theory and research* (pp. 821-859). New York: Russell Sage.

Carlson, C. I., Cooper, C. R., & Spradling, V. Y. (1991). Developmental implications of shared versus distinct perceptions of the family in early adolescence. *New Directions for Child Development, 51,* 13-31.

Chase, I. D. (1975). A comparison of men's and women's intergenerational mobility in the United States. *American Sociological Review, 40,* 483-505.

Cherlin, A. (1988). *The changing American family and public policy.* New York: Urban Institute Press.

Cherlin, A., & Furstenberg, F. F., Jr. (1994). Stepfamilies in the United States: A reconsideration. *Annual Review of Sociology, 20,* 359-381.

Clark, R. (1983). *Family life and school achievement: Why poor black children succeed or fail.* Chicago: University of Chicago Press.

Clausen, J. A. (1993). *American lives: Looking back at the children of the Great Depression.* New York: Free Press.

Clay, D. C., & Schwarzweller, H. (Eds.). (1991). *Research in rural sociology and rural development (Household strategies).* Greenwich, CT: JAI.

Cohen, S., & Wills, T. A. (1985). Stress, social support, and the buffering hypothesis. *Psychological Bulletin, 98*(2), 310-357.

Coleman, J. C. (1974). *Relationships in adolescence.* Boston: Routledge & Kegan Paul.

Coleman, J. S. (1988). Social capital in the creation of human capital. *American Journal of Sociology, 94*(Suppl.), S95-S120.

Coleman, J. S. (1990). *Foundations of social theory.* Cambridge, MA: Harvard University Press.

Coleman, J. S. (1994). Social capital, human capital, and investment in youth. In A. C. Petersen & J. T. Mortimer (Eds.), *Youth unemployment and society* (pp. 34-50). New York: Cambridge University Press.

Coleman, J. S., Campbell, E. Q., Hobson, C. J., McPartland, J., Mood, A. M., Weinfeld, F. D., & York, R. L. (1966). *Equality of educational opportunity.* Washington, DC: U.S. Office of Education.

Compas, B. E. (1987). Coping with stress during childhood and adolescence. *Psychological Bulletin, 101*(3), 393-403.

Compas, B. E., Davis, G. E., Forsythe, C. J., & Wagner, B. M. (1986). Assessment of major and daily stressful events during adolescence: The Adolescent Perceived Events Scale. *Journal of Consulting and Clinical Psychology, 55*(4), 534-541.

Conger, R. D., & Elder, G. H., Jr., in collaboration with Lorenz, F. O., Simons, R. L., & Whitbeck, L. B. (Eds.). (1994). *Families in troubled times.* New York: Aldine.

Crimmins, E. M., Easterlin, R. A., & Saito, Y. (1991). Preference changes among American youth: Family, work, and goods aspirations, 1976-86. *Population and Development Review, 17*(1), 115-133.

Cronbach, L. J. (1987). Statistical tests for moderator variables: Flaws in analyses recently proposed. *Psychological Bulletin, 102,* 114-117.

Csikszentmihalyi, M., & Larson, R. (1984). *Being adolescent: Conflict and growth in the teenage years.* New York: Basic Books.

D'Amico, R. J. (1984). Does employment during high school impair academic progress? *Sociology of Education, 57,* 152-164.

Deci, E. L. (1975). *Intrinsic motivation.* New York: Plenum.

Delongis, A., Coyne, J. C., Dakof, G., Folkman, S., & Lazarus, R. S. (1982). Relationships of hassles, uplifts, and major life events to health status. *Health Psychology, 1,* 119-136.

Demo, D. H., & Acock, A. C. (1988). The impact of divorce on children. *Journal of Marriage and thr Family, 50,* 619-648.

Dennehy, K., & Mortimer, J. T. (1992). Work and family orientations of contemporary adolescent boys and girls. In J. Hood (Ed.), *Work, family, and masculinities* (pp. 87-107). Newbury Park, CA: Sage.

Dillman, D. A. (1983). Mail and other self-administered questionnaires. In P. H. Rossi, J. D. Wright, & A. B. Anderson (Eds.), *Handbook of survey research* (pp. 359-377). New York: Academic Press.

Duckett, E., Raffaelli, M., & Richards, M. H. (1989). "Taking care": Maintaining the self and the home in early adolescence. *Journal of Youth and Adolescence, 18,* 549-565.

Eagly, A. H., & Crowley, M. (1986). Gender and helping behavior: A meta-analytic review of the social psychological literature. *Psychological Bulletin, 100,* 283-308.

Eberly, M. B., Montemayor, R., & Flannery, D. J. (1993). Variation in adolescent helpfulness toward parents in a family context. *Journal of Early Adolescence, 13,* 228-244.

Eccles, J. S., Buchanan, C. M., Flanagan, C., Fuligni, A., Midgley, C., & Yee, D. (1991). Control versus autonomy during early adolescence. *Journal of Social Issues, 47,* 53-68.

Eckenrode, J., & Gore, S. (1990). *Stress between work and family.* New York: Plenum.

Eder, D. (1985). The cycle of popularity: Interpersonal relations among female adolescents. *Sociology of Education, 58,* 154-165.

Elder, G. H., Jr. (1974). *Children of the Great Depression.* Chicago: University of Chicago Press.

Elder, G. H., & Caspi, A. (1990). Studying lives in a changing society: Sociological and personological explorations. In A. I. Rabin, R. A. Zucker, R. Emmons, & S. Franks (Eds.), *Studying persons' lives* (pp. 201-247). New York: Springer.

Elder, G. H., & Rockwell, R. C. (1979). Economic depression and postwar opportunity in men's lives: A study of life patterns and health. In R. G. Simmons (Ed.), *Research in community and mental health* (Vol. 1, pp. 249-303). Greenwich, CT: JAI.

Elder, G. H., Jr., Caspi, A., & Van Nguyen, T. (1986). Resourceful and vulnerable children: Family influences in hard times. In R. K. Silbereisen, K. Eyferth, & G. Rudinger (Eds.), *Development as action in context* (pp. 167-186). Berlin: Springer-Verlag.

Elder, G. H., Jr., Conger, R. D., & Foster, E. M. (1990). *Rural youth in the household economy: An exploration of required helpfulness.* Paper presented at the biennial meeting of the Society for Research in Adolescence, Atlanta.

Elder, G. H., Jr., Foster, E. M., & Ardelt, M. (1994). Children of the household economy. In R. D. Conger & G. H. Elder, Jr., in collaboration with F. O. Lorenz, R. L. Simons, & L. B. Whitbeck (Eds.), *Families in troubled times* (pp. 127-148). New York: Aldine.

Elder, G. H., Jr., Liker, J. K., & Cross, C. E. (1984). Parent-child behavior in the Great Depression: Life course and intergenerational influence. In P. B. Baltes & O. G. Brim (Eds.), *Life-span development and behavior* (Vol. 6, pp. 109-159). New York: Academic Press.

Elder, G. H., Jr., Nguyen, T. V., & Caspi, A. (1985). Linking family hardship to children's lives. *Child Development, 56,* 361-375.

Elder, G. H., Jr., & O'Rand, A. M. (1995). Adult lives in a changing society. In K. S. Cook, G. A. Fine, & J. S. House (Eds.), *Sociological perspectives on social psychology* (pp. 452-475). Boston: Allyn & Bacon.

Elder, G. H., Jr., Robertson, E. R., & Ardelt, M. (1994). Families under economic pressure. In R. D. Conger & G. H. Elder, Jr., in collaboration with F. O. Lorenz, R. L. Simons, & L. B. Whitbeck (Eds.), *Families in troubled times* (pp. 79-104). New York: Aldine.

Elliott, D. S., & Voss, H. L. (1974). *Delinquency and dropout.* Lexington, MA: Lexington Books.

Erikson, E. H. (1959). *Identity and the life-cycle.* New York: International Universities Press.

Erikson, E. H. (1968). *Identity, youth, and crisis.* New York: Norton.

Finch, M. D., & Mortimer, J. T. (1985). Adolescent work hours and the process of achievement. In A. C. Kerckhoff (Ed.), *Research in sociology of education and socialization* (Vol. 5, pp. 171-196). Greenwich, CT: JAI.

Finch, M. D., Mortimer, J. T., & Ryu, S. (in press). Transition into part-time work: Health risks and opportunities. In J. Schulenberg, J. Maggs, & K. Hurrelmann (Eds.), *Health risks and developmental transitions during adolescence.* Cambridge: Cambridge University Press.

Finch, M. D., Shanahan, M. J., Mortimer, J. T., & Ryu, S. (1991). Work experience and control orientation in adolescence. *American Sociological Review, 56,* 597-611.

Flinn, W. L. (1982). Communities and their relationships to agrarian values. In W. B. Browne & D. F. Hadinger (Eds.), *Rural policy problems: Changing dimensions* (pp. 19-32). Lexington, MA: Lexington Books.

Friedmann, H. (1978). World market, state, and family farm: Social bases of household production in an era of wage labor. *Comparative Studies in Society and History, 20,* 545-586.

Furstenberg, F. F., Jr. (1981). *National survey of children.* Philadelphia: Temple University, Institute for Social Research.

Furstenberg, F. F., Jr. (1988). Child care after divorce and remarriage. In E. M. Hetherington & J. D. Arasteh (Eds.), *Impact of divorce, single parenting, and stepparenting on children* (pp. 245-261). Hillsdale, NJ: Lawrence Erlbaum.

Garmezy, N. (1988). Longitudinal strategies, causal reasoning and risk research: A commentary. In M. Rutter (Ed.), *Studies of psychosocial risk: The power of longitudinal data* (pp. 29-44). Cambridge: Cambridge University Press.

Gecas, V. (1989). The social psychology of self-efficacy. *Annual Review of Sociology, 15,* 291-316.

Gecas, V., & Nye, F. I. (1974). Sex and class differences in parent-child interaction: A test of Kohn's hypothesis. *Journal of Marriage and the Family, 36,* 742-749.

Gecas, V., & Schwalbe, M. L. (1986). Parental behavior and adolescent self-esteem. *Journal of Marriage and the Family, 48,* 37-46.

Gecas, V., & Seff, M. A. (1991). Families and adolescents: A review of the 1980s. In A. Booth (Ed.), *Contemporary families: Looking forward, looking back* (pp. 208-225). Minneapolis, MN: National Council on Family Relations.

Giele, J. Z. (1988). Gender and sex roles. In N. J. Smelser (Ed.), *Handbook of sociology* (pp. 291-323). Newbury Park, CA: Sage.

Gilligan, C. (1982). *In a different voice*. Cambridge, MA: Harvard University Press.

Goldscheider, F. K., & Goldscheider, C. (1993). *Leaving home before marriage: Ethnicity, familism, and generational relationships*. Madison: University of Wisconsin Press.

Goldscheider, F. K., & Waite, L. (1989, August). *The domestic economy: Husbands, wives, and children*. Paper presented at the annual meeting of the American Sociological Association, San Francisco.

Goldstein, H. (1989). Models for multilevel response variables with an application to growth curves. In R. D. Bock (Ed.), *Multilevel analysis of educational data* (pp. 107-125). San Diego: Academic Press.

Goodnow, J. J. (1988). Children's household work: Its nature and functions. *Psychological Bulletin, 103*, 5-26.

Goodnow, J. J. (1995). Differentiating among social contexts: By spatial features, forms of participation, and social contracts. In P. Moen, G. H. Elder, Jr., & K. Luscher (Eds.), *Examining lives in context: Perspectives on the ecology of human development* (pp. 269-301). Washington, DC: American Psychological Association.

Goodnow, J. J., & Delaney, S. (1989). Children's household work: Task differences, styles of assignment, and links to family relationships. *Journal of Applied Developmental Psychology, 10*, 209-226.

Goodnow, J. J., & Warton, P. M. (1991). The social bases of social cognition: Interactions about work and their implications. *Merrill-Palmer Quarterly, 37*, 27-58.

Granovetter, M. S. (1974). *Getting a job*. Cambridge, MA: Harvard University Press.

Greenberger, E. (1983). A researcher in the policy arena: The case of child labor. *American Psychologist, 38*, 104-111.

Greenberger, E. (1984). Children, families, and work. In N. D. Reppucci, L. A. Weithorn, E. P. Mulvey, & J. Monahan (Eds.), *Children, mental health, and the law* (pp. 103-122). Beverly Hills, CA: Sage.

Greenberger, E. (1988). Working in teenage America. In J. T. Mortimer & K. M. Borman (Eds.), *Work experience and psychological development* (pp. 21-50). Boulder, CO: Westview.

Greenberger, E., & Steinberg, L. D. (1986). *When teenagers work: The psychological and social costs of adolescent employment*. New York: Basic Books.

Greenberger, E., Steinberg, L. D., Vaux, A., & McAuliffe, S. (1980). Adolescents who work: Effects of part-time employment on family and peer relations. *Journal of Youth and Adolescence, 9*, 189-202.

Gross, E. (1971). Plus ça change . . .? The sexual structure of occupations over time. In A. Theodore (Ed.), *The professional woman* (pp. 39-51). Cambridge, MA: Schenkman.

Hallinan, M. T. (1994). School differences in tracking: Effects on achievement. *Social Forces, 72*, 799-820.

Harkins, E. B. (1978). Effects of empty nest transition on self-report of psychological and physical well-being. *Journal of Marriage and the Family, 40*, 549-556.

Hauser, R. M., Tsai, S. L., & Sewell, W. H. (1983). A model of stratification with response error in social and psychological variables. *Sociology of Education, 56*, 20-46.

Heinz, W. R. (1992). Introduction: Institutional gatekeeping and biographical agency. In W. R. Heinz (Ed.), *Institutions and gatekeeping in the life course* (pp. 9-27). Weinheim: Deutscher Studien Verlag.

Hendershot, G. E., & Placek, P. J. (1981). The validity and reliability of birth expectations: Evidence from the National Survey of Family Growth and the National Natality Survey. In G. E. Hendershot & P. J. Placek (Eds.), *Predicting fertility: Demographic studies of birth expectations* (pp. 61-74). Lexington, MA: D. C. Heath.

Hetherington, E. M. (1989). Coping with family transitions: Winners, losers, and survivors. *Child Development, 60,* 1-14.

Hirshleifer, J. (1993). The affections and the passions. *Rationality and Society, 5,* 185-202.

Hogan, D. P. (1978). The variable order of events in the life course. *American Sociological Review, 43,* 573-586.

Holland, J. L. (1976). Vocational preferences. In M. D. Dunnette (Ed.), *Handbook of industrial and organizational psychology* (pp. 521-570). Chicago: Rand McNally.

Hood, J. C. (1993). *Men, work, and family.* Newbury Park, CA: Sage.

Hormuth, S. E. (1984). Transitions in commitments to roles and self-concept change: Relocation as a paradigm. In V. L. Allen & E. van de Vliert (Eds.), *Role transitions: Explorations and explanations* (pp. 109-124). New York: Plenum.

Jaccard, J., Turrisi, R., & Wan, C. K. (1990). *Interaction effects in multiple regression.* Newbury Park, CA: Sage.

Jacobs, J. (1991). The dynamics of young men's career aspirations. *Sociological Forum, 6*(4), 609-639.

Jessor, R., & Jessor, S. L. (1977). *Problem behavior and psychosocial development: A longitudinal study of youth.* San Diego: Academic Press.

Johansson, G., & Aronsson, G. (1991). Psychosocial factors in the workplace. In G. M. Green & F. Baker (Eds.), *Work, health, and productivity* (pp. 179-197). New York: Oxford University Press.

Jöreskog, K. G., & Sörbom, D. (1989). *LISREL 7 user's reference guide.* Chicago: Scientific Software, Inc.

Kalleberg, A. L. (1996). Changing contexts of careers: Trends in labor market structures and some implications for labor force outcomes. In A. C. Kerckhoff (Ed.), *Generating social stratification: Toward a new generation of research* (pp. 343-358). Boulder, CO: Westview.

Kalliopuska, M. (1992). Grouping of children's helping behavior. *Psychological Reports, 71,* 747-753.

Kandel, D. B. (1989). Issues of sequencing of adolescent drug use and other problem behaviors. *Drugs and Society, 3,* 55-76.

Kandel, D. B., Davies, M., & Raveis, V. H. (1985). The stressfulness of daily social roles for women: Marital, occupational and household roles. *Journal of Health and Social Behavior, 26,* 64-78.

Kennedy, R. E., Jr. (1989). *Life choices* (2nd ed.). New York: Holt, Rinehart & Winston.

Kerckhoff, A. C. (1995). Social stratification and mobility processes: Interactions between individuals and social structures. In K. S. Cook, G. A. Fine, & J. S. House (Eds.), *Sociological perspectives on social psychology* (pp. 476-496). Boston: Allyn & Bacon.

Kohn, M., & Schooler, C. (1974a). *Study of occupations (Adult version).* Chicago: University of Chicago, National Opinion Research Center.

Kohn, M., & Schooler, C. (1974b). *Study of occupations (Child version).* Chicago: University of Chicago, National Opinion Research Center.

Kohn, M. L. (1969). *Class and conformity: A study in values.* Homewood, IL: Dorsey.

Kohn, M. L. (1977). Reassessment, 1977. In M. L. Kohn, *Class and conformity: A study in values* (2nd ed., pp. xxv-lx). Chicago: University of Chicago Press.

Kohn, M. L. (1981). Personality, occupation, and social stratification: A frame of reference. In D. J. Treiman & R. V. Robinson (Eds.), *Research in social stratification and mobility* (Vol. 1, pp. 267-297). Greenwich, CT: JAI.

Kohn, M. L., & Schooler, C. (1973). Occupational experience and psychological functioning: An assessment of reciprocal effects. *American Sociological Review, 84,* 24-52.

Kohn, M. L., & Schooler, C. (1983). *Work and personality: An inquiry into the impact of social stratification.* Norwood, NJ: Ablex.

Kohn, M. L., Slomczynski, K. M., & Schoenbach, C. (1986). Social stratification and the transmission of values in the family: A cross-national assessment. *Sociological Forum, 1,* 73-102.

Kumka, D. S. (1984). *Values and occupational choice: A case for consistency.* Unpublished doctoral dissertation, University of Minnesota.

Laird, N. M., & Ware, J. H. (1982). Random effects models for longitudinal models. *Biometrics, 38,* 963-974.

Lasch, C. (1977). *Haven in a heartless world: The family besieged.* New York: Basic Books.

Lasley, P. (1994). Rural economic and social trends. In R. D. Conger & G. H. Elder, Jr., in collaboration with F. O. Lorenz, R. L. Simons, & L. B. Whitbeck (Eds.), *Families in troubled times* (pp. 57-78). New York: Aldine.

Laursen, B., & Collins, W. A. (1994). Interpersonal conflict during adolescence. *Psychological Bulletin, 115,* 197-209.

Lawrence, F. C., & Wozniak, P. H. (1987). Rural children's time in household activities. *Psychological Reports, 61,* 927-937.

LeCroy, C. W. (1989). Parent-adolescent intimacy: Impact on adolescent functioning. *Adolescence, 23,* 137-147.

Leik, R. (1986). *OpenCode: Program for coding open-ended responses.* Minneapolis, MN: Folkware.

Lempers, J. D., Clark-Lempers, D., & Simons, R. L. (1989). Economic hardship, parenting, and distress in adolescence. *Child Development, 60,* 25-39.

Lepore, S. J. (1992). Social conflict, social support, and psychological distress: Evidence of cross-domain buffering effects. *Journal of Personality and Social Psychology, 63*(5), 857-867.

Lerner, R. (1984). *On the nature of human plasticity.* Cambridge, England: Cambridge University Press.

Lewin-Epstein, N. (1981). *Youth employment during high school.* Washington, DC: National Center for Educational Statistics.

Liem, J. H., & Liem, G. R. (1990). Understanding the individual and family effects of unemployment. In J. Eckenrode & S. Gore (Eds.), *Stress between work and family* (pp. 175-204). New York: Plenum.

Lin, N., Ensel, W. M., & Vaughn, J. C. (1981). Social resources and strength of ties: Structural factors in occupational status attainment. *American Sociological Review, 46,* 393-405.

Lindsay, P., & Knox, W. E. (1984). Continuity and change in work values among young adults: A longitudinal study. *American Journal of Sociology, 89,* 918-931.

Linton, R. (1942). Age and sex categories. *American Sociological Review, 7,* 589-603.

Linville, P. W. (1985). Self complexity and affective extremity: Don't put all of your eggs in one cognitive basket. *Social Cognition, 3*(1), 94-120.

Lodahl, T. M., & Kejner, M. (1965). The definition and measurement of job involvement. *Journal of Applied Psychology, 49,* 24-33.

Long, J. F., & Wetrogan, S. I. (1981). The utility of birth expectations in population projections. In G. E. Hendershot & P. J. Placek (Eds.), *Predicting fertility: Demographic studies of birth expectations* (pp. 29-50). Lexington, MA: D. C. Heath.

Lorence, J., & Mortimer, J. T. (1985). Job involvement through the life course: A panel study of three age groups. *American Sociological Review, 50,* 618-638.

Lueptow, M., McClendon, J., & McKeon, J. W. (1979). Father's occupation and son's personality: Findings and questions for the emerging linkage hypothesis. *Sociological Quarterly, 20,* 463-475.

Luthar, S. S. (1991). Vulnerability and resilience: A study of high-risk adolescents. *Child Development, 62,* 600-616.

Maccoby, E. E., & Jacklin, C. N. (1974). *The psychology of sex differences.* Stanford, CA: Stanford University Press.

Maccoby, E. E., & Martin, J. (1983). Socialization in the context of the family: Parent-child interaction. In E. M. Hetherington (Ed.), *Handbook of child psychology: Vol. 4. Socialization, personality and social development* (pp. 1-101). New York: John Wiley.

Mainquist, S., & Eichorn, D. (1989). Competence in work settings. In D. Stern & D. Eichorn (Eds.), *Adolescence and work: Influences of social structure, labor markets, and culture* (pp. 327-367). Hillsdale, NJ: Lawrence Erlbaum.

Manning, W. D. (1990). Parenting employed teenagers. *Youth & Society, 22,* 184-200.

Marini, M. M. (1978). The transition to adulthood: Sex differences in educational attainment and age at marriage. *American Sociological Review, 43,* 483-507.

Marini, M. M. (1984). The order of events in the transition to adulthood. *Sociology of Education, 57,* 63-84.

Marini, M. M., & Brinton, M. C. (1984). Sex typing in organizational socialization. In B. F. Reskin (Ed.), *Sex segregation in the workplace* (pp. 192-232). Washington, DC: National Academy Press.

Marini, M. M., Shin, H. C., & Raymond, J. (1989). Socioeconomic consequences of the process of transition to adulthood. *Social Science Research, 13,* 89-135.

Markus, H., Cross, S., & Wurf, E. (1990). The role of the self-system in competence. In R. J. Steinberg & J. Kolligan, Jr. (Eds.), *Competence considered* (pp. 205-226). New Haven, CT: Yale University Press.

Markus, H., & Nurius, P. (1986). Possible selves. *American Psychologist, 41,* 954-969.

Marsh, H. W. (1991). Employment during high school: Character building or a subversion of academic goals? *Sociology of Education, 64,* 172-189.

Masten, A. S., & Brasewell, L. (1991). Developmental psychotherapy: An integrative framework for understanding behavior problems in children and adolescents. In. P. R. Martin (Ed.), *Handbook of Behavior Therapy and Psychological Science: An Integrative Approach* (pp. 35-0567). New York: Pergamon.

McHale, S. M., Bartko, W. T., Crouter, A. C., & Perry-Jenkins, M. (1990). Children's housework and psychosocial functioning: The mediating effects of parents' sex-role behaviors and attitudes. *Child Development, 61,* 1413-1426.

McLaughlin, S. D., Melber, B. D., Billy, J. O. B., Zimmerle, D. M., Wings, L. D., & Johnson, T. R. (1988). *The changing lives of American women.* Chapel Hill: University of North Carolina Press.

McLean, R. A., Sanders, W. L., & Strong, W. W. (1991). A unified approach to mixed linear models. *The American Statistician, 45,* 54-64.

McLoyd, V. C. (1990). The impact of economic hardship on black families and children: Psychological distress, parenting, and socioemotional development. *Child Development, 61,* 311-346.

McNeil, L. (1984). *Lowering expectations: The impact of student employment on classroom knowledge.* Madison: Wisconsin Center for Educational Research.

Menaghan, E. (1991). Work experiences and the family interaction process: The long reach of the job? *Annual Review of Sociology, 17,* 419-444.

Meyer, R. M., & Wise, D. A. (1982). High school preparation and early labor force experiences. In R. B. Freeman & D. A. Wise (Eds.), *The youth labor problem: Its nature, causes and consequences* (pp. 277-347). Chicago: University of Chicago Press.

Milkman, R. (1987). *Gender at work: The dynamics of job segregation by sex during World War II.* Urbana, IL: University of Illinois Press.

Miller, J., & Garrison, H. H. (1982). Sex roles: The division of labor at home and in the workplace. *Annual Review of Sociology, 8,* 237-262.

Miller, J., & Young, S. (1990). The role of allowances in adolescent socialization. *Youth & Society, 22*(2), 137-159.

Modell, J. (1980). Normative aspects of American marriage timing since World War II. *Journal of Family History, 5,* 210-234.

Modell, J. (1989). *Into one's own: From youth to adulthood in the United States, 1920-1975.* Berkeley: University of California Press.

Moen, P. (1992). *Women's two roles.* Westport, CT: Auburn House.

Moen, P., & Wethington, E. (1992). The concept of family adaptive strategies. *Annual Review of Sociology, 18,* 233-251.

Montemayor, R. (1983). Parents and adolescents in conflict: All families some of the time and some families all of the time. *Journal of Early Adolescence, 3,* 83-103.

Mortimer, J. T. (1974). Patterns of intergenerational occupational movements: A smallest-space analysis. *American Journal of Sociology, 79,* 1278-1299.

Mortimer, J. T. (1976). Social class, work and the family: Some implications of the father's occupation for familial relationships and sons' career decisions. *Journal of Marriage and the Family, 38,* 241-254.

Mortimer, J. T. (1996). Social psychological aspects of achievement. In A. C. Kerkoff (Ed.), *Generating social stratification: Toward a new generation of research* (pp. 17-36). Boulder, CO: Westview.

Mortimer, J. T., Dennehy, K., & Lee, C. (1991). *Work experience and other influences on adolescents' occupational values: Evidence from a prospective study.* Report for the National Center for Research on Vocational Education.

Mortimer, J. T., Dennehy, K., Lee, C., & Finch, M. D. (1994). Economic socialization in the American family: The prevalence, distribution and consequences of allowance arrangements. *Family Relations, 43,* 23-29.

Mortimer, J. T., & Finch, M. D. (1986). The effects of part-time work on self-concept and achievement. In K. Borman & J. Reisman (Eds.), *Becoming a worker* (pp. 66-89). Norwood, NJ: Ablex.

Mortimer, J. T., Finch, M., Dennehy, K., Lee, C., & Beebe, T. (1994). Work experience in adolescence. *Journal of Vocational Education Research, 19*(1), 39-70.

Mortimer, J. T., Finch, M. D., & Kumka, D. (1982). Persistence and change in development: The multidimensional self-concept. In P. B. Baltes & O. G. Brim, Jr. (Eds.), *Life-span development and behavior* (pp. 263-313). New York: Academic Press.

Mortimer, J. T., Finch, M. D., & Maruyama, G. (1988). Work experience and job satisfaction: Variation by age and gender. In J. T. Mortimer & K. Borman (Eds.), *Work experience and psychological development through the life span* (pp. 109-155). Boulder, CO: Westview.

Mortimer, J. T., Finch, M. D., Ryu, S., Shanahan, M. J., & Call, K. T. (in press). The effects of work intensity on adolescent mental health, achievement, and behavioral adjustment: New evidence from a prospective study. *Child Development.*

Mortimer, J. T., Finch, M. D., Shanahan, M. J., & Ryu, S. (1992a). Work experience, mental health and behavioral adjustment in adolescence. *Journal of Research on Adolescence, 2,* 25-58.

Mortimer, J. T., Finch, M. D., Shanahan, M. J., & Ryu, S. (1992b). Adolescent work history and behavioral adjustment. *Journal of Research on Adolescence, 2,* 59-80.

Mortimer, J. T., & Kumka, D. S. (1982). A further examination of the "occupational linkage hypothesis." *Sociological Quarterly, 23,* 3-16.

Mortimer, J. T., & Lorence, J. (1979a). Work experience and occupational value socialization: A longitudinal study. *American Journal of Sociology, 84,* 1361-1385.

Mortimer, J. T., & Lorence, J. (1979b). Occupational experience and the self-concept: A longitudinal study. *Social Psychology Quarterly, 42,* 307-323.

Mortimer, J. T., & Lorence, J. (1995). The social psychology of work. In K. S. Cook, G. A. Fine, & J. S. House (Eds.), *Sociological perspectives on social psychology* (pp. 497-523). Boston: Allyn & Bacon.

Mortimer, J. T., Lorence, J., & Kumka, D. S. (1986). *Work, family, and personality: Transition to adulthood.* Norwood, NJ: Ablex.

Mortimer, J. T., Pimentel, E. E., Ryu, S., Dennehy, K., & Lee, C. (in press). Part-time work and occupational value formation in adolescence. *Social Forces.*

Mortimer, J. T., & Shanahan, M. J. (1991, August). *Adolescent work experience and relations with peers.* Paper presented at the annual meeting of the American Sociological Association, Cincinnati.

Mortimer, J. T., & Shanahan, M. J. (1994). Adolescent work experience and family relationships. *Work and Occupations, 21,* 369-384.

Mortimer, J. T., Shanahan, M., & Ryu, S. (1993). The effects of adolescent employment on school-related orientation and behavior. In R. K. Silbereisen & E. Todt (Eds.), *Adolescence in context: The interplay of family, school, peers and work in adjustment* (pp. 304-326). New York: Springer-Verlag.

Nett, E. M. (1988). *Canadian families: Past and present.* Toronto: Butterworth.

Nidorf, J. F. (1985). Mental health and refugee youths: A model for diagnostic training. In T. C. Owen (Ed.), *Southeast Asian mental health: Treatment, prevention, services, training, and research* (pp. 391-427). Washington, DC: National Institute for Mental Health.

Paikoff, R. L., with Collins, W. A. (1991). Editor's notes. *New Directions in the Family During Adolescence, 51,* 1-11.

Parcel, T. L., & Menaghan, E. G. (1994). *Parents' jobs and children's lives.* Hawthorne, NY: Aldine de Gruyter.

Pearlin, L. I., & Kohn, M. L. (1966). Social class, occupation, and parental values: A cross-national study. *American Sociological Review, 31,* 446-479.

Pearlin, L. I., & McCall, M. E. (1990). Occupational stress and marital support: A description of microprocesses. In J. Eckenrode & S. Gore (Eds.), *Stress between work and family* (pp. 39-60). New York: Plenum.

Pearlin, L. I., Menaghan, E. G., Lieberman, M. A., & Mullan, J. T. (1981). The stress process. *Journal of Health and Social Behavior, 22,* 337-356.

Pedhazur, E. J. (1982). *Multiple regression in behavioral research: Explanation and prediction.* New York: CBS College Publishing.

Peskin, H., & Livson, N. (1972). Pre- and postpubertal personality and adult psychologic functioning. *Seminars in Psychology, 4,* 343-355.

Peters, J., & Haldeman, V. (1987). Time used for household work: A study of school-age children from single-parent, two-parent, one earner, and two earner families. *Journal of Family Issues, 2,* 212-225.

Petersen, A. C., Sargiani, P., & Kennedy, R. (1991). Adolescent depression: Why more girls? *Journal of Youth and Adolescence, 20,* 247-272.

Petersen, A. C., & Taylor, B. (1980). The biological approach to adolescence: Biological change and psychological adaptation. In J. Adelson (Eds.), *Handbook of adolescent psychology* (pp. 117-158). New York: Wiley.

Peterson, J. L., & Zill, N. (1986). Marital disruptions, parent-child relationship, and behavior problems in children. *Journal of Marriage and the Family, 48,* 295-307.

Phillips, S., & Sandstrom, K. (1990). Parental attitudes toward "youthwork." *Youth & Society, 22,* 160-183.

Piotrkowski, C. (1979). *Work and the family system.* New York: Free Press.

Piotrkowski, C. S., & Crits-Christoph, P. (1981). Women's jobs and family adjustment. *Journal of Family Issues, 2*(2), 126-147.

Quinn, R. P., & Staines, G. L. (1979). *The 1977 Quality of Employment Survey.* Ann Arbor: University of Michigan, Survey Research Center, Institute for Social Research.

Raudenbush, S. W., & Chan, W. S. (1993). Application of hierarchical linear model to the study of adolescent deviance in an overlapping cohort design. *Journal of Consulting and Clinical Psychology, 61,* 941-951.

Reskin, B. (1993). Sex segregation in the workplace. *Annual Review of Sociology, 19,* 241-270.

Richards, M. H., & Larson, R. (1989). The life space of socialization of the self: Sex differences in the young adolescent. *Journal of Youth and Adolescence, 18,* 617-626.

Ridgeway, C., & Walker, H. (1994). Status structures. In K. S. Cook, G. A. Fine, & J. S. House (Eds.), *Sociological perpsectives on social psychology* (pp. 281-310). Boston: Allyn & Bacon.

Rindfuss, R. R. (1991). The young adult years: Diversity, structural change, and fertility. *Demography, 28*(4), 493-512.

Rindfuss, R. R., Cooksey, E. C., & Sutterlin, R. L. (1990). *Young adult occupational achievement: Early expectations versus behavioral reality.* Paper presented at the World Congress of Sociology, Madrid.

Rindfuss, R. R., Swicegood, C. G., & Rosenfeld, R. (1987). Disorder in the life course: How common and does it matter? *American Sociological Review, 52,* 785-801.

Rosen, B. D., & Aneshensel, C. S. (1978). Sex differences in the educational-occupational expectation process. *Social Forces, 57,* 164-186.

Rosenbaum, J. E., & Kariya, T. (1991). Do school achievements affect the early jobs of high school graduates in the United States and Japan? *Sociology of Education, 64,* 78-95.

Rosenberg, M. (1957). *Occupation and values.* Glencoe, IL: Free Press.

Rosenberg, M. (1965). *Society and the adolescent self-image.* Princeton, NJ: Princeton University Press.

Rossi, A. (1989). A life-course approach to gender, aging, and intergenerational relations. In K. W. Schaie & C. Schooler (Eds.), *Social structure and aging* (pp. 207-236). Hillsdale, NJ: Lawrence Erlbaum.

Rowlinson, R. T., & Felner, R. D. (1988). Major life events, hassles, and adaptation in adolescence: Confounding in the conceptualization and measurement of life stress and adjustment revisited. *Journal of Personality and Social Psychology, 55*(3), 432-444.

Rutter, M. (1983). Stress, coping, and development: Some issues and some questions. In N. Garmezy & M. Rutter (Eds.), *Stress, coping, and development in children* (pp. 1-41). New York: McGraw-Hill.

Rutter, M. (1990). Psychosocial resilience and protective mechanisms. In J. Rolf, A. S. Masten, D. Cicchetti, K. H. Nuechterlein, & S. Weintraub (Eds.), *Risk and protective factors in the development of psychopathology* (pp. 181-214). New York: Cambridge University Press.

Savin-Williams, R. C., & Berndt, T. J. (1990). Friendship and peer relations. In S. S. Feldman & G. R. Elliott (Eds.), *At the threshold: The developing adolescent* (pp. 277-307). Cambridge, MA: Harvard University Press.

Scheck, D. C., Emerick, R., & El-Assal, M. M. (1973). Adolescents' perceptions of parent-child relations and the development of internal-external control orientations. *Journal of Marriage and the Family, 35,* 643-654.

Schulenberg, J., & Bachman, J. G. (1993, March). *Long hours on the job? Not so bad for some adolescents in some types of jobs: The quality of work and substance use, affect and stress.* Paper presented at the annual meeting of the Society for Research on Child Development, New Orleans.

Sewell, W. H. (1975). *Education, occupation and earnings: Achievement in the early career.* New York: Academic Press.

Sewell, W. H., & Hauser, R. M. (1972). Causes and consequences of higher education: Models of the status attainment process. *American Journal of Agricultural Economics, 52,* 651-661.

Sewell, W. H., & Hauser, R. M. (1976). Causes and consequences of higher education: Models of the status attainment process. In W. H. Sewell, R. M. Hauser, & D. Featherman (Eds.), *Schooling and achievement in American society* (pp. 9-27). New York: Academic Press.

Shanahan, M. J., Elder, G. H., Jr., Burchinal, M., & Conger, R. D. (1994, August). *Rural context and the adolescent work experience: New research findings.* Paper presented at the annual meeting of the American Sociological Association, Washington, DC.

Shanahan, M. J., Elder, G. H., Jr., & Burchinal, M. (1995). *Adolescent earnings and self-conceptions in urban and rural ecologies.* Paper presented at the annual meeting of the Society for Research in Child Development, Indianapolis.

Shanahan, M. J., Elder, G. H., Jr., Burchinal, M., & Conger, R. D. (1996). Adolescents working and relating to parents: A developmental perspective. *Child Development, 67.*

Shanahan, M. J., Finch, M. D., Mortimer, J. T., & Ryu, S. (1991). Adolescent work experience and depressive affect. *Social Psychology Quarterly, 54,* 299-317.

Shanahan, M. J., & Mortimer, J. T. (in press). Understanding the positive consequences of psychosocial stressors. In B. Markovsky, M. Lovaglia, & R. Simon (Eds.), *Advances in group processes* (Vol. 13). Greenwich, CT: JAI.

Simmons, R. G. Comfort with the self. In S. Stryker (Ed.), *Self, affect and society.* (Unpublished manuscript)

Simmons, R. G., & Blyth, D. A. (1987). *Moving into adolescence: The impact of pubertal change and school context.* Hawthorne, NY: Aldine de Gruyter.

Smetana, J. G., Yau, J., Restrepo, A., & Braeges, J. L. (1991). Conflict and adaptation in adolescence: Adolescent-parent conflict. In M. E. Colten & S. Gore (Eds.), *Adolescent stress: Causes and consequences* (pp. 43-65). Hawthorne, NY: Aldine de Gruyter.

Spaeth, J. L. (1976). Cognitive complexity: A dimension underlying the socioeconomic achievement process. In W. H. Sewell, R. M. Hauser, & D. L. Featherman (Eds.), *Schooling and achievement in American society* (pp. 103-131). New York: Academic Press.

Spencer, M. B., Dornbusch, S. M., & Mont-Reynaud, R. (1990). Challenges in studying minority youth. In S. S. Feldman & G. R. Elliott (Eds.), *At the threshold: The developing adolescent* (pp. 123-146). Cambridge, MA: Harvard University Press.

Steel, L. (1991). Early work experience among white and nonwhite youth. *Youth & Society, 22,* 419-447.

Steinberg, L. (1987). Recent research on the family at adolescence: The extent and nature of sex differences. *Journal of Youth and Adolescence, 16*(3), 191-197.

Steinberg, L. (1990). Autonomy, conflict, and harmony in the family relationship. In S. S. Feldman & G. R. Elliott (Eds.), *At the threshold: The developing adolescent* (pp. 255-276). Cambridge, MA: Harvard University Press.

Steinberg, L., & Dornbusch, S. M. (1991). Negative correlates of part-time employment during adolescence: Replication and elaboration. *Developmental Psychology, 27,* 304-313.

Steinberg, L., & Silverberg, S. B. (1986). The vicissitudes of autonomy in early adolescence. *Child Development, 20*(6), 1017-1025.

Steinberg, L. D., Fegley, S., & Dornbusch, S. M. (1993). Negative impact of part-time work on adolescent adjustment: Evidence from a longitudinal study. *Developmental Psychology, 29,* 171-180.

Steinberg, L. D., Greenberger, E., Garduque, L., Ruggiero, M., & McAuliffe, S. (1982). High school students in the labor force: Some costs and benefits to schooling and learning. *Education Evaluation and Policy Analysis, 4,* 363-372.

Steinberg, L. D., Greenberger, E., Garduque, L., Ruggiero, M., & Vaux, A. (1982). Effects of work in adolescent development. *Developmental Psychology, 18,* 385-395.

Stern, D., & Nakata, Y. F. (1989). Characteristics of high school students' paid jobs, and employment experience after graduation. In D. Stern & D. Eichorn (Eds.), *Adolescence and work: Influences of social structure, labor markets, and culture* (pp. 189-234). Hillsdale, NJ: Lawrence Erlbaum.

Stevens, C. J., Puchtell, L. A., Ryu, S., & Mortimer, J. T. (1992). Adolescent work and boys' and girls' orientations to the future. *Sociological Quarterly, 33*(2), 153-169.

Sullivan, M. (1989). *Getting paid: Youth crime and work in the inner city.* Ithaca, NY: Cornell University Press.

Suls, J. (1989). Self-awareness and self-identity in adolescence. In J. Worell & F. Danner (Eds.), *The adolescent as decision-maker: Applications to development and education*. San Diego: Academic Press.

Super, D. E. (1957). *The psychology of careers*. New York: Harper & Row.

Sweeting, H., & West, P. (1994). The patterning of life events in mid- to late adolescence: Markers for the future? *Journal of Adolescence, 17*, 283-304.

Thoits, P. A. (1983). Dimensions of life events that influence psychological distress: An evaluation and synthesis of the literature. In H. B. Kaplan (Ed.), *Psychosocial stress: Trends in theory and research* (pp. 33-103). New York: Academic Press.

Thoits, P. A. (1991). On merging identity theory and stress research. *Social Psychology Quarterly, 54*(2), 101-112.

Thoits, P. A. (1995). Stress, coping, and social support processes: Where are we? What next? *Journal of Health and Social Behavior*, Special issue, 53-79.

Thrall, C. (1978). Who does what: Role stereotype, children's work, and continuity between generations in the household division of labor. *Human Relations, 32*(3), 249-265.

Tilly, L. A., & Scott, J. W. (1978). *Women, work and family*. New York: Holt, Rinehart & Winston.

Treiman, D. J., & Terrell, K. (1975). Sex and the process of status attainment: A comparison of working women and men. *American Sociological Review, 40*, 174-200.

U.S. Bureau of Employment Security. (1950). *Job guide for young workers* (June series). Washington, DC: Government Printing Office.

U.S. Bureau of Labor Statistics. (1968). *Employment and earnings statistics for the U.S., 1909-1967*. Washington, DC: Government Printing Office.

U.S. Bureau of Labor Statistics. (1985, March). *Employment and earnings*. Washington, DC: Government Printing Office.

U.S. Bureau of the Census. (1982a). *1980 census of population: Alphabetical index of industries and occupations* (Series PHC80-R3, final ed.). Washington, DC: Government Printing Office.

U.S. Bureau of the Census. (1982b). *Census of population and housing, 1980 (Summary tape file 3)*. Washington, DC: Government Printing Office.

U.S. Department of Commerce, Bureau of the Census. (1940). *Census of the population: Vol. 3. The labor force: Industry, employment and income, Part 1: United States summary*. Washington, DC: Government Printing Office.

U.S. Department of Commerce, Bureau of the Census. (1950). *Census of the population: Vol. 2. Characteristics of the population, Part 1: United States summary*. Washington, DC: Government Printing Office.

U.S. Department of Commerce, Bureau of the Census. (1960). *Census of the population: Vol. 1. Characteristics of the population, Part 1: United States summary*. Washington, DC: Government Printing Office.

U.S. Department of Commerce, Bureau of the Census. (1980). *Census of population, detailed population characteristics: U.S. summary, Section A*. Washington, DC: Government Printing Office.

U.S. Department of Commerce, Social and Economic Statistics. (1970). *Census of population, detailed characteristics: U.S. summary*. Washington, DC: Government Printing Office.

Vondracek, F. W., Lerner, R. M., & Schulenberg, J. E. (1986). *Career development: A life-span developmental approach*. Hillsdale, NJ: Lawrence Erlbaum.

Voydanoff, P. (1987). *Work and family life*. Newbury Park, CA: Sage.

Wagenaar, A. C., & Perry, C. L. (1994). Community strategies for the reduction of youth drinking: Theory and application. *Journal of Research on Adolescence, 4,* 319-345.

Waite, L. J., & Goldscheider, F. K. (1991). *New families, no families? The transformation of the American home.* Berkeley: University of California Press.

Ware, J. G., Johnston, S. A., Davies-Avery, A., & Brook, R. H. (1979). Current HIS mental health battery. (r.19879/3-Hew) Appendix E. In *Conceptualization and measurement of health for adults in the Health Insurance Study: Vol. 3. Mental health.* Santa Monica, CA: RAND.

Weiner, B. (1979). A theory of motivation for some classroom experiences. *Journal of Educational Psychology, 71,* 3-25.

Weiss, R. S. (1979). *Going it alone: The family life and social situation of the single parent.* New York: Basic Books.

Weiss, R. S. (1990). Bringing work stress home. In J. Eckenrode & S. Gore (Eds.), *Stress between work and family* (pp. 17-38). New York: Plenum.

Werner, E. E. (1987). Vulnerability and resiliency in children at risk for delinquency: A longitudinal study from birth to young adulthood. In J. D. Burchard & S. N. Burchard (Eds.), *Prevention of delinquency* (pp. 16-43). Newbury Park, CA: Sage.

Westoff, C. F. (1981). The validity of birth intentions: Evidence from U.S. longitudinal studies. In G. E. Hendershot & P. J. Placek (Eds.), *Predicting fertility: Demographic studies of birth expectations* (pp. 51-59). Lexington, MA: D. C. Heath.

Wharton, A., & Erickson, R. (1993). Managing emotions on the job and at home: Understanding the consequences of multiple emotional roles. *Academy of Management Review, 18,* 457-486.

Wheaton, B. (1990). Where work and family meet: Stress across social roles. In J. Eckenrode & S. Gore (Eds.), *Stress between work and family* (pp. 153-174). New York: Plenum.

White, L. (1994). Coresidence and leaving home: Young adults and their parents. *Annual Review of Sociology, 20,* 81-102.

White, L. K., & Brinkerhoff, D. B. (1981a). Children's work in the family: Its significance and meaning. *Journal of Marriage and the Family, 43,* 789-798.

White, L. K., & Brinkerhoff, D. B. (1981b). The sexual division of labor: Evidence from childhood. *Social Forces, 60,* 170-181.

Willits, F. K., Bealer, R. C., & Timbers, V. L. (1990). Popular images of "rurality": Data from a Pennsylvania survey. *Rural Sociology, 55,* 559-578.

Windle, M. (1992). A longitudinal study of stress buffering for adolescent problem behaviors. *Developmental Psychology, 28*(3), 522-530.

Yamoor, C. M., & Mortimer, J. T. (1990). An investigation of age and gender differences in the effects of employment on adolescent achievement and well-being. *Youth & Society, 22,* 225-240.

Zelizer, V. (1985). *Pricing the priceless child: The changing social value of children.* New York: Basic Books.

Zill, N., & Peterson, J. L. (1982). Learning to do things without help. In L. M. Laosa & I. E. Sigel (Eds.), *Families as learning environments for children* (pp. 343-367). New York: Plenum.

Index

About the Editors

Jeylan T. Mortimer is Professor of Sociology and Director of the Life Course Center at the University of Minnesota. Since 1987, she has directed the Youth Development Study, with funding from NIMH, NIA, the National Center for Research on Vocational Education, and the William T. Grant Foundation. She is the author of *Work, Family, and Personality, Transition to Adulthood* (with J. Lorence and D. Kumka), *Work Experience and Psychological Development Through the Life Span* (coedited with K. Borman), and *Youth Unemployment and Society* (coedited with A. Petersen).

Michael D. Finch is Associate Professor of Health Services Research, Policy and Administration in the School of Public Health, University of Minnesota. His current interests include work and adolescent development, long-term care for the elderly, and health insurance. He is co-investigator (with Jeylan T. Mortimer) of the Youth Development Study. His recent publications appear in *Social Forces, The Gerontologist, Journal of the American Geriatrics Society, Family Relations, Child Development,* and *The American Journal of Medicine.*

About the Contributors

Pamela J. Aronson is a graduate student in the Department of Sociology at the University of Minnesota. She has worked for the Youth Development Study as survey manager since 1993. Her studies focus on the gender identities of young women during the transition to adulthood.

Margaret Burchinal is Director of the Design and Statistical Computing Unit at the Frank Porter Graham Child Development Center and a Research Assistant Professor in the psychology department at the University of North Carolina at Chapel Hill. She is interested in longitudinal methodology and cognitive development, with special emphasis on estimating individual growth curves, and in the impact of early child care experiences on children's development.

Kathleen Thiede Call, a sociologist, is an Assistant Professor at the University of Minnesota's Institute for Health Services Research. Her dissertation, "Arenas of Comfort and Stress in Adolescence: Evidence from a Prospective Longitudinal Study," is based on data from the Youth Development Study. Her research interests include social psychology, life course development, and, more recently, issues of access to health care.

Rand D. Conger is Professor of Sociology at Iowa State University, Director of the NIMH-funded Center for Family Research in Rural Mental Health, and Co-Principal Investigator of the Iowa Youth and Families Project. His interests include family research methods, family stress and individual well-being, context and family processes, and child and adolescent development. He currently serves on the NIMH's Behavioral Sciences Task Force.

Glen H. Elder, Jr. is Howard W. Odum Distinguished Professor of Sociology and Research Professor of Psychology at the University of North Carolina at Chapel Hill, where he directs the Social Change Project on life course studies. He is coeditor of *Children in Time and Place* (Cambridge University Press, 1994) and *Families in Troubled Times* (Aldine, 1994).

Michael Hacker earned his undergraduate degrees in sociology and philosophy at the University of Minnesota. He is currently pursuing the Master in Social Work degree at Augsburg College and working for a volunteer youth shelter in Minneapolis.

Ellen Efron Pimentel is Assistant Professor of Sociology at the University of Illinois, Chicago. Her postdoctoral research was conducted at the University of Minnesota using the Youth Development Study data. Her research interests include demography, marriage and family, and gender, with much of her work focusing on East Asia.

Seongryeol Ryu has been a data manager and analyst for the Youth Development Study since 1989. His interests include social psychology and methodology. He recently completed his dissertation, "Socioeconomic Change in the Family and Adolescent Achievement Orientations," based on the YDS data.

Michael J. Shanahan is Assistant Professor of Human Development and Family Studies at Pennsylvania State University. His research examines connections between the economy and human development and includes studies of adolescent work and social development, poverty and children's mental health, and cohort studies of attainment and well-being. He is coeditor of *Comparisons in Human Development: Understanding Time and Context* (Cambridge University Press, 1995b).

Carol Zierman has a BS in sociology from the University of Minnesota, where she was an undergraduate research assistant for the Youth Development Study and conducted her senior research project using project data. She is currently a Research Associate with the Amherst H. Wilder Foundation's Research Center and coauthor of *What Works in Preventing Rural Violence: Strategies, Risk Factors and Assessment Tools* and *Minnesota Statewide Survey of Persons Without Permanent Shelter, Volume I: Adults and Children* and *Volume II: Unaccompanied Youth.*